# YOUTH AND SEXUALITY IN THE TWENTIETH-CENTURY UNITED STATES

When did the sexual revolution happen? Most Americans would probably say the 1960s. In reality, young couples were changing the rules of public and private life for decades before. By the early years of the twentieth century, teenagers were increasingly free of adult supervision, and taking control of their sexuality in many ways. Dating, going steady, necking, petting, and cohabiting all provoked adult hand-wringing and advice, most of it ignored. By the time the media began announcing the arrival of a "sexual revolution," it had been going on for half a century.

*Youth and Sexuality in the Twentieth-Century United States* tells this story with fascinating revelations from both personal writings and scientific sex research. John C. Spurlock follows the major changes in the sex lives of American youth across the entire century, considering how dramatic revolutions in the culture of sex affected not only heterosexual relationships but also gay and lesbian youth, and same-sex friendships. The dark side of sex is also covered, with discussion of the painful realities of sexual violence and coercion in the lives of many young people. Full of details from first-person accounts, this lively and accessible history is essential for anyone interested in American youth and sexuality.

**John C. Spurlock** is Professor of History at Seton Hill University in Greensburg, Pennsylvania. He is the author of *New and Improved: The Transformation of American Women's Emotional Culture*, and *Free Love: Marriage and Middle-Class Radicalism in America, 1825–1860*.

# YOUTH AND SEXUALITY IN THE TWENTIETH-CENTURY UNITED STATES

*John C. Spurlock*

Routledge
Taylor & Francis Group

NEW YORK AND LONDON

First published 2016
by Routledge
711 Third Avenue, New York, NY 10017

and by Routledge
2 Park Square, Milton Park, Abingdon, Oxon OX14 4RN

*Routledge is an imprint of the Taylor & Francis Group, an informa business*

*Library of Congress Cataloging-in-Publication Data*
Spurlock, John C., 1954–
    Youth and sexuality in the twentieth-century United States / John C.
Spurlock. — 1 Edition.
        pages cm
    Includes bibliographical references and index.
    1. Youth—United States—Sexual behavior.    2. Sex customs—United
States—History—21st century.    3. Youth—Psychology.    I. Title.
    HQ796.S685 2015
    306.70835—dc23
    2015003908

ISBN: 978-1-138-81748-7 (hbk)
ISBN: 978-1-138-81749-4 (pbk)
ISBN: 978-1-315-74559-6 (ebk)


Typeset in Bembo
by Apex CoVantage, LLC

For Ruth and Esther

# CONTENTS

# ACKNOWLEDGMENTS

Over the many years that this book has taken shape I have benefited from the encouragement of friends and colleagues. Some of my earliest discussions took place with James W. Reed and Susan Ferentinos. Many colleagues read portions of this work and returned valuable insights, including David del Mar, Lizzie Reis, Robert Johnston, Lia Paradis, Adrian Perez Melgosa, Jennifer Halpern, Judith Garcia Quismondo, Lara Kelland, and Rebecca Davis. Tracey Laszloffy and Rebecca Harvey offered insights from their work in family therapy. I had the privilege of writing several articles for an encyclopedia edited by James T. Sears. His steady engagement with me helped move me toward a broader understanding of adolescent sexualities.

Seton Hill University (SHU) supported my work with a sabbatical leave and funding for travel. That support came along with encouragement from the academic dean and provost, Mary Ann Gawelek, and the chair of the Humanities Division, Michael Arnzen. Seton Hill University library provided a steady stream of interlibrary loan items thanks to Judith Koveleskie and Eileen Moffa, among others. Bill Black helped me find my way around the SHU archives.

The Schlesinger Library and the Radcliffe Institute for Advanced study supported my work with travel and research grants in 2002 and 2010, and the Smith College archives supported my work with a travel and research grant in 2010.

Many of the ideas for this book took shape during my semester teaching at the University of Montenegro, Filozofksi Fakultet. During that time, and consistently since then, Janko Andrijasević, has taken a supportive interest in my work. I have also benefited from my return trips to Montenegro, where I have presented some of the concepts in this work at the Anglo-American Studies Conference, chaired by Marija Krivokapić. At Routledge I was fortunate to have a supportive editor and editorial assistant in Kimberly Guinta and Genevieve

Aoki, respectively. The anonymous reviewers for Routledge gave thorough and highly useful assessments of the entire manuscript.

Michael Sims has taken time to read portions of this work and has also given me a forum for my ideas and my reflections on the process of writing. Students who have taken courses with me on Sex in America and Modern Love have added to the stream of discussion. Michael Ballew and Paul Spurlock helped make available photos for the book from the family archive.

Other help and encouragement is harder to classify but still vital. In this regard I want to especially mention Zhiping Mi. My daughters, Ruth and Esther, have been my most enthusiastic supporters, although they also probably worried that this book would be finished while they were still adolescents.

# ILLUSTRATIONS

# INTRODUCTION

Adults in the 1920s who worried about the exploits of "flaming youth" would have felt reassured by acquaintance with Yvonne Blue and Lucille Lowder, born in 1911 and 1912, respectively. Yvonne grew up in middle-class Chicago. Lucille lived a few hundred miles away but in another world, on a homestead in Colorado. For both girls, however, school, church, and girlfriends (and, in Lucille's case, farm chores) took up most of their time. Yvonne had only girls as guests at her 13th birthday party. She and her two best girlfriends planned to form a literary club (which they later changed to a pirate club). For Lucille, girlfriends also mattered. As the youngest rider on her school bus, she sat in the small seat next to the driver. "Margaret Sears and her brothers and sisters, and Gilbert Downing . . . started going to our school," Lucille recalled in a reflection written late in life. "Margaret and Gilbert had a daily fight over who was going to sit next to me. She usually won." In fact, Margaret and Lucille would become lifelong friends, remaining in touch into old age even though usually separated by huge distances. For both Lucille and Yvonne, their early teenage years seemed to be shaped more by an older tradition of romantic friendships among girls and young women than by the contemporary "revolt of modern youth."[1]

Yvonne and Lucille lived during a time of rapid change in American social life and a still more rapid change in the sexuality of young Americans. Both girls sensed these shifts. Yvonne wrote about friends of hers who were "loud and boy-crazy" or even so consumed with the topic of boys as to be "perverted." She recounted that when walking to school one day along with one of her boy-crazy friends, "millions of boys yelled 'Hi Teddy!'" while they ignored Yvonne. Lucille, for her part, recalled a fifteen-year-old who "was madly in love with a cowboy, and got pregnant." She went away to a pregnancy home to have the baby, and when she returned had to live with her father. Both Lucille and Yvonne would go on to have boyfriends and date for a few years before they met the men who would become their husbands.[2]

The experiences of Yvonne and Lucille point toward one of the major transitions in youthful sexuality in the twentieth century. During the early decades of the century, girls and boys tended to form early emotional attachments to same-sex friends. The heterosexual play that became an ever more pervasive feature of adolescent life generally arrived later. The early and persistent heterosexual interests of young people that we assume as normal (or at least normative) today only appeared after a decades-long shift during the early twentieth century, from a world dominated by family and homosocial relations to one of heterosexual conviviality largely removed from family oversight.

This study began at the end of the twentieth century. During work on an earlier book, I became fascinated with the way high school girls wrote about their experiences of social life at high school and their growing sense of themselves as sexual beings. To better understand the lives of girls and boys in this period, I found that I had to search both backward and forward to explain the shifts in sexual awareness and experience for youth in the early twentieth century. The result is a hybrid of historical scholarship. Like a work of historical synthesis, in this book, I offer a periodization for the century as a whole, and I attempt to draw in the best scholarship for each period.[3] My references, and in many cases my text, point to the outstanding work of historians of sexuality.

What follows, however, is not primarily a synthesis of the work of others. I have tried to find my own way and to think through the issues that I've identified in the self-writing and in the sexual studies from the last century. Consequently, the claims that I make shape this work as they would in a more narrowly focused monograph. Taking an approach that is both wide-ranging and thesis-driven has enabled me to follow my insights into the lives of American youth over longer periods and to see how the structure of sexuality shifted throughout the century. The themes that I pursue in these chapters may come with an emphasis that sets them apart—slightly in some cases, more dramatically in others—from the work of my colleagues in this field.

As the twentieth century opened, a new form of heterosexual conviviality had already exploded onto the streets of the urban centers across the United States. Working-class youth used their spare income to seek recreation in amusement parks, movie theaters, and dance halls and created the wild new fad known as the "date." By the second or third decade of the century, middle-class youth had begun to assimilate the same practice. Underlying this new, public heterosociality, however, was a persistent homosociality that in some ways made the former possible. By the time of the Great Depression, both the new heterosociality and the parallel homosocial networks declined in favor of longer-term heterosexual companionships. "Going steady," or steady dating, replaced the ephemeral relations typical of the date.

Popular memory views the decades after mid-century as a time of sexual revolution. In my reading, however, adolescent sexuality had already settled into a very durable pattern. With the weeks- or years-long steady relations, youthful Americans improvised a new kind of transitional sexuality, something I have compared to companionate marriage. Boys and girls spent more and more time together, and some of that time they turned over to sex play. In this game girls gave more physical intimacy in exchange for greater emotional intimacy from their boyfriends. This quid pro quo would eventually become the typical way that girls, and to a lesser extent boys, became sexually active in the United States. Even with the decline of some of the rituals of "going steady" (along with the disappearance of the term), the practice has proved extremely stable. It still shapes adolescent socializing today.

## Voices and Evidence

Studies of sexuality had already begun before the twentieth century opened, and they continued to grow in number and sophistication as the century proceeded. Analysis of these studies has made them even more interesting and useful, by allowing historians to employ them while fully aware of the ideas and assumptions that shaped them. Studies of youthful sexuality began by the 1920s, with 249 by 1933.[4] In what follows these serve as useful guides to many of the social scripts elaborated among the young. Sexual research served a variety of agendas. But as this work grew, it also became more rigorous within the context of social science, and grew more valuable by offering multiple insights into the lives of the young. No study emerges here as containing a central "truth" of adolescent sexuality. Reported statistical percentages serve first as good estimates, then become better estimates only with corroboration. Still, sexual science offers fundamental insights that shape the later chapters of this book.

The chapters that follow include a variety of accounts that come as directly as possible from young people themselves, including oral histories and diaries. This can never offer the same kind of knowledge that surveys of large groups can. The most common diary writers are middle-class girls and young women. But their words offer texture to our understanding of how abstract social trends played out within real lives. The voices of girls and young women are particularly helpful. They not only participated in the changes of this period, in some ways they were the change. What seemed like a sudden realization in the 1920s that youth had shifted away from courtship toward a more convivial, lighthearted approach to lovemaking came when "fresh-faced" and "respectable" adolescent girls and young women began to allow new, and often very public, forms of intimacy. The news of a sexual revolution in the 1960s came not with reports that boys had changed their willingness to have sex before marriage but that girls had.

Personal writings also help overcome some blind spots in the social science literature. Even in the period following Alfred Kinsey's mid-century publications, homosexual male and female experiences only slowly found a place in research on youth. Oral histories have to some degree allowed historians to regain these voices of youthful sexuality. Similarly, homosociality, after a few important studies in the 1920s, dropped off the agenda of social research on youth.[5] Diaries, however, show that girls continued to feel drawn to other girls throughout the 1920s and 1930s and that the attenuation of homosocial relations followed later shifts in heterosexual conviviality.

This book seeks to provide as broad an understanding of youthful sexuality as possible. But, it rests on sources that are overwhelmingly white and middle-class, mainly northern and urban, and this is true for both the personal writings and the social science literature. Some of the experiences of the young might qualify as common or unifying. Education, urbanization, and social mobility all tended to draw young people into a national youth culture. Marketing, from at least the 1940s, also treated youth (teenagers) as a homogeneous group, and so contributed to the breakdown in differences.[6] Still, these trends moved slowly and imperfectly during the century. Divisions and diversity have remained. Whenever possible, I include studies or voices from beyond these limitations.

## Adolescence and Youth

For the great majority of American children, biological adolescence takes place between ages 10 and 20. The physical changes for boys and girls at puberty— the maturation of the testes and the ovaries—with their associated hormonal changes seem like obvious signals for the beginning of adolescent lives. Sexual feelings and sex play can begin earlier than puberty or much later, but puberty remains the most common starting point for sexual sensations. Yet many more changes than just hormones come into play. Masturbation usually begins about this time for boys. For most children, as they pass puberty, sex play becomes more typical, more common, and more intense.

I use the term *youth* alongside *adolescence* in this work not so much to set the boundaries for this study as to indicate the blurriness of those boundaries. Until the twentieth century, youth was defined more by its end marker—marriage and (for men at least) independent work. Childhood and youth had no commonly accepted boundary, except perhaps in religious traditions with a confirmation or coming-of-age ritual. Most older children became full-time workers while still living at home. Even for middle-class boys, the end of formal schooling might come relatively early, replaced with a position as a clerk. College education could begin in the middle-teen years for a boy who had excelled in his studies.

In the twentieth century, however, the beginning of "youth" came to depend more and more on institutional definitions. As age-graded schooling became the standard in urban areas in the late nineteenth century, ever-larger portions of American children experienced an important transition sometime around age 12 when state laws ended mandatory schooling. Age grading meant that most children either ended their school years at age 12 or moved into a distinct, higher level of education. The use of the term *teenager* came to be associated with a new phase of development. High school education became common for American youth in the decades after the turn of the twentieth century, first for girls and then for boys. But only in the years following the beginning of the Great Depression did a majority of American teenagers have at least some high school education.

Schooling, and changes in state laws and the economy that limited employment for children, gave adolescence and youth a much clearer beginning point. But these shifts also blurred the end point. The experience of adolescence can extend well beyond the high school years. Even though college-age youth usually have the status of young adults, they also retain many of the characteristics of adolescence. For middle-class youth, the college years extend their dependence on family resources and delay their full participation in work and family formation. On the other hand, college students frequently live semi-independently in college housing. As far as sexual issues go, college often extends the practices that young people have experienced in high school. For the middle class, college often serves as the finishing school of adolescence. For this work, I have set the end boundary of youth at the point where individuals take on adult roles such as marriage and parenthood or living and working independently.

Even if we think of adolescence as containing biological or psychological imperatives that will play out in any setting, it should also be evident that youth requires the mastery of a range of social roles.[7] We see this most clearly among self-aware young people consciously assessing who they are and how they relate to other young people. So, for instance, a novel from the 1920s shows the protagonist observing others and testing himself in the fluid relations that he experiences as he grows up. A half-century later Rachel Rafael reviews relations with girlfriends, parents, and boys in the pages of her diaries, struggling to understand the interplay of role, status, and desire.[8] Adolescence requires the assimilation and mastery of particular scripts that will serve the individual through high school and college and beyond.

## Sexuality

Adolescent sexuality comprises all the ways that youth learn to play with one another within the context of the newly awakened desire that follows puberty and within the new social settings elaborated by older children. Especially in early adolescence, sex play probably has more to do with play than with sex. As boys and girls move out of their same-sex groups and begin to socialize in mixed sex groups and then to form couples, new demands accumulate about how to act. Prudence, discussing her teenaged peers with a graduate student in the 1940s, complained that "some of the high school boys act so childish when you go out for a date." In front of their friends, the boys cut up and make their dates feel uncomfortable. Prudence concluded that "the fellows ought to know how to act." Yet the boys, just like Prudence, were trying out scripts. As Prudence practiced heterosexual socializing, the boys tested how in public settings they might communicate to friends their loyalty to their same-gender peers.[9]

During adolescence, play with others can unexpectedly fill with novel sensations. One girl, a late bloomer in comparison to many of her peers in the 1920s, was already in college when she wrote of "longing for the sheer physical excitement" she now associated with "crude, primitive love-making." Yet Marion Taylor's awakening desire had to match her understanding and mastery of scripts that helped her relate to, and enjoy, the company of college boys. Although she felt a bit foolish about it, she admitted to her diary, "I am learning to 'jolly' and 'small talk,' to 'flirt' in an embryonic, amateurish sort of way!"[10] Much of the painful review and acquisition of social skills comes through discussion with peers—close friends who provide counsel and support and sometimes insight into how to conduct one's self. Another important contribution to conviviality is social learning—watching others, imitating them, learning from their example. In all these ways, sexuality does not merely arrive at puberty. Young people learn sexuality as well as acquire it from their hormones.

Even as they experience physical changes, adolescents have to learn adolescence. The chapters that follow try to make sense of this new world of youth. Already at the outset we see working-class youth shaping new social scripts around the practice of dating, and making some types of sexual practices—kissing, fondling—more common and more public. Dating, in turn, will be adapted and elaborated as middle-class youth practice it and as more years in youth are devoted to schooling. The period of greatest improvisation comes early in the century. By mid-century, most of the scripts of adolescent sexuality will be well established and widely understood. Adolescents later in the century seem more intent on accommodating new possibilities to existing scripts than to creating new ones.

## Homosociality

The kind of social learning that allows the young to gain a sense of self and to negotiate their social setting often takes place in groups. The opinions and responses of peers always carry great weight and perhaps even greater weight for adolescents who face new, insistent challenges. For some the attitudes of friends have far more impact than does information from any other source. Children readily play with anyone available, but they tend to cluster into single-sex groups. For American children today, beginning at about puberty, single-sex groups have less dominance and mixed groups become common and even typical. Yet even with this shift toward mixed-sex socializing, same-gender peers still provide the most important role models for teenagers, and often give them information with the highest value for the individual. Status usually comes from the judgment of one's same-sex peers.

Homosociality refers to relations among same-sex peers and to same-sex friendships that may have deep emotional meaning for the friends. Even casual observers of the young will be familiar with these kinds of friendships and group relations, and most of us will recall how much our high school and college friendships meant to us. Within the context of social changes taking place during the twentieth century, homosociality has played a vital role in the development of adolescent sexuality. In the nineteenth century, Americans of all classes tended to segregate themselves by gender. In the twentieth century, sorting by gender declined, perhaps more for youth than for younger or older people. Among the most dramatic changes for adolescent sexuality has been the shift from reliance on same-sex peers to socializing in mixed groups. Similarly, the value of same-sex friendships as sources of emotional meaning and support declined in the twentieth century.

The attenuation of homosocial relations and networks has shaped the organization of adolescent sexuality. As we shall see, adolescents early in the twentieth century frequently, perhaps typically, resorted to same-sex peers to understand the new world of desire they found themselves drawn toward. In many cases, these friendships continued to provide the most important connections for young people until almost the end of youth. These homosocial relations were taken for granted even by social scientists of the early twentieth century who still warned against warm friendships that lasted too long (how long remained a question). But for most youth, same-sex peers provided the support and comfort that enabled them to manage the new desires and emotions, and the new social demands, of adolescence. Sometimes these friends were the first lovers, allowing for exploration of desire.

As the century moved on, friendships remained but their role and importance declined. Boys and girls had to take on new social roles and meet the challenges of heterosexuality earlier in their teenaged years. Beginning by the 1930s, same-sex friendships lost time and intensity to mixed-group socializing and to heterosexual relations that looked more and more like engagements or even temporary marriages.

## Sexual Marginalization

The homosocial relations that flourished until the 1930s gave greater space for the young to explore their sexuality without the demands of heterosexual performance. During the period when dating in its "classic" form held sway for middle-class youth, many adolescents fell outside the circle of popularity and thus dated little. For some, this was a hardship as they yearned for a better social life. But for girls attracted to girls, or boys to boys, this offered a grace period when they could spend time with desired peers. Even physical expressiveness remained possible and perhaps even relatively common as boys and girls learned the roles available to desire.

By the 1930s, dating as it had developed in the early twentieth century had declined and would disappear by mid-century. The shift toward long-term heterosexual relations appears to have changed the lives of youth whose sexuality would not fit into the heterosexual mold. Heterosexual couples not only became the social standard, they became the norm. Most high school students went steady. Students without a steady partner became socially marginalized. This put pressure on youth who preferred the company of same-sex peers. Harry Beckner recalls growing up in Nebraska in the 1940s and 1950s: "In high school you had to fit the mode or you were queer, so I played the straight line. But I wasn't interested in girls."[11] Gay youth either found ways to mimic the heterosexual couple formula, or else they had to accept a marginal role in the social life of their schools and communities.

I use terms such as *marginalized* in the work that follows as carefully as possible. The social scripts created for adolescent sexuality in the twentieth century actively excluded some kinds of relations among same-sex youth. I have attempted to draw in the stories of gay, lesbian, and other youth who do not fit neatly into the roles assigned by heterosexual conviviality. My terminology will fall short in some cases, because it cannot reflect the variety of sexualities that makes up the life of youth.[12]

## Disordered Desire

Michael Kimmel has shown that into the twenty-first century, manhood is a performance for the sake of other men.[13] As Harry Beckner and others recalled from their youth in early- and mid-twentieth-century America, for a boy, the worst slur was to be called "queer." This might have nothing to do with sexual orientation. Rather, the term gave a judgment on masculinity—a boy's ability to compete with other boys in ways that were often crude and physical. For girls, however, gaining the reputation of being a "slut" carried a far different weight. Girls might be assigned this reputation from having larger breasts or sharper tongues than other girls had; they may have fooled around with someone's boyfriend at a party. Or, they might simply have been new in town. Once assigned, the role carried with it the presumption of disordered desire—someone whose sexuality had no boundaries, who would do what other girls would not, and who would use their sexuality to steal the boyfriends of other girls.

The couple system may have shaped the belief in the slut. When dating prevailed, girls competed for dates. But only the most popular girls dated consistently—most girls had to expect to be left out. As steady dating became more popular, fewer girls were on the outside, but their status required the fidelity of their boyfriends. Any girl who seemed capable of violating the boundaries of the couple system became a threat to all other girls.

The slut belief system carried on, and even amplified, the sexual double standard. It also retains within it the weight of a class standard. Earlier in the century, boys often expected girls of a lower economic class to provide more sexual favors. As one young man put it bluntly in the late 1940s, "It is all right for a boy to go as far as he wants, but not with the girl he is to marry or with a girl in his own class."[14] The sexual double standard, then, also existed as a class double standard. Even though by mid-century, class differences in sexual experience had narrowed, the role of the slut remained.

## Sexual Violence

Adults presume the innocence of the young—innocence in the sense that sexual acts are new for children and that they discover sexual pleasure as much from awkward curiosity as from desire. For many children, however, sexual knowledge begins when they are used as objects of adult desire. From early in the twentieth century, physicians and the new experts in social science identified statutory rape and incest as problems of poverty and ethnicity. Although anecdotal evidence still linked sexual violence and other social ills, the same evidence seemed to cordon off middle-class children from the possibility of such acts. Until after the middle of the twentieth century, sexual science offered no guide to the prevalence of rape and incest. The only exception was the work by Kinsey, which still fell short of revealing much about sexual debut that was not consensual. Until feminist social scientists in the 1960s and later began to study the roles of coercion in sexuality, incest and rape remained unspeakable acts, matters for criminal courts but unrelated to "normal" life. These were seen as rare in general and were considered almost entirely alien to white and middle-class families.

As a consequence of this willful ignorance, the impact of sexual violence on the shape or organization of adolescent sexuality never becomes apparent. Even now there are no firm statistics on the topic, although a reasonable, even conservative conclusion from work in the last decades of the twentieth century would be 10 percent of adolescents (a higher percentage for girls, lower for boys) have begun sex lives without consent. Even today the personal meaning of these experiences remains in question. Psychologists have for decades identified incest and childhood rape with difficulties in forming sexual relations. Girls may become heedless of their reputations and use sex as a tool, without regard to their own desires. "Basically," recalled one girl writing in the 1990s, "everyone was a one-nighter, even if we fucked several different times, because I didn't have a clue about how to start a friendship when the booze wore off." Or, in some cases, girls can only associate sex with the abuse. Another girl, molested as a child, discovered time and again that as she became physically expressive with boys: "I would freak out. See his [the molester's] face, smell him like it was totally happening again."[15]

Evaluating the role of sexual violence on the organization of adolescent sexuality must remain speculative. In what follows I have raised the issue of sexual violence and the state of understanding of it in the period covered in various chapters. I have also made some suggestions about the way a group of adolescents dealing secretly with sexual trauma might respond to the sexual culture in their high schools, and in turn influence that organization.

The topics presented earlier serve as a guide to what follows. I try to pull these into a coherent narrative about youthful sexuality in the United States. At times the themes will flow together, at other times remain distinct and related only by proximity. In historical terms, the last century is close to us, just as adolescence will seem like a recent adventure to some readers. But even the recent past of adolescence and the twentieth century still demand all our skills of analysis and our historical imagination.

## Notes

1. Yvonne Skinner, "Papers of Yvonne Blue Skinner," n.d., MC459 M-26, Schlesinger Library, Radcliffe Institute for Advanced Study, Harvard University, May 10, 1924; Lucille (Lowder) Spurlock, "My Story," typescript, n.d., personal collection of the author, 24. The terms that appear in quotes in this paragraph were both well known and widely used during the 1920s, both taken from the titles of best-selling books of the period. Warner Fabian, *Flaming Youth* (New York: Boni and Liveright, 1923); and Ben B. Lindsey and Wainwright Evans, *The Revolt of Modern Youth* (New York: Boni and Liveright, 1925).

2. Skinner, July 17, August 4, 1926, February 4, 1927; Lowder, "My Story," 25. In Yvonne's case, her future husband was the behavioral psychologist B. F. Skinner. Lucille married Lawton Spurlock in 1941.

3. The most powerful work on the theory of sexuality has flowed from the insights of Michel Foucault, *The History of Sexuality. Volume 1, an Introduction* (New York: Vintage, 1990). His work has raised many questions for historical inquiry into sexuality. Jennifer Terry, *An American Obsession: Science, Medicine, and Homosexuality in Modern Society* (Chicago: University of Chicago Press, 1999) provides one of the best examples of the study of sexuality within a Foucauldian framework.

4. Steven Mintz, *Huck's Raft: A History of American Childhood* (Cambridge, MA: Belknap, 2006), 223. Historical work on the study of sexuality include Julia A. Ericksen, *Kiss and Tell: Surveying Sex in the Twentieth Century* (Cambridge, MA: Harvard University Press, 1999); and Vern L Bullough, *Science in the Bedroom: A History of Sex Research* (New York: Basic Books, 1994).

5. John C. Spurlock, "From Reassurance to Irrelevance: Adolescent Psychology and Homosexuality in America," *History of Psychology* 5 (February 2002): 38–51.

6. Susan Maria Ferentinos, "An Unpredictable Age Sex, Consumption, and the Emergence of the American Teenager, 1900–1950" (PhD diss., Indiana University, 2005), http://wwwlib.umi.com/dissertations/fullcit/3204295.

7. Social script theory has had an important impact on my thinking about sexuality and on the ways I have developed this current study. The introduction by Edward Laumann (and others), in *The Social Organization of Sexuality : Sexual Practices in the United States*, paperback ed. (Chicago: University of Chicago Press, 2000) is one recent discussion of the application of social script theory to the study of sexuality. Adna Marion LeCount, "A Study of Certain Boy-girl Relationships in a Group of High School Seniors" (EdD project, Teachers College, Columbia University, 1950), 275.

8. Rachel Rafael's experiences are examined in Chapter 4. The novel I refer to is discussed in Chapter 2: Robert Carr, *The Rampant Age* (Garden City, NY: Doubleday, Doran and Co., 1928).

9. Opal Wolford, "The Dating Behavior and the Personal and Family Relationships of High School Seniors with Implications for Family Life Education" (PhD diss., Cornell University, 1948).

10. Marion Taylor, "The Papers of Dorothy Sherman Pencharz," Diaries, Schlesinger Library, Radcliffe Institute, Harvard University, Cambridge, MA.

11. Will Fellows, ed., *Farm Boys: Lives of Gay Men from the Rural Midwest* (Madison: University of Wisconsin Press, 1996), 72.

12. In her introduction, Susan Maria Ferentinos, *Interpreting LGBT History* (Lanham, MD: Rowman & Littlefield, 2015) offers a valuable discussion and guide to the difficulties of terminology in capturing the experience of youth outside of a heteronormative context.

13. Michael S Kimmel, *Guyland: The Perilous World Where Boys Become Men* (New York: Harper, 2008).

14. Winston Ehrmann, *Premarital Dating Behavior* (New York: Henry Holt, 1959), 275.

15. The two quotes come from the Girl Zines collection, Sophia Smith Special Collections, Smith College, box 1: Abuse, issue #3, 40–41: "Scream of Love," by Violet I.; Aphrodite's Trousers, issue #2, essay by Claire.

# 1

# WORK, PLAY, AND SEX PLAY

BLINKER:    Where do you see these—these men? At your home?
FLORENCE:   Of course not. I meet them just as I did you. Sometimes on the boat,
            sometimes in the park, sometimes on the street.
BLINKER:    Do you allow them [to kiss you]?
FLORENCE:   Some. Not many. They won't take you out anywhere unless you do.
BLINKER:    Why don't you entertain your company in the house where you
            live?
FLORENCE:   If you could see the place where I live you wouldn't ask that.
                                                *O'Henry, "Brickdust Row" (1906)*

Blinker, in O'Henry's story, represents the adult world that dimly but inevitably recognizes that a new sexuality has taken shape among urban young people. Florence takes a certain delight in shocking him, telling him that she goes out unaccompanied and intends to meet men when she does; she expects men to treat her, and she makes her own decisions about kissing them as repayment. In a few words, and without any sense of shame, she describes the new rituals of heterosexual "dating" and "treating," both considered provocative and morally tainted practices by middle-class adults. American youth, in a single generation, elaborated a new, distinctive heterosexuality. Youthful sexuality changed in profound ways more than once during the twentieth century, but the most rapid and profound transformations came during the half-century after 1900. We can quickly gain a sense of how much changed, and how rapidly, by a short examination of the lives of two young women living in the 1890s.

Rahel Golub left that Russian Pale of Settlement in 1892, at age 12, to join her father in America. She worked at one sweatshop after another to supplement their savings so that the whole family could be reunited on the Lower East Side in New York City. The work affected her health. Often sick, she became an object of concern for her family. A neighbor in their tenement suggested she had a cure for Rahel's persistent illness. Not long after this her mother sent her on the usual shopping errands but had her go out of her way to buy sugar at a shop she had not visited before. Two days later, her mother asked her, "Well, what do you think of that young man?" Rahel had hardly noticed the youth who had handed over the sack of sugar.

That Saturday she saw the young man, Israel, for the second time in her life when he came to her home with his uncle. "I shrank behind my mother and a cousin," Rahel recalled. Once past the formal introductions, everyone sat down, with her father and the boy's uncle sitting across from one another "and at once began a lively conversation to which the rest of us sat and listened respectfully." As the conversation continued, and the uncle raised the issue of making a match, Israel asked Rahel to go for a walk. Observing him, she thought, "It seemed quite natural that he should sit with his neck shrunk into his collar and keep his hat on like the two older men and be quite as old-fashioned as they were." Once outside on their walk, Israel seemed pleasant enough. Two days later the uncle sent a message saying that his family was prepared to make an "alliance." A match-maker followed this message, and soon an engagement ceremony.[1]

The experiences of another girl a few years later, far to the west of the Lower East Side, offered a startling contrast to Rahel's courtship. Blanche Drew and her cousin Suzanne caused a stir among the young men of Ethel, Missouri, during Blanche's visit there. They vied to spend time with the cousins at Suzanne's house, with as many as eight young men there at one time. Blanche and Suzanne, of course, loved all the attention. But Suzanne's mother had a different sense of how the girls managed their social lives. She complained to Blanche's stepmother that she was at a loss to know what to do. "Every night she and Suzanne have the parlor full of company—I really don't know how to keep track of all the boys they entertain—I am at my wit's end to know what to do."[2]

Blanche and Rahel lived in different worlds, even if those worlds were contained in the same nation. Neither girl could have changed places with the other one. And their experiences of boys seemed completely unrelated. Blanche would have protested an arranged marriage, even if her family could have conceived of such an idea. Rahel's family would never have permitted an unfamiliar boy to pay a visit, even if their tiny flat could have accommodated it. Yet both girls participated in courtship rituals with many common features. Boys came to the girls' homes, where family and friends could watch over the couple and provide opinions as needed, or even if not needed. Although Blanche's aunt felt that she had lost control over her niece's social life, she still knew all about Blanche's activities and had at least the possibility of seeing and meeting all the boys who came to visit her home. Traditional courtship took place in the home, with family either involved or nearby.

Yet in spite of its pervasiveness, family-centered courtship had already begun to disappear by the time Rahel's family settled in America. The change happened most dramatically in Rahel's world. Girls began to resist and reject the marriages arranged by family and neighbors—as Rahel eventually did herself. Along with arranged marriage, the practice of chaperonage and domestic courtship also collapsed as older boys and girls began to meet outside their families' homes to play together in new ways. These new, improvised practices responded to the same shifts in American society that distinguished one segment of childhood as adolescence. Adolescence first became visible in American society as the problem of delinquent boys. Adolescent sexuality also made its appearance as a problem, but as a girl problem.

## Youth, Work, Family

"There are many city neighborhoods," Jane Addams wrote in 1909, "in which practically every young person who has attained the age of fourteen years enters a factory."[3] She wrote at a time when almost 2 million 10- to 15-year-olds worked in the nonfarm sector. In the late nineteenth century, everywhere in the United States, children followed their parents into the kitchens and fields of family farms or into factories, cutting rooms, and even mines to work alongside parents. But when the girl or the boy became a full-time seamstress, factory hand, or apprentice, the child became a contributor to the family income and took her or his place in the family strategy for survival. The child became a young man or woman, a youth, someone with a path to becoming an adult with at least nominal independence. Only a tiny fraction of American young people, mainly middle- and upper-class boys and girls, could ignore the need to earn wages. For the great majority of Americans, work was the common experience of youth.[4]

Even for younger children, wage labor could take a large share of the week. A chart of recommended limits on child employment from the beginning of the twentieth century suggested no more than 15 hours of work per week for eight- to nine-year-olds. The streets of every large city teemed with children peddling wares and with newsies hawking the latest edition of competing dailies. "Their very number makes one stand aghast," wrote children's advocate Jacob Riis. After child labor laws set limits on the ages of young workers in the 1890s, Riis found on his tour of sweatshops that many children as young as 12 automatically said they were 14 or 15, sometimes even unasked, to avoid legal complications. Boys not only hawked papers but "shined," ran errands, worked as printers' devils, and took on every occupation their size allowed. Girls worked in factories, managed pushcarts, or, if needed, watched even younger children so their mothers could work. As late as the 1930s, investigators interviewing girls in the Massachusetts reformatory found that they had "entered gainful employment" at a mean age of 14.9 yrs.[5]

Although reformers in the Progressive Era lamented the hollow looks of girl seamstresses in New York's garment factories and the breaker boys in Pennsylvania's anthracite mines, rural children also began work on the family farm as soon as they could help. M. D. Rice, in Georgia, went to work as a child. "I 'member I was allus strong for a kid and laid off corn ground for Daddy when I wasn't but twelve years old. . . . Wasn't long atter that I was doin' a man's work 'long with Daddy." Poor southerners shared poverty and backbreaking work in common even if race divided them. A researcher among black sharecroppers in rural Mississippi described one who began "slopping hogs—at the age of 7. Then he learned to cut wood for the stove, and later to milk the cows and feed the mules. At 12 his father and older brother taught him how to plow, but he was 15 before he had full responsibility as a plow hand." Rural poverty and the hardships of farm life, whether in Galician shtetls or villages on the Middle Border, continued to drive families off the land. Sharecroppers in North Carolina, unable to scrape a living from the soil and caught between landlords and furnishing merchants, entered the textile mills springing up across the New South. For much the same reasons, French Canadians crossed into New England to work in New Hampshire's Amoskeag mill.[6]

Labor for children began early in their lives and seemingly consumed their youth. Yet their work rarely took them far from home. The example of farm children is the clearest and least surprising. Work meant work around the house, in the kitchen and garden, and eventually (for the boys) in the fields with fathers, brothers, kin, and neighbors. Yet work in cities and village factories also took place in familiar surroundings. Rahel Golub, as a 12-year-old seamstress, earned her first sweatshop wages with her father. When she found other work, she never had to stray far from her neighborhood and, in fact, only went to a distant part of the city later when her health forced her to enter a hospital. One of Riis's photos shows a family of Bohemian cigar makers—a mother, a father, and a child—all working together in the family's tiny tenement room, with another young child nearby. Children who worked in the streets usually worked on their own street, or nearby, and they ran with crowds of children who were siblings or neighbors. David Nasaw's list of well-known people who worked as newsies in early-twentieth-century New York included the Marx brothers and the Warner brothers.[7]

Just as the family provided the context for work, the movement from childhood to youth to adulthood operated through the interplay of family and work. Youth began, with no set boundary, as the child began to contribute to the family income from his or her meager wages and probably left school to make more time for work. Children and youth continued to live at home and only left to establish their own households, typically in their late teens to mid-20s.[8]

## Bad Boys and Adolescents

As the twentieth century dawned, however, urban youth began to push beyond this world bound by family, neighborhood, and work. The rapid industrialization of the United States following the Civil War transformed the countryside along with the cities. But the cities rapidly gained on rural areas in population as immigrants arrived and often settled in their search for work. H. W. Lytle and John Dillon's pre–World War I tract on white slavery played on the theme of innocent young women, new arrivals to the city, taken into the whirl of social life in the big city and suddenly losing themselves without kin or real friends to protect them. These youth might arrive from the countryside, where Blanche and Suzanne lived or the one where Rahel was born. In the decades leading up to World War I, 18 million immigrants arrived in the United States and settled overwhelmingly in America's industrial cities. Urban life became more crowded and more diverse. And as families either arrived or grew rapidly, urban life also became much younger.[9]

Children living in the cities were visible not just to curious reformers, reporters, and social workers who searched them out in their workplaces. Children spent a lot of time on the streets, playing, working, and finding mischief. Older children who worked for wages, after making contributions to the family fund, had income enough to escape the crowded apartments where family members and boarders lived and to partake of whatever excitement they could find on the sidewalks of New York or Chicago. "They demand pleasure," Jane Addams wrote of these youth, "as the right of one who earns his own living."[10]

However natural or predictable the youthful fascination with excitement might seem in retrospect, in the late nineteenth century, middle-class city dwellers reacted with suspicion and concern. Youth became visible as a problem. In 1904 G. Stanley Hall would make *adolescence* the standard term in social science, and ultimately in general usage, for late childhood. Adolescence, Hall wrote, was a "new birth," marked by rapid growth, restless energy, and awkwardness. He also joined the new term to the search for excitement and trouble. Among other animal species, he wrote, youth "is the age when males engage in conflicts for females and develop organs of combat . . ." Among human creatures, the restlessness and combativeness of this period led to social problems: "adolescence is preeminently the criminal age."[11]

If the new criminal class belonged to a certain age range, it also belonged almost exclusively to one gender. Adolescents were boys "overborne by their own undirected and misguided energies," Jane Addams wrote in 1909. As the paragraph continues, she refers only to boys with their "obstreperousness," their "impulsive misdeeds," their "appetites." She catalogued the trouble boys found as they "followed their vagrant wills unhindered:" setting fires, stealing, throwing stones at trains, loafing on the docks, petty larceny (like cutting telephone wires under a sidewalk and selling them), "'wandering spells,'" carrying and using guns, taking cocaine, playing tricks. Harpo Marx recalled of his early-twentieth-century boyhood that "[i]ndividually and in gangs we accounted for most of the petty thievery and destruction of property on the upper East Side."[12]

The category that applied most generally to "boy crimes" was "incorrigibility," and might include fighting, begging, gambling, or even loafing. "When the child ceases to be a source of income because he will not work and has to be supported," wrote Jacob Riis, the "father surrenders him as a truant and incorrigible." One mother took her son to court on this charge because he continued to play dice, smoke, and keep bad company.[13] By the late nineteenth century, for a growing portion of Americans, the sight of boys together—urban working-class boys—signaled trouble. When they gathered with other boys, young males in the city seemed only a bad inspiration away from criminal offense. Bad boys—delinquent, mischievous, high-spirited, even criminal—called attention to the teenage years as a distinct phase in human life. By 1900 a whole profession of child savers had arisen to intervene in the lives of young people. Beginning with Illinois in 1899 a separate court system tried to deal with problem youth, and youth organizations and summer camps were opened to ameliorate the urban environment that seemed to wear down the spirits and health of children.[14] Hall's 1904 work marked the beginning for social science of identifying youth as a developmental stage with distinctive issues. But it also marked the end of the obsession with bad boys. By the time Hall's work appeared, girls seemed much more of a problem than boys did.

## The Girl Problem

Girls together never carried the promise of trouble the way a gathering of boys could. One early criminologist stated flatly that women "are less criminal than men . . ." "As these overworked girls stream along the street," Jane Addams wrote, we "see only the self-conscious walk, the giggling speech, the preposterous clothing." From our comfortable distance, these urban youth seem free-spirited and adventurous. Yet they lived surrounded by constraints of time, poverty, and family resistance. Tradition, whether in Sicily or in the Pale of Settlement, demanded that girls become women at marriage, moving seamlessly from the protection of their fathers to the protection of their husbands. Girls could go to socials at ethnic clubs or attend carefully chaperoned dances at a settlement house. The girls whose world stretched from home to church or synagogue might bend to family expectations. But if she went to work, she more likely wanted to go her own way. Just like the boys, working girls wanted time for recreation, even a little excitement.[15] The collision with traditional values happened in every neighborhood, probably in every tenement. Once outside their family circle, girls created modern heterosexuality.

As children made their own way, they made their own matches. Elizabeth Ewen has shown that by the late nineteenth century, in traditional regions like the Russian Pale, families and neighbors had already begun to take a larger role in courtship than the traditional matchmaker. In the New World, even the influence of family and neighbors steadily declined. The formal call, in which the young man visited a young woman at her home, with family in attendance, became another casualty of urban life. "My mother and dad don't believe girls should go out alone," wrote one Hungarian girl. "They want me to keep steady company with only one boy [and he must be Hungarian] and then marry him . . . what does [my father] want us to do, pack up and go to his village in Hungary to live?[16]

Whether they escaped poverty in the countryside or poverty in Europe, in America's cities they also sought to escape from their tenement flats and the family-centered social rituals. After a long day at work "the young girl naturally craves a share in the profusion of pleasure which she sees everywhere on sale," wrote two social work investigators. Frances Donovan, a middle-class journalist, experienced the lure of recreation for herself. At the end of a day's work as a waitress, "although I was tired . . . I was in a mood for anything, anything but home . . . after the excitement of such a day, I felt that to dance in a cabaret to the music of a jazz band was just the sort of recreation that I would appreciate." Girls saved from their small wages whatever was left after the contribution to the family funds in order to buy nice hats and dresses, makeup, perhaps some rose water, so they could have opportunity for a little fun at a theater or dance hall.[17]

Most girls, however, were not on their way to theatre, movie, or cabaret by themselves. Louise De Koven Bowen's study of department store girls in Chicago found that of 173 who lived at home, 126 paid all of their wages "into the family exchequer." The majority of these girls and young women had little time for recreation, and they could afford dances and 5- and 10-cent theaters only if "invited."[18] In other words, girls depended on boys—who typically kept more of their earnings for themselves—to pay at least some of the costs of a night on the town. Kathy Peiss, Ruth Alexander, Mary Odem, and other historians have shown the central role of commercial pleasures to the emergence of a modernized heterosexuality. Whether in Jane Addams's Chicago or Jacob Riis's New York, in California, or even in smaller cities in the Midwest, when girls and boys appeared together in public places they carried a charge of sexual potential.[19]

Middle-class investigators early in the century emphasized the snares of even healthy recreation "when presented in vulgar form or when combined with evil companions and drinking." These included "dancing in halls or other public places not carefully supervised, as well as in resorts and hotels," "suggestive moving pictures and 'sex dramas,' . . . which, further, provide opportunity for indecent behavior because of the comparative darkness during performances; 'joy rides' with casual acquaintances, which so frequently end in immoral conduct." Restaurants, cafes, and skating rinks could be added to the list. One work, compiled to lift the veil of secrecy from the white slave trade, warned that "the ordinary ice cream parlor is very likely to be a spider's web for [a girl's] entanglement." "The amusement parks are now becoming a serious menace to our young people," wrote a missionary working among prostitutes in Chicago. "All over these places Satan has his agents stationed, seeking victims." Amusement parks made explicit the erotic excitement available for dating couples—not only the tunnel of love, with its mandatory kiss just before the boats returned to the start, but also rides meant to mix people together or turn them onto their backs and so to send women's skirts up around their thighs.[20]

From the point of view of purity crusaders, dance halls had a special role as "the ante-room to hell itself." Adolescents had always enjoyed dancing. Working-class young people put together "affairs" in their neighborhoods; ethnic social clubs, or even settlement houses, might sponsor dances. Just after the turn of the century, new dances and popular music spurred a dance craze that swept across the country. By the early twentieth century, even small cities and rural towns had halls that attracted "wild young people." Larger cities had many. Historian Randy McBee notes that New York had 500 dance halls by 1910; Chicago had 218 dance halls in

1917, and another 718 saloons with a room or other space for dancing. For city girls, "the dance hall, with its lights, gay music, refreshments, and attractive surroundings, seems every thing that is bright and beautiful." Unlike the traditional affairs or the dances sponsored by settlement houses, big cities offered "numberless places where one may dance and find partners, with none too scrupulous a supervision." One investigator recognized the dancers as children at play, but with alcohol and sex as part of the mix. "Couples stand very close together, the girl with her hands around the man's neck, the man with both his arms around the girl or on her hips; their cheeks are pressed close together, their bodies touch each other; the liquor which has been consumed is like setting a match to a flame." The names given to the dances, such as "On the Puppy's Tail," "Shaking the Shimmy," "The Dip," "The Stationary Wiggle," made evident their erotic intent.[21]

Adolescent girls and boys might show up at these establishments separately, but they came looking for partners. A "spieler" served both as an assistant to the instructor and as a prod to socializing. "He dances with the wall flowers," wrote a wary reformer, "and he is expected to keep everybody happy and everybody busy." Jane Addams lamented the many "young men, obviously honest young fellows from the country" who "look eagerly up and down the rows of girls, many of whom are drawn to the hall by the same keen desire for pleasure and social intercourse . . ." When she told one young man that the dance hall was an unlikely setting for meeting a "nice girl," he responded plaintively, "'But I don't know any other place where there is a chance to meet any kind of girl.'"[22]

As historian Beth Bailey has discussed, the custom of the date—the social excursion in which a boy and girl go out together in search of amusement—originated with urban youth on the streets of the nation's cities. But the date seems almost too formal a description to match what must have seemed random and chaotic at the time. Maimie Pinzer recalled young men coming to her department store in the afternoon to make dates for the evening. Perhaps more typical than the prearranged outing by self-identified couples would have been a group of girls in their best dresses and feathered hats as they made their way to the Slovak club hall, or the movie theater, or the dance hall, meeting a similar group of boys dressed in clean shirts and their best shoes. The "cliquey alliances" that girls and boys formed served as homosocial reference groups for "adventure with members of the other sex." At dance halls like the Strand in New York City, girls passed their evenings dancing with the boys but also chatting for long periods with one another. As boys and girls became better acquainted, the date might supplement these group excursions but probably replaced them only for older youth. Consistently, however, the boys had more money than did the girls. So dating, for girls, meant finding boys who would pay their way. As one girl put it, "the boys you 'pick up' 'treat.'"[23]

One girl explained to a social reformer the gendered rituals of a typical date. On a trip with a girlfriend to Bowery Bay on the East River, they were followed by two men who showed their interest by tipping their hats. Next they asked them to dance. And then, "'[t]hey treated—She had beer and I had a lemon soda.'" Dating always included the practice of treating. Boys and young men paid for admissions and bought drinks. If the "pickup" was only for an evening, the girl might try to slip away before the return home. But, if "she is not clever, some one of her partners of the evening may exact tribute," the interviewer wrote, referring to the sex play that went along with working-class dating.[24] This might have been no more intimate than the kissing games played by middle-class youth, but often it included fondling and occasionally intercourse.

Clothing often figured among the "treats" that men provided. Referring to girls working as retail clerks, reformer Mabel Dedrick posed the question, "How can these girls dress themselves the way they are required to nowadays in these stores and do it honorably on the salary that many of them receive?" Another Chicago reformer lamented the temptation of department store girls: "Constantly surrounded by the articles which are so dear to the feminine heart." From the middle-class viewpoint, the lust for fashion clouded a girl's judgment. An early-twentieth-century youth worker for the YWCA lamented "a certain sham maturity" among working girls: "A girl of 16 on her first job too often dresses, acts, and lives out the part of a woman of 25 or 30." Social researcher Anne Bingham claimed to know of many such cases like that of a 16-year-old who, "partly because she longed for pretty clothes . . . began promiscuous relations with men from whom she received from $3 to $5."[25]

In her study of waitresses, Frances Donovan found that the women had to dress well for their employers as well as their boyfriends. "That a woman should spend all her money for clothes is most significant. The love of dress is unquestionably one of the most disorganizing factors in modern city life because of its individualistic character." Recent work by historians has shown that women of different classes, races, and regions expressed desire through their choices of clothing. They dressed not only to impress potential employers or to compete for boyfriends but also for themselves. Without "pretty clothes," Frances Donovan wrote, "a girl can not hope to realize her personality." Donovan's insight is uncharacteristically sympathetic to the situation of working girls.[26]

## The Dangers of Adolescent Sexuality

Adolescent sexuality first assumed an identity in the United States primarily as a problem for working-class girls and their families. Loss of reputation might result in loss of marriage prospects. But this outcome probably felt less threatening to working girls struggling with long workdays and little hope for improved circumstances. Their desire to have a little fun would have seemed more compelling than the attractions of a marriage years in the future. The risk of pregnancy, however, probably had a stronger claim on the attention of girls. Men who treated often sought sex, but the girls and young women had to negotiate the terms. Kissing and other sexual activity might substitute for "going the limit."[27] If she went the limit and pregnancy resulted, the girl had to make, or accept, adult decisions. This could mean single parenthood (often within a family and culture that associated this condition with shame), abortion, or early marriage. Middle-class reformers responded to the new sexuality of American girls with legal changes and new institutions.

If adolescent sexuality first appeared as a problem, it was a problem with well-defined social features. Even though urban and rural premarital pregnancy rates were about the same in the late nineteenth century (23 percent in 1900), their proximity to social workers and charities meant that pregnant white, working-class girls would be seen as victims of urban conditions. In 1883 the Florence Crittenton Anchorage opened in New York City as a refuge for unmarried, pregnant women. These homes spread to cities across the nation and inspired similar institutions sponsored by the Salvation Army, the Catholic Church, and African American organizations. The Anchorage gave shelter and some work training to young women, and during their residence in the home the young mothers were encouraged to keep their children. As the nineteenth century moved toward a close, the Anchorage dealt with ever younger residents, their average age falling from 22 to 15.[28]

During the 1880s the Women's Christian Temperance Union took up the cause of female children when it launched a campaign to change the age of consent laws. Most states followed the common law standard, which set 10 years as the age of consent for girls. In many states, legislators opposed these changes. They feared that "sensual" or "immoral" girls who had long since lost their virtue would entrap young men who would become victims of their own "normal" drives. Nevertheless, the women's groups exploited "a narrative of sexual danger to female virtue" that probably coincided with an older tradition of consent laws protecting the chastity of daughters and future wives. By the late 1890s almost every state had raised the age of consent to 16 or older.[29]

The age of consent laws gave some legal protection to girls, but they could not protect girls from themselves. Girls who persisted in seeking the amusements of city life and in enjoying treating and sex play might seem like a nuisance in public but authorities might take a far more serious view. Troublemaking boys had consumed the imagination of legal reformers in the late nineteenth century, but at least boys were expected to cause trouble. After the turn of the century, delinquent girls assumed much greater attention from authorities. Between 1910 and 1920 many states expanded older reformatories for girls and young women and built 23 new ones. By 1924 there were 57 "training schools" for girls across the country, including segregated institutions in the South.[30]

Reform schools existed for boys as well as girls, but the criminal conduct of boys and girls differed markedly. One study of Chicago showed that in the late nineteenth century the immigrant boys brought into juvenile court were generally charged with stealing, while the girls faced the ambiguous charge of immorality. This did not necessarily mean that she had performed a sex act (much less had done so for pay). "Rather," as Steven Scholossman and Stephanie Wallach note, "the girl only had to show 'signs' in her appearance, conversation, and bearing that she had probably had intercourse in the past or might do so in the near future." Before, and continuing after the century turned, New York City enacted a wide range of ordinances aimed at controlling young women. Beginning in 1886, "incorrigible girl" statutes gave parents the use of the justice system to help them control daughters who were "willfully disobedient' or 'in danger of becoming morally depraved."[31] The authority of parents was further strengthened by the Mann Act (1910), which gave the federal government broad powers to interfere with the movement of young women for any "immoral purpose." A big part of the workload of the newly formed Bureau of Investigation was to find and return runaway daughters.[32]

Sex play could end with arrest, a court appearance, and even time in a reformatory. Maimie Pinzer's mother had her arrested after she spent a few nights with a young man she had met while working at a Philadelphia department store. The next day her mother asked the Commonwealth of Pennsylvania to declare 13-year-old Maimie "incorrigible," which led to Maimie's transfer to a Magdalen home for one year. The same attitudes prevailed in the South, where Cora Corman was picked up for vagrancy. She had worked in mills from age 13. After her shift she went out to theaters. She not only had two steady boyfriends but also had relations with other men. Authorities placed her in the Samarcand training school, in North Carolina.[33]

The practice of treating had begun in the late nineteenth century, as a more or less equitable exchange of drinks among working-class men. The transformation of the practice into a youthful heterosexual ritual seemed far less equitable, at least to the reformers who documented the practice. The exchange of gifts, clothes, dinners, or movie admissions for sex play looked to many reformers of the time too much like prostitution. One reformer wrote that there were many "adolescent girls who involve themselves in immoral relations more or less indiscriminately, believing that if they do not accept money they keep themselves without the sphere of prostitution."[34] "Clara" for instance, at 13, began spending time and having sex with men. She never took money for sex, but the men paid for her room. "Angelina" went to work in a chocolate factory at about age 15, and "in the factory she very soon fell in with several immoral girls, from whom she learned to pick up men. Though she went about only with men whom she 'liked and not for money,' one young fellow gave her inexpensive clothes and trinkets." She later had sex with him when he promised marriage, but then he left her. A few years later she spent time with various men. "Although she did not actually prostitute," investigators wrote, "she allowed men to pick her up, give her a meal in a cheap restaurant, or take her to a dance."[35] To middle-class reformers, girls and young women seemed very vulnerable to economic power.

Investigators also readily found young women who moved from garment factory or stenography school to brothel. The cautionary tales in "From Dance Hall to White Slavery," as shown in figure 1.1, included stories of vulnerable young women who fall in with bad companions and lose themselves. But as historian

The tragic climax of this young life was not reached in one
step, but led there by easy stages through the
fascination of the dance hall. (The
Tragedy of the Young Mother.)

FIGURE 1.1 "The tragic climax of this young life" from H. W. Lytle and John Dillon, *From Dance Hall to White Slavery: The World's Greatest Tragedy* (Chicago: C. C Thompson, 1912).

Alice Clement has shown, the low wages paid to women made prostitution a reasonable, even attractive, option for some young women. Maimie Pinzer, who at 13 ran afoul of Pennsylvania's incorrigibility statue, spent several years of her youth and early adulthood living with a lover and dating other men to supplement their income. Working-class neighbors might disapprove of prostitution, but they could still accept the prostitutes who practiced in the tenements and the local candy or cigar stores. From the perspective of those who lived near the prostitutes, the economic calculation that might lead to sex work made much better sense than it did to middle-class reformers.[36]

## Coercion and Rape

"Once the girls are earning," wrote one investigator, "one often finds the most curious indifference and lack of information on the part of parents as to where the girls work, under what conditions, the attitude of employers, the kind of working companions, etc." Often enough, as girls left behind older forms of social control they also abandoned the protections afforded by those controls. Older boys and men might encourage or coerce them to have sex. Accounts by women offer many examples of being seduced and abandoned and of bosses who extracted favors for employment. Department store sales clerks were "at the mercy of 'the man higher up' in her department; if he makes advances to her that she does not accept, he can tell her that her services are not longer required." Polly Adler, who later became a famous brothel proprietress, first had sex when her boss asked her to Coney Island. On the way, they stopped at his home. He made advances, which she resisted. He knocked her out and raped her.[37]

Accounts of coerced sex and rape appear so abundantly in studies from the early decades of the century that we have to recognize this as one of the underlying realities in the social experience of sexuality, especially for girls. In his study of sexual crimes in New York City, Stephen Robertson found that 85 percent of cases of rape, abduction, sodomy, seduction, and carnal abuse involved minor females. A 1934 study of 1,400 sex crime cases in New York provides a broad survey of the dangers to girls in the urban environment. Public amusements played a leading role in the narrative, with many stories set in automobiles (Mary: "she accepted his invitation to go riding in his automobile. When she asked to be taken home, he refused unless she had relations with him . . . the man beat her and then raped her."), amusement parks (Tessie meets two men at an unnamed amusement park, goes to their bungalow where they both assault her), and movie houses (Angelica, 13, met a friendly young man of 24, who took her to a movie, then took her to his room and forced her to have sex). But amusement parks and motion-picture theaters seem, in the end, to have offered opportunities to meet men rather than venues for sex with them. Even automobiles, which appeared in most contemporary accounts of sexual danger, were the scene of coercive sex in only 54 instances (about 8 percent) in one compilation. In contrast, girls' own homes came third on the list, with 194 instances. And, while the dangers of meeting seductive strangers figured prominently in the warnings about sexual predators, friends, or acquaintances accounted for 34 percent of the men responsible for first sex experiences of the girls studied.[38]

A substantial minority of those "acquaintances" were relatives of the girls. The study presented 20 cases of incest, and most of those were father–daughter incest. Helen was raped by her father at age 15, and then more times subsequently. Dorothy was five when her father began using her sexually. Mary's father fondled her for years until age 14 when he raped her. Of the 1,400 cases studied, fathers, brothers, uncles, stepfathers, or mother's boyfriends accounted for 7.5 percent of the first illicit sex experiences of the girls. Another study from the 1930s, of girls in reform school, found that 5.8 percent of first sex experience had taken place with a father, a stepfather, or another relative. Early studies, like the ones cited here, investigated special populations, and the authors made no claim to represent the experiences of girls and adolescents in general. All we can claim from these studies is that among delinquent populations of girls, incestuous rape accounted for a significant minority of the sexual initiations of girls. Considering the strong social sanctions related to incest, we can speculate that these percentages understated the lived experiences of these girls. In Linda Gordon's study of abuse cases in Boston, incest accounted for roughly 10 percent of the cases that agencies saw, with little change during the twentieth century.[39]

Studies of delinquent populations and of social service recipients localized incest among the poor and working class. The hardships faced by the poor offer some form of explanation for incidents of family breakdown and violations of sexual boundaries. Yet recent work by historian Lynn Sacco strongly suggests that incest reached into every strata of society. Accounts of trials of father–daughter incest among the middle-class dropped off after 1890 in the nation's newspapers, replaced by stories that featured the poor, immigrants, and African Americans as the perpetrators. Both legal and medical experts seem to have concluded that white, middle-class incest was an impossibility. Yet, during this same period, bacteriological tests for gonorrhea had become simple and accurate. Vulvovaginitis, a condition associated with venereal infection, was noted in growing numbers among girls. By 1927 a medical journal claimed that it was the second-most-common disease in children, after measles. And the condition crossed class boundaries, appearing even in the middle-class nuclear households that physicians assumed stood as the bulwark against sexual chaos. For much of the first half of the twentieth century, medical and psychiatric literature found ways of minimizing or dismissing reports of incest or of redefining the act.[40]

Even though a significant minority of youth experienced sexual violence, these traumas remained personal. Short of criminal action, perpetrators remained free of consequences. Courts regarded sexual conduct in girls as criminal behavior (grounds for a stint at a reformatory) but ignored it in boys. Disregarding age of consent laws, juries often considered older girls as fully capable of giving consent. Girls relied on other girls as sources of solace. One woman, a waitress whom Frances Donovan gave the name "Lillie," confided to Donovan about being raped as a young teenager by a boarder who lived over her uncle's shop. But their talk took place many years after the event, and Lillie made little of it—or tried to. Sexual coercion and violence remained an unspoken theme of adolescence as American youth began to share common experiences that crossed regional and class boundaries.[41]

## Other Worlds

Middle-class youth seemed to live in a different world, one that resisted the public and enthusiastic heterosexuality of their working-class peers. Boys and young men might be close companions for years before marriage. Middle-class girls increasingly went to school beyond the mandatory seven years of elementary education. Whether they boarded at private seminaries or stayed at home, they lived surrounded by female family members and friends. Middle-class youth valued a "culture of friendship" that would flourish in the single-sex academies and colleges that sprang up in the late nineteenth century. Although female friendships in the first flush of passionate "smashing" might disrupt college life, passionate friendships rarely disturbed civil peace.[42] Among women these relationships could persist as lifelong partnerships or continue as important dimensions in the lives of married women. Or, the friendship might attenuate after the marriage, as it typically did for men, and finally fall into the background of a woman's life. In any case, strong and even passionate friendships had strong cultural support as the twentieth century dawned. Adolescence seems to have required a special friend.

Even in the middle class, however, boys and girls spent time together. Younger children mixed more or less freely, until the boys went away to apprenticeships, work, or school. Children and youth learned dances, and girls and boys met for social occasions. Boys and girls played kissing games like post office, forfeits, and go to Rome. Girls together for a party would talk about boys and would try conjuring tricks to learn what kind of men they would marry. As they grew older, of course, more formal courtship came into play. At least initially under family supervision, boys and young men would make a visit, or call, to the home of the young woman whom they wished to meet.[43]

By the second decade of the twentieth century, however, these middle-class norms had begun to break down. With housing in large cities at a premium, young professionals had to share rooms. Even couples with middle-class aspirations might find themselves without a parlor and so resort to the entryway to their apartment house or to riding the subway and bus for time together. When her companion asks why she does not have men call on her at her home, Florence, in the O'Henry story "Brickdust Row," tells him, "If you could see the place where I live you wouldn't ask that." A *New York Times* writer in 1920 quoted from a friend's account of a ride on the Hudson River Line: "Why, coming on and off the boat, they were the kind of people that you'd expect to see at a concert or—or teaching school. And then, my dear, those nice looking girls would let the men kiss them right on the deck, just as if they were—were shop girls, and east side immigrants."[44]

Rural youth in the late nineteenth century also found time for mixed play without adult interference. Boys and girls had opportunities to meet at church events, parties, or sleigh rides. Figure 1.2 shows a group of young people on what might be a church picnic. Although dancing was banned in some areas due to religious opposition, it became popular where allowed. "The dancing was a revelation to me," Hamlin Garland wrote of his youth on the Great Plains, "of the beauty and grace latent in the awkward girls and hulking men of the farms." He recalled a donation party at which the young people organized a dance and made music by singing and clapping. Calling remained an important part of courtship, as boys grew to men and sought more attention from the young women whom they admired. Along with opportunities for group play, rural youth also enjoyed more time alone for "sparking." An early-twentieth-century educator wrote about the "[c]oquetry, flirting, and playing at love" among the young.

**FIGURE 1.2** An excursion. This group has formed into couples, with the most affection shown between the two boys in the front. Arkansas, early twentieth century, before 1920.
*Source*: Michael Ballew collection.

"The term 'spooning' was current during this period and described the permissible and expected, if not altogether approved, behavior during courtship and engagement."[45]

Many of the early-twentieth-century southern families studied by I. A. Newby negotiated both rural and industrial demands as they moved from sharecropping to millwork. In general, boys had freedom to seek the attention of, and woo, whom they pleased. Girls, however, were viewed as too emotional. Families closely watched them and tried to control their romantic prospects. Nora Oates recalled how young people made use of their meager resources to play at courtship. On payday the boys would go to "see their best girlfriends. . . . They would chew their gum and rattle the change in their pants pockets." With no movie houses, they had to improvise with box parties or lawn socials. Boys might send notes to girls they liked, using younger boys as messengers. Oates recalls first receiving a note when she was 15, with an invitation to meet a boy at the Wednesday evening church service. Wednesday, Saturday, and Sunday nights were the principal "dating" nights, another man recalled of his youth in the mills. These dates, in fact, proceeded much more like traditional calls, with boys going to girls' homes and staying until 9:00 or 9:30, well beyond the reasonable bedtime.[46] Dating, in the urban sense, depended on picture shows or dance halls or parks; the mill villages, like many small towns across the country, still lacked commercial amusements.

Black youth at the turn of the century lived in worlds as diverse as their white counterparts. Adolescents in middle-class black families would have assumed the identity of respectability and chastity. For poor and working-class African Americans, both poverty and racism could work against these middle-class standards. Young women working as domestics often encountered harassment and even coercion by white male employers. In New York City, black youth had opportunities for public amusements much like their white counterparts. But for young black women, there seemed to be greater likelihood than for white women that ordinary socializing could leave them vulnerable to charges of prostitution. Cheryl Hicks recounts the case of Mable Hampton who was arrested at her employer's home while waiting with a friend to go out to a cabaret on a double date. In another example, two women were arrested as they left a dance hall in the early-morning hours. Like white girls, black girls could fall in love or into sin with the boys and men in their lives, sometimes to supplement their wages, sometimes as part of the complex exchanges of treating. Evelyn Pitts, for instance, had sexual relations with two or three men from age 17 for several years but never took money for it. Another young woman began working as a prostitute full-time at age 17, thereby increasing her income from $7 a month to $10 a week.[47]

Evidence for the class divide among rural African Americans comes from a slightly later period, but is consistent with what we know of urban youth. "Victorian regulation," according to sociologist Charles Johnson who lived in the black belt during the Depression years, only applied to the very religious and the well-off among rural blacks. Consequently, "comparatively few restrictions are placed on the conduct of the adolescent." Johnson lamented the proliferation of attractions and distractions that gave Depression-era rural youth opportunities much like turn-of-the-century urban youth—beer halls, honky-tonks ("where cheap whisky is sold and 'hot' music is made available for dancing by dropping a nickel in the slot"), movies, taverns, and bootlegging joints. Sex experimentation usually began around age 14, and for many girls in their later teens, pregnancy and marriage followed hard upon one another.[48]

Yet attitudes toward sexual issues followed class rather than race. Poor whites living in the Ozarks, for instance, had little concern about premarital pregnancy. "Lawful wedlock," wrote a middle-class observer living in the Ozarks, "is supposed to cancel all previous laxities, anyhow, and a mother whose child is born a month or two after her marriage does not appear to lose caste." At the same time, middle-class black families, even in the rural South, taught stricter standards with regard to premarital chastity.[49] As the century moved toward its third and fourth decades, groups of young people separated by class, race, and even geography began to act more like one another, and to imitate one another's practices for play and sexual exploration.

## Other Sexualities

Near the middle of the century, Alfred Kinsey and associates published their groundbreaking studies on human sexuality. According to their survey, 37 percent of men had, at some point after the beginning of adolescence, experienced a sex act with another man. When asked about preadolescent or early adolescent sex play such as exhibitionism and mutual masturbation, almost half (48 percent) of those interviewed recalled some acts that could be classified as homosexual. And among the preadolescent boys interviewed, 60 percent recalled some sex play of this kind. On reflection, it is surprising that this proportion should have been so low. Large families, cramped quarters, and sleeping arrangements that combined children with parents, siblings, cousins, and often visitors, meant that children in both urban and rural settings regularly slept with other children and adults. And children, as we have seen, spent a great deal of time with other children and away from adults. In rural areas boys on break from work or at the local swimming hole had opportunities to explore sexual play with male companions. Cornelius Utz, growing up early in the century in northwestern Missouri recalled, "[O]ne way or another, I had sex-play with six of my seven brothers—fondling and masturbating each other to orgasm, dry-fucking by pressing against each other." This happened at night while they slept together, as though in a dream. They never discussed it. For most children, this kind of sexual exploration fell away during adolescence and often was forgotten in a sentimental reconstruction of childhood.[50]

Of course, some boys never became interested in girls. The possibility of a man who would live outside of a conventional marriage, who would seek only the company and the sexual favors of other men, had already become a topic of discussion in medical literature by the turn of the century. Kinsey only dealt in sexual acts, with an underlying assumption that biology produced identities—a man only interested in men, or one only interested in women, and gradations in between these extremes. But work both within sexual science and in history since mid-century has shown that identity makes many more demands on our understanding than just knowing whom one has sex with. For working-class men in the early twentieth century, the role taken in a sex act was crucial. Manhood meant taking the active role in anal or interfemoral sex, or being the recipient of fellatio. Effeminate men, the "fairies" or "queens" who had established communities in many large cities, stood as sexual "others."[51]

Rural Americans often understood that some men and women were different in some ways, that they lived apart from conventional small-town society. These individuals might find a kind of acceptance as eccentrics. Urban youth had some choice in terms of the sexual roles they could play, and even some community. Boys might date girls and cruise areas of the city where they could find sex as "trade," that is, straight men who engaged in sex acts with gay men. Urban amusements not only shaped heterosexual dating but also provided a setting for homosexual meetings and seduction. One 18-year-old recalled going to an amusement park near Portland, Oregon, where he met a 20-year-old who paid for his rides and bought him candy. As they relaxed together, the older youth began to fellate the younger.[52]

But as boys grew older, continuing companionship with other boys and adolescents could become a problem as more and more friends began dating girls. Homosociality might find an outlet at the YMCA, which had as its founding principle the value of male companionship. The YMCA served mainly young professionals who were leaving youth behind to meet the challenges of adulthood. Still, the Y allowed youth to find other boys and young men who might share their sexual interests. Along with the erotic suggestiveness of physical training and sports, young men roomed together. YMCAs in most cities became centers for gay cruising. In 1912 a scandal broke out in Portland, Oregon, over a homosexual "ring" at the city's YMCA, with connections to many prominent men in the community. Fifty men were eventually indicted in the investigation. For most cities, however, the Y remained a safe place for men to meet one another and to cruise for trade. Many men later recalled having their first sex with another man there.[53]

Young men from the country often used the YMCA as a means of making the transition to urban life. For many, this could mean an introduction to gay life or a chance to explore sexuality before settling into a conventional life. Youth who remained in the country, however, had more difficulty finding social roles that made room for gay sexuality. One group that moved in and out of urban settings was the hoboes or transient workers who traveled from area to area in search of work. In this subculture men often partnered with boys or adolescents who had left home for life on the road. These couples tended to reproduce the gender roles of settled society. The older man, known as the "wolf" or "jocker" typically took the active role in sex acts. The youth—"lamb" or "punk"—in addition to taking the passive role in sex, ran errands, cooked, and cleaned clothes. Emotional bonds might well arise between the partners, and the young man benefited from the advice and protection of the older man.[54]

Some working-class boys and men earned money with casual or regular sex work. Early in the century newsies could supplement their meager day's earnings by a short encounter with older boys or men. Working-class youth might make some money by playing the dominant role for well-off effeminate men. In some cities, young men also could work as sex partners for older men. These adolescents could settle on a bench in Battery Park, in New York, for instance, and wait for a man interested in anal or oral sex. The boys might, or might not, have thought of themselves as queer but probably distinguished themselves from older queens or fairies. The men who picked them up probably thought of themselves as sexually "normal"—that is, interested in sex in the active role.[55]

The new sexuality of the early twentieth century may have made homoerotic relations somewhat easier for youth. As the socializing of youth moved out of the home and the supervision of family, casual relations among young people became more common in general. Homosocial groups remained important for much of the early part of the century. Groups of boys and girls might meet and mingle, but the relations among same-sex peers would remain vital to American youth. These could often provide the setting for deep emotional bonds and even physical intimacy. Only after dating declined in importance did the social space for queer sexualities begin to contract for American youth.

## Toward an American Youth

By the late nineteenth and early twentieth centuries, education appeared to more and more social commentators as the surest means of healing social wounds and of saving American youth. Along with G. Stanley Hall, writers such as Arthur MacDonald, an early criminologist, and Edward Ross, the theorist of social control, looked to free public education to ameliorate "the poverty, misery, and vice of the next generation." During the twentieth century, extended education would apply not only to the fortunate few in the middle and upper classes but would also reach a widening circle of American youth. This common experience of education beyond elementary school would become one of the principle forces shaping a distinctive American youth culture.[56]

By the late nineteenth century, public education already had a long and complex history in the United States. The system depended on state law and local funding, so different regions inevitably provided widely different opportunities for students. Most rural areas required only a few months of attendance during a school year (and in some areas only a few weeks), typically half the amount of time that urban schools required. Although age-graded schools had become typical in towns and cities after the mid-nineteenth century, many rural districts still relied on a single teacher to provide instruction for all students together in a single-room school. States usually required attendance to age 14. More education had little utility for young people, most of whom had too much work to take time for school. Many rural areas and even small towns lacked high schools, so students who wanted to continue had to board in nearby cities.[57]

Yet the same trends that led to the creation of juvenile justice systems and the criminalization of promiscuity also fostered the expansion of the education system. Already by the end of the century some state legislation attempted to limit child labor. This movement gained momentum during the Progressive years in the early twentieth century. From 1900 to 1930, the proportion of 10- to 15-years-olds earning wages fell from 25 percent for boys and 10 percent for girls to 6.4 and 2.9 percent, respectively. Even though child labor laws had limited success until the Great Depression, they operated in concert with the growing belief in the value of continued education and the desire to protect children from dangers inherent in city life and the workplace. In 1890, less than 7 percent of teenaged youth were in Grades 9 to 12, but by 1920 the proportion had risen to one-third. By 1930 slightly more than half of high school-aged children attended high school.[58]

By 1890, most states had systems that were primarily coeducational, and in 28 states all schools mixed boys and girls. Because far more girls than boys could be spared from wage labor, girls outnumbered boys in high school. In 1890, girls accounted for 65 percent of high school graduates. Pictures of high school classrooms from the era show desks filled mainly by girls, sometimes with only one boy in the room. A boy aged 13 to as late as 20, wrote education professor Irving King, "is swamped with the rising tide of vital energy within himself—swamped also in the midst of a complex world of social relationships and duties, whose inner workings and compromises he as yet knows nothing about . . ." Recalling his own childhood in New York, Michael Gold put it more simply: "School is a jail for children." Many boys responded to the unwelcome constraints of Grades 9 and above by forming school gangs or by dropping out—of children who entered 9th grade, only about 11 percent completed 12th grade.[59]

As the century advanced, however, sex ratios slowly evened out in American high schools. Even if a college-preparatory curriculum of algebra and Latin seemed irrelevant to most young people, extended education by the early twentieth century had begun to shape youth culture. In both large and small cities, and later in towns across the country, high schools provided a range of activities in which similar-aged peers worked and played together. The "extracurriculum" that grew into such an important element of high schools included clubs, dances, student government, and publications. For students, however, by far the most important meaning of these activities was the possibility of spending time with peers. Older children still enjoyed time to play together. Dances sponsored by the high school soon became a regular feature of the town social scene, even though in some small towns religious opposition delayed the trend. Early in the century a Sunday school teacher worried that in her rural town "on the floor of [the school] gymnasium were taught and practiced all the latest new steps, trots, and bunny-hugs that Satan has invented." Perhaps the most important development in the extracurriculum to assimilate young males was the development of school sports. By the 1920s most schools administrators had accepted and integrated sports into school programs.[60]

By the early twentieth century, high school attendance had begun to grow into a common and eventually typical experience for American youth. The classes, and the activities beyond the classroom, provided the foundation for something that had not existed before, a common youth culture. High school brought together middle- and working-class youth, exposed them to a curriculum that had broad similarities from one school to the next and from one state to the next. Sports, publications, dances grew spontaneously from the needs and desires of young people themselves. With the common youth culture that eventually became almost universal in the United States, there also grew a consistent organization of sexual activity.

## A New Sexuality?

Our survey of American young people at the dawn of the twentieth century, separated as they were by class, ethnicity, education, urban or rural residence, makes clear that any generalizations about "American youth" or "American adolescents" would be facile at best. Still less could we claim that this age group practiced a common sexuality. But, by the turn of the twentieth century, we find all of the elements that will become adolescent sexuality as the century progressed. The respectable call of sheepish young men at the homes of protected young women had already lost most of its claim on the lives of urban, working-class youth. The roaming groups of 12- to 20-year-olds, looking for fun at soda fountains or movie theaters had become far more typical. City streets seemed to swarm with dates— boys and girls, young men and women, looking for fun. The attraction of dating for youth seems clear when backward-looking authors such as M. V. O'Shea and T. W. Shannon lamented the loss of middle-class norms that confined the mutual inspection of prospective life partners to the orderly middle-class home.[61] Finally, for older youth, dates could lead to steady dating, which seems to have drawn from the practice of both dating and of formal courtship.

Whether they led to courtship or not, dates included sex. Even middle-class youngsters had their kissing games. Rural youth, black and white, made use of opportunities for shared solitude. But kissing, fondling, and other sex play became public in the city. Along with the regular equation of sex play with dating there appeared another practice in urban youth culture. Treating required a delicate balance between generosity and parsimony, both for the boy or the young man with his slender means and the girl or young woman with her reputation. If for parents or social workers treating risked taking the girl into prostitution, for the girls the danger existed of gaining a reputation for giving too much for too little.

To a great extent, girls and boys developed their own, distinctive codes of reputation. Strong friendships have always characterized youth, and these friendships have typically been with same-gender peers, that is, homosocial. Urban boys and adolescents formed gangs based on geography, each gang taking about two city blocks as its territory. Jacob Riis surveyed the exploits of the Rag Gang, Rock Gang, Stable Gang, Short Tails, and Whyos. They disturbed the peace with their social outings almost as much as their fights with other gangs. Even though the working-class sexuality that seemingly shaped adolescent practice for most of the twentieth century was almost extravagantly heterosexual, homosocial relations continued to play a vital part in the lives of American youth until mid-century. Girls moved in groups with other girls. Whether at work, settlement houses, or the ladies' rooms at the dance halls, they held intense discussion to sort out the difficult terrain of modern urban sexuality. Boys also relied on their peers as they formed groups to go out in the evenings looking for fun and girls. Boys and young men either went to dance halls with their same-sex peers or else sought them out once they arrived. Groups of young men also often performed mass or ensemble dances to establish their comfort with the dance hall environment.[62] Twentieth-century heterosexuality followed and depended on strong homosocial networks.

One other dimension of sexuality that arrived in the century almost fully developed was the management of unwanted pregnancy. The Florence Critten-ton Homes, and similar refuges for unmarried mothers, probably served a small minority of unwed pregnant girls and young women. Abortion, legal and available after the 1880s only in some states and only for the women who could gain the support of a board of physicians, was still widely available from clandestine practitioners.[63] And as the century advanced, adoption, both legal and clandestine, provided a source of relief both for unwed mothers and for childless couples.

All of these elements of a distinctive, adolescent sexuality spread from city to suburb to countryside in the first two decades of the century. By the 1920s middle-class and working-class youth would create a distinctive peer culture. At the core of this peer culture were the new rituals of adolescent sex play.

## Notes

1. Ruth Cohen, *Out of the Shadow: A Russian Jewish Girlhood on the Lower East Side* (Ithaca, NY: Cornell, 1995), 199–207.
2. Susan Maria Ferentinos, "An Unpredictable Age: Sex, Consumption, and the Emergence of the American Teenager, 1900–1950" (PhD diss., Indiana University, 2005), http://wwwlib.umi.com/dissertations/fullcit/3204295.

3. Jane Addams, *The Spirit of Youth and the City Streets* (Chicago: University of Chicago Press, 1972), 107.

4. Howard Chudacoff, *Children at Play: An American History* (New York: New York University Press, 2008), 88.

5. G. Stanley Hall, *Adolescence: Its Psychology and its Relations to Physiology, Anthropology, Sociology, Sex, Crime, and Religion* (New York: D. Appleton, 1904), 1:263; Jacob Riis, *How the Other Half Lives: Studies among the Tenements of New York* (New York: Penguin, 1997), 135; Riis, *The Children of the Poor* (New York: Scribner's, 1915), 96, 111; and S. Glueck and E. Glueck, *Five Hundred Delinquent Women* (New York: Alfred A. Knopf, 1934), 81.

6. I. A. Newby, *Plain Folk in the New South: Social Change and Cultural Persistence, 1880–1915* (Baton Rouge: Louisiana State University Press, 1989), 2; and Tamara Hareven, *Family Time and Industrial Time: The Relationship between the Family and Work in a New England Industrial Community* (Cambridge: Cambridge University Press, 1982).

7. Riis, *How the Other Half Lives*, 104, 105; David Nasaw, *Children of the City: At Work and Play* (New York: Doubleday, 1985), 69; and Riis, *Children*, 111.

8. Only 3 percent of the urban population at the turn of the century lived alone. Tamara Hareven, *Family Time and Industrial Time: The Relationship between the Family and Work in a New England Industrial Community* (Cambridge: Cambridge University Press, 1982), 154.

9. H. W. Lytle and John Dillon, *From Dance Hall to Whites Slavery: The World's Greatest Tragedy* (Chicago: Charles C Thompson, 1912), https://archive.org/stream/fromdancehalltow00lytl#page/n7/mode/2up; and Steven Mintz, *Huck's Raft: A History of American Childhood* (Cambridge, MA: Belknap, 2006), 200.

10. Addams, *Youth and the City*, 54.

11. Hall, *Adolescence*, xiii–xv:1, 132, 325.

12. Addams, *Youth and the City*, 51–52; and Nasaw, *Children of the City*, 23.

13. Addams, *Youth and the City*, 57–58; and Riis, *Children*, 109.

14. W. Douglas Morrison, *Juvenile Offenders* (New York: D. Appleton, 1897), 6, 117; Leslie Paris, *Children's Nature: The Rise of the American Summer Camp* (New York: New York University Press, 2010); and Anthony Platt, *The Child Savers: The Invention of Delinquency* (Chicago: University of Chicago Press, 1969), 3–4.

15. Morrison, *Juvenile Offenders*, 48; and Addams, *Youth and the City*, 8–10.

16. Elizabeth Ewen, *Immigrant Women in the Land of Dollars: Life and Culture on the Lower East Side, 1890–1925* (New York: Monthly Review Press, 1985), 228–232; Cohen, *Out of the Shadow*, 199–207, 225; Elizabeth Clement, *Love for Sale: Courting, Treating, and Prostitution in New York City, 1900–1945* (Chapel Hill: University of North Carolina Press, 2006), 34; and Ferentinos, "Unpredictable Age," 131–132.

17. Robert A. Woods and Albert J. Kennedy, *Young Working Girls: Summary of Evidence from Two-thousand Social Workers* (Boston: Houghton Mifflin, 1913), 6; and Frances Donovan, *The Woman who Waits* (Boston: Richard G. Badger, 1920), 50.

18. Louise de Koven Bowen, *The Department Store Girl: Based on Interviews with 200 Girls* (Chicago: Juvenile Protection Agency of Chicago, 1911), 2, 11.

19. Kathy Peiss, *Cheap Amusements: Working Women and Leisure in Turn-of-the-Century New York* (Philadelphia: Temple University Press, 1986); Mary Odem, *Delinquent Daughters: Protecting and Policing Adolescent Female Sexuality in the United States, 1885–1920* (Chapel Hill: University of North Carolina Press, 1995); Ruth Alexander, *The Girl Problem: Female Sexual Delinquency in New York, 1900–1930* (Ithaca, NY: Cornell University Press, 1998); and Sharon Wood, *The Freedom of the Streets: Work, Citizenship, and Sexuality in a Gilded Age City* (Chapel Hill: University of North Carolina Press, 2005).

20. Anne T. Bingham, *Determinants of Sex Delinquency in Adolescent Girls: Based on Intensive Studies of 500 Cases* (New York: New York Probation and Protective Association, 1923), 24; Woods and Kennedy, *Young Working Girls*, 107; Ernest Bell, *Fighting the*

*Traffic in Young Girls* (Chicago, 1911), 71; the quote is from Florence Mabel Dedrick in Bell, *Fighting the Traffic*, 111; Clement, *Love for Sale*, 53–54. For contemporary images of the amusement park, see the silent films, *It* and *The Crowd*, both from the late 1920s.

21. Bell, *Fighting the Traffic*, 112; Leora Blanchard, *Teen-age Tangles: A Teacher's Experience with Live Young People* (Philadelphia: Union Press, 1923), 46; and Louise de Koven Bowen, *The Public Dance Halls of Chicago*, rev. (Chicago: Juvenile Protective Association of Chicago, 1917), 3, 4, 5, 8, http://memory.loc.gov/cgi bin/query/r?ammem/musdi:@field(DOCID+@lit(M025); Woods and Kennedy, *Young Working Girls*, 107; Bell Lindner Israels, "The Way of the Girl," *The Survey*, July 3, 1901, 486; Randy McBee, *Dances and Dancing, Girlhood in America: An Encyclopedia* (New York: ABC-CLIO, 2001), 174–182; and Randy McBee, *Dance Hall Days: Intimacy and Leisure among Working-Class Immigrants in the United States* (New York: New York University Press, 2000).

22. Israels, "Way of the Girl," 495; and Addams, *Youth and the City*, 11–12.

23. Beth Bailey, *From Front Porch to Back Seat: Courtship in Twentieth-Century America*, John Hopkins Paperbacks ed. (Baltimore: Johns Hopkins University Press, 1989); Maimie Pinzer, *The Maimie Papers*, ed. Ruth Rosen and Sue Davidson (Old Westbury, NY: Feminist Press, 1977), 193; Woods and Kennedy, *Young Working Girls*, 8; Clement, *Love for Sale*, 56–57, 61–63; and Israels, "Way of the Girl," 487.

24. Israels, "Way of the Girl," 487, 489.

25. YWCA publications in the early twentieth century cautioned girls and young women against buying shoes that were fashionable but hard on the feet; Woods and Kennedy, *Young Working Girls*, 8; Bell, *Fighting the Traffic*, 13; Bowen, *Department Store Girls*, 5; Ferentinos, "Unpredictable Age," 29–30; Donovan, *Woman who Waits*, 209; and Bingham, *Determinants of Sex Delinquency*, 7. For discussions of dress and desire, see the excellent studies by Kelly Schrum, *Some Wore Bobby Sox: The Emergence of Teenage Girls' Culture, 1920–1945* (New York: Palgrave MacMillan, 2004); and Susan K. Cahn, *Sexual Reckonings: Southern Girls in a Troubling Age* (Cambridge, MA: Harvard University Press, 2007).

26. Donovan, *Woman who Waits*, 208–209.

27. Clement, *Love for Sale*, 66.

28. Constance Nathanson, *Dangerous Passage: The Social Control of Sexuality in Women's Adolescence* (Philadelphia: Temple University Press, 1991); Michael W. Sedlak, "Young Women and the City: Adolescent Deviance and the Transformation of Educational Policy, 1870–1960," *History of Education Quarterly* 23 (Spring 1983): 5, 8; Regina Kunzel, *Fallen Women, Problem Girls: Unmarried Mothers and the Professionalization of Social Work, 1890–1945*, new ed. (New Haven, CT: Yale University Press, 1995); and Deborah L. Rhodes, "Adolescent Pregnancy and Public Policy" *Political Science Quarterly* 108 (Winter 1993–1994): 639.

29. Carolyn Cocca, *Jailbait: The Politics of Statutory Rape Laws in the United States* (Albany: State University of New York Press, 2004), 11, 14–15; and Odem, *Delinquent Daughters*, 71.

30. Steven Schlossman and Stephanie Wallach, "The Crime of Precocious Sexuality: Female Juvenile Delinquency in the Progressive Era," *Harvard Educational Review* 48 (February 1978): 70; and Cahn, *Sexual Reckonings*, 45–46.

31. Schlossman and Wallach, "Precocious Sexuality," 72.

32. Jessica R. Pliley, *Policing sexuality: the Mann Act and the making of the FBI* (Cambridge, Massachusetts: Harvard University Press, 2014), 131-154.

33. Pinzer, *Maimie Papers*, 193–196; Cahn, *Sexual Reckonings*, 60; and Alexander, *The Girl Problem*, 34, 50.

34. Many examples of the ploys used by procurers to gain the trust of innocent girls, especially girls from the country new to the city, in Don Romesburg, "Wouldn't a

Boy Do?: Placing Early-Twentieth-Century Male Youth Sex Work into Histories of Sexuality," *Journal of the History of Sexuality*, 2009, 367–392; Bell, *Fighting the Traffic*; and H. W. Lytle and John Dillon, *From Dance Hall to White Slavery: The World's Greatest Tragedy* ([Chicago]: C. C Thompson, 1912). Woods and Kennedy, *Young Working Girls*, 85; and Clement, *Love for Sale*, 52.

35. Miriam Van Waters, *Youth in Conflict* (New York: Republic Publishing, 1925), 13; Glueck and Glueck, *Five Hundred Delinquent Women*, 53–54; and Woods and Kenndy, *Young Working Girls*, 105–112, provide an extended discussion of treating.

36. Lytle and Dillon, *From Dance Hall to White Slavery*; Clement, *Love for Sale*, 76, 106; and Pinzer, *The Maimie Papers*, 193–196.

37. Bingham, *Determinants of Sex Delinquency*, 15; Riis, *Children*, 43; Bowen, *Department Store Girl*, 6; and Polly Adler, *A House Is not a Home* (New York: Rinehart and Co, 1950), 24–25.

38. Stephen Robertson, *Crimes against Children: Sexual Violence and Legal Culture in New York City, 1880–1960* (Chapel Hill: University of North Carolina Press, 2005), 2; and J. A. Goldberg and R. Goldberg, *Girls on City Streets: A Study of 1400 Cases of Rape* (New York: American Social Hygiene Association, 1935), 13, 33–37, 88, 294–295, 301.

39. Goldberg and Goldberg, *Girls on City Streets*, 191–193, 294–295; Glueck and Glueck, *Five Hundred Delinquent Women*, 91; Pinzer, *Maimie Papers*, 193; and Linda Gordon, *Heroes of their own Lives: The Politics and History of Family Violence: Boston, 1880–1960* (Urbana: University of Illinois Press, 2002), 207.

40. Lynn Sacco, *Unspeakable: Father-Daughter Incest in American History* (Baltimore: Johns Hopkins, 2009), 90–91; Erna Olafson, David L. Corwin, and Roland C. Summit, "Modern History of Child Sexual Abuse Awareness: Cycles of Discovery and Suppression," *Child Abuse & Neglect* 17 (1993): 7–24; Elizabeth Wilson, "Not in This House: Incest, Denial, and Doubt in the White Middle Class Family," *Yale Journal of Criticism* 8 (1995): 35–58.

41. Shclossman and Wallach, "The Crime of Precocious Sexuality," 65–94; Robertson, *Crimes against Children*, 39 and throughout chap. 1; and Donovan, *The Woman who Waits*, 34.

42. E. Anthony Rotundo, *American Manhood: Transformations in Masculinity from the Revolution to the Modern Era* (New York: Basic Books, 1993), 75–85; Carroll Smith-Rosenberg, "The Female World of Love and Ritual: Relationships between Women in Nineteenth-Century America." *Signs: Journal of Women in Culture and Society* 1, no. 1 (1975): 19–27; Catherine Kelly, *In the New England Fashion: Reshaping Women's Lives in the Nineteenth Century* (Ithaca, NY: Cornell University Press, 2002); and Nancy Sahli, "Smashing: Women's Relationships before the Fall," *Chrysalis* 8 (1979), 17–27. The close relations among men extended throughout the college years for men in college fraternities. See Helen Lefkowitz Horowitz, *Campus Life: Undergraduate Cultures from the End of the Eighteenth Century to the Present* (New York: A.A. Knopf, 1987), chap. 1 to 3.

43. Ann Marie Kordas, "Girl Troubles: Female Adolescent Sexuality in the United States, 1850–1950" (PhD diss., Philadelphia: Temple University, 2002), 59.

44. The transition in courtship is traced in Ellen Rothman, *Hands and Hearts: A History of Courtship in America* (Cambridge, MA: Harvard University Press, 1987); and Beth Bailey, *From Front Porch to Back Seat*. Helen Bullitt Lowry, "Wanted: A New O' Henry; Passing of Middle Class Parlor and the Eighteenth Amendment to Steamboat Regulations," *New York Times*, June 20, 1920, Arts and Leisure, n.p.

45. Michael Gordon, "Was Waller Ever Right? The Rating and Dating Complex Reconsidered," *Journal of Marriage and Family* 43 (February 1981): 70–71; Hamlin Garland, *A Son of the Middle Border* (New York: Grosset and Dunlap, 1914), 182–185, 223; and Ira S. Wile, ed., *The Sex Life of the Unmarried Adult: An Inquiry into and an Interpretation of Current Sex Practices* (New York: Vanguard, 1934), 124.

46. Newby, *Plain Folk*, 289–290.

47. Cheryl D. Hicks, *Talk with You Like a Woman: African American Women, Justice, and Reform in New York, 1890–1935*, Gender and American Culture (Chapel Hill: University of North Carolina Press, 2010), 210–218.

48. Charles S. Johnson, *Growing up in the Black Belt: Negro Youth in the Rural South* (New York: Schocken, 1941), 65, 153, 185, 225–238.

49. Vance Randolph, *The Ozarks: An American Survival of Primitive Society* (New York: Vanguard, 1931), 53–54; and Johnson, *Black Belt*, 229–230.

50. Alfred Kinsey, *Sexual Behavior in the Human Male* (Bloomington: Indiana University Press, 1998), 169; Kinsey's data showed no differences between the two generations interviewed in his study (413–414, 623). Colin R. Johnson, *Just Queer Folks: Gender and Sexuality in Rural America*, Sexuality Studies (Philadelphia: Temple University Press, 2013), 58–59; and Will Fellows, ed., *Farm Boys: Lives of Gay Men from the Rural Midwest* (Madison: University of Wisconsin Press, 1996), 38.

51. Johnson, *Just Queer Folks*, 125–128; Michel Foucault, *The History of Sexuality*, vol. 1, *An Introduction* (New York: Vintage, 1990); Linda Fish and Rebecca Harvey, *Nurturing Queer Youth: Family Therapy Transformed* (New York: Norton, 2005), 52; George Chauncey, Jr., "Christian Brotherhood or Sexual Perversion? Homosexual Identities and Construction of Sexual Boundaries in the World War I Era," in *Hidden from History: Reclaiming the Gay and Lesbian Past*, ed. Martin B. Duberman, Martha Vicinus, and George Chauncey (New York: New American Library, 1989), 296–304.

52. Peter Boag, *Same-Sex Affairs: Constructing and Controlling Homosexuality in the Pacific Northwest* (Berkeley: University of California Press, 2003), 99–100.

53. Boag, *Same-Sex*, chap. 1; and John Donald Gustav-Wrathall, *Take the Young Stranger by the Hand: Same-Sex Relations and the YMCA* (Chicago: University of Chicago, 1998), 161, 168–173.

54. Nels Anderson, *The Hobo: The Sociology of the Homeless Man* (Chicago: University of Chicago Press, 1923), 137, 145–150; and Boag, *Same-Sex*, 21–33.

55. Romesburg, "Wouldn't a Boy Do?"; and George Chauncey, *Gay New York: Gender, Urban Culture, and the Makings of the Gay Male World, 1890–1940* (New York: Basic Books, 1994), 89–90.

56. Arthur MacDonald, *Abnormal Man, Being Essays on Education and Crime and Related Subjects* (Washington, DC: Government Printing Office, 1893), 14, 41, 167; and Edward A. Ross, *Social Control: A Survey of the Foundations of Order)* New York: Macmillan, 1901).

57. David Tyack, *Learning Together: A History of Coeducation in American Public Schools* (New York: Russell Sage Foundation, 1992), 82, 114–118, 136; Riis, *Children*, 92; Chudacoff, *Children at Play*, 36; and Blanchard, *Teen-age Tangles*, 101.

58. Tyack, *Learning Together*, 173; Chudacoff, *Children at Play*, 86, 98; Theodore Sizer, *Secondary Schools at the Turn of the Century* (New Haven, CT: Yale University Press, 1964), 9. This chapter makes only modest departures from the work of Joseph Kett, *Rites of Passage: Adolescence in America, 1790 to the Present* (New York: Basic Books, 1977), in chapter 8, who points to a range of institutional changes, including juvenile justice and schooling, that brought adolescence into being. Also, John Modell, *Into One's Own: From Youth to Adulthood in the United States, 1920–1975* (Berkeley: University of California Press, 1991), 37, and throughout, develops the theme of the extension of adolescence into the early 20s as a result of extended schooling. A recent study of these same themes comes from Sarah Chinn, *Inventing Modern Adolescence: The Children of Immigrants in Turn-of-the-Century America* (New Brunswick, NJ: Rutgers University Press, 2009).

59. Tyack, *Learning Together*, 104, 110, 114, 193; Hall, *Adolescence*, 2:619–620; Michael Gold, *Jews without Money* (New York: Liveright, 1930), 36; Newby, *Plain Folk*, 502–503; and Irving King, *The High School Age* (Indianapolis, IN: Bobbs-Merrill, 1914), 89.

60. Reed Ueda, *Avenues to Adulthood: The Origins of the High School and Social Mobility in an American Suburb* (Cambridge: Cambridge University Press, 1987), 132–134; August B. Hollingshead, *Elmtown's Youth* (New York: John Wiley and Sons, 1949), 145; Blanchard, *Teen-age Tangles*, 97–98; and Tyack, *Learning Together*, 193, 229.

61. M. V. O'Shea, *The Trend of the Teens* (Chicago: F. J. Drake, 1920); and T. W. Shannon, *The Laws of Sex Life and Heredity or Eugenics* (Marietta, OH: S. A. Mullkin, 1917).

62. Riis, *Children*, 168–175; Nasaw, *Children of the City*, 33–34; Clement, *Love for Sale*; and McBee, *Dance Hall Days*, 134, 136.

63. Leslie Reagan, *When Abortion Was a Crime: Women, Medicine, and Law in the United States, 1867–1973* (Berkeley: University of California Press, 1997).

# 2

# THE NEW YOUTH AND THE DOMESTICATION OF DATING

From the perspective of the early twenty-first century, the heterosexual conviviality that flourished in the 1920s can seem both quaint and tame. As middle-class children adopted the working-class practices that replaced calling, dating became less provocative, more domesticated. By the end of the 1920s adult authorities had begun to view dating, and even petting, as normal rituals leading to courtship. But in this period, and so rapidly as to astonish contemporaries, middle-class and working-class youth together established freedom from adult supervision as a basic entitlement of youth. Sex play became a normal part of adolescent lives. Extended education provided the context for a youth peer culture that included heterosexual conviviality. British cultural anthropologist Geoffrey Gorer considered dating unique among world cultures as well as "the most singular feature of American social life."[1] But parallel to the new heterosexuality of American youth there was a network of intense homosocial relationships. Until at least the 1930s, the heterosexual and homosocial relations of American youth existed symbiotically, each sustaining the other. This new sexuality, although short-lived in its "classic" 1920s form, permanently recast the boundaries of sexuality for American youth.

## The Social and Physical Context

By the 1920s certain long-term shifts in the organization and function of middle-class families had become apparent. Family size in the United States generally had shrunk but more for professional and business families, with two or three children becoming typical for the middle class by 1920. Sociologists at the time, and historians since, have noted that these families became more affectionate and that children had more freedom to express themselves. One educator summed up this trend in recommending that parents of adolescents "must relax discipline, and govern by invisible leading strings." The emerging profession of child guidance sided with adolescent children in struggles over recreation and parental control. Historian Kathleen Jones has shown that counseling professionals "argued that children were often more aware of the qualities needed for success in modern society than were tradition-bound parents."[2] And the long period of economic expansion following World War I meant that there were more middle-class families and that they could devote more resources to their children. By 1930 child advice literature recommended that families provide allowances. Consequently, older children had the freedom and the resources to take advantage of the consumer economy to express themselves through their clothing and the fads they pursued. But as the family became more open to individual expression, it also became less central to socialization, to preparing children for roles in society. Other institutions assumed some roles that had formerly belonged to the family.[3]

During the 1920s, high school became the central experience for most American adolescents. Teenagers attending high school spent as much time with teachers and peers as they did with their families. In Middletown, (Muncie, Indiana) Merrill and Helen Lynd found by 1924 that high school enrollment accounted for 25 percent of total school enrollment. Taken for granted by the business class in Middletown, high school education had also gained wider acceptance in the city's working class. The national graduation rate for 18-year-olds would pass 50 percent only in 1940, but high school attendance grew at a breakneck pace. In 1920 about one-fourth of 14- to 17-year-olds were enrolled in school, but by 1930 the proportion had doubled. Until the Depression, working-class boys could find work during their teenage years that proved more appealing than school and more valuable for their families. Even so, by 1928 boys accounted for 44 percent of high school graduates.[4]

High school demanded more schoolwork and new forms of social performance at a time of rapid physical change. From early adolescent years, the simple reality of growing, sometimes very rapidly, could create acute discomfort. Girls typically experienced a growth spurt before the boys, so had to manage self-images that depended on external and shifting judgments about height, weight, and body type. As Joan Jacobs Brumberg has documented, weight became an obsession for teenaged girls beginning in the 1920s. "I'm so tired of being fat!" lamented one 17-year-old in 1927. She joined a host of other girls in the 1920s who wanted to change their appearance. Another 14-year-old in 1928 speculated in her diary about how she appeared to boys, pretty sometimes and ugly at others. She had grown tall too fast, she believed, and although she wanted to have a slender figure like her sister's, she impatiently referred to herself as an "ox."[5]

As if to aggravate the strangeness of the changing inner world of self and the outer world of society, children continued in age-graded classrooms where differences among them in physical growth and educational achievement would appear in sharp contrast. Rather than tall boys finding peers who were a bit older, they had to make do with the same desks as everyone else, at least until sports practice. A fictional teenager from one of the period's best sellers regards his good friend Buck during French class: "The square-jawed devil-may-care desperado of the pool room and open Ford was now merely a well-built young man with a rather low brow, trying with the pitiful earnestness of a big collie dog to grasp the complexities of irregular French verbs."[6] Still, as the century continued, school grade became an important marker for adolescence. Rather than physical maturity, grade in school determined when young people entered the dizzy world of heterosexual play.

For teachers and administrators, heterosexual play inevitably created problems. Teachers in one study in 1928 identified their main problems as "heterosexual activity," stealing, masturbation, and "obscene notes and pictures." Sex education had already entered some public school curricula by the 1920s—social hygiene was taught in about half of schools by 1922—although with no national standards. Many administrators and teachers preferred not to deal with it, in spite of the obvious concerns raised by sexual issues in school. One woman principal asked that her superintendent talk to her boys "on the general subject of morality, and he said it was the place of the school doctor; the doctor said it was the place of the parents . . ." A model curriculum from the period recommended that sexuality be integrated into other courses, such as biology, and from an early age, with study of plant and then animal reproduction to support more personal questions such as "Who am I?" and the attraction between boys and girls. But a study in 1927 of schools with integrated curricula found that "eugenics and heredity" were more common topics than "reproduction" or the "social aspects" of human sexuality were.[7]

With little or ambivalent help from family and school for understanding their new sense of self, teenagers depended more and more on their friends. Everyone, seemingly, needed a close friend and a small reference group or clique to mediate her or his relation to the wider peer groups at junior high and high schools. Work and traditional courtship provided a pathway to adult responsibilities. High school—and for some, college—postponed adulthood and full engagement in the work world. The sexuality of this period of adolescence was a complicated game, in anthropologist Geoffrey Gorer's account, one in which the players understood the rules. But the peer group determined the winners and losers.[8]

## The Date

The most visible element of the new sexuality was the date. As we saw in the last chapter, dating had flourished among urban, working-class youth for at least two decades before 1920. Prior to World War I, however, middle-class children still tended toward family-centered socializing. One middle-class teenaged girl noted in 1912 that after a dance put on by a friend she took a cab with two other girls and a boy "without any chaperon, except the cabman, which was very shocking."[9] Ten years later young people without adult supervision, in groups and in couples, had become common almost everywhere in the United States. By the early 1930s large majorities of high school students began dating by their sophomore year.[10]

The date, and a whole culture of dating, became so pervasive among middle-class youth during the 1920s that one early historian of adolescent culture asserted that middle-class youth had invented the practice.[11] But by the 1920s working-class youth had already made dates—couples together without chaperones—a common sight on city streets and in public amusements. This example may have served as an important forum of social learning for middle-class youth who began to take up the practice in the years after World War I. Also, as working- and middle-class youth mixed more and more in urban high schools, working-class practices would have become easier for middle-class youth to copy.

Another line of influence probably came from the colleges which expanded rapidly during the 1920s. By 1930 almost 20 percent of Americans 18 to 22 were attending some school beyond high school. College men who could afford to had typically made trips into nearby towns and cities to find sexual play with working-class women or prostitutes. As coeducation became a common feature of higher education by the 1920s, working-class practices discovered on these "slumming" trips may have shaped the social life at college. Sexual conquest became an integral element of a college man's identity. With the working-class girls in town, this meant intercourse. With the young women who were his social peers, this meant gaining as much as possible, although probably not inter-course. College women, for their part, domesticated the sexual practices of the coeducational campus. They could date a series of men, pet, and go out alone or in groups. But sexual intercourse became the bright line that separated good girls from bad and college women from local working-class women.[12] The fraterni-ties and sororities took the lead in formalizing the peer dating of the colleges, and fraternity chapters in high schools may have helped spread this new form of heterosexual play among younger adolescents.

Middle-class and small-town couples not only joined working-class ado-lescents in the movie houses and dance halls; they also added new spaces to the adolescent social terrain. The high school extracurriculum institutionalized socializing, providing adult-supervised activities to keep high school youth away from the local dance halls. But school dances also gave students opportunities for strolling, visiting, loitering, and joy riding when the dances ended. Even reli-gious youth took the new independence for granted. An academic who worked with churchgoing young people reflected on their attitude toward chaperones. "The boy or girl who can drive a car, ride a horse, shoot, swim, skate, and sail a boat alone is rather a hard person to convince that he or she needs an older person present during 'dates' to protect his or her reputation."[13]

We can examine the middle-class domestication of dating by comparing two first dates 10 years apart. Both of these were blind dates. In 1920 one of Marion Taylor's former teachers arranged for a young man to escort her home after her graduation. She was excited at the prospect but disappointed when he showed up and turned out to be short, with a bullet head. "I don't know how to meet the ordinary little gallantries," she recorded. "He sprang at me to help me on with my cloak. . . . And he edged around for the outside of the sidewalk, and I forgot that the gentleman is supposed to do that and I nearly knocked him off because I started to walk on the outside too. . . . And crossing the street he would seize my arm in a vise-like grip and shove me over." They had nothing to talk about. When he took her home, she just wanted him to leave, but instead, they sat for a time in the front room. She recounted, "I made various lame remarks and there were several harrowing pauses."[14]

Almost 10 years later expectations for dating had changed. Edyth Weiner, age 14, attended a dance with an escort arranged by her sorority sisters. The older boy drank too much and became sick. Afterwards, they went riding in his car, with other couples in the back seat. "All the kids in back were necking like the devil," wrote Edyth, but her date, probably still drunk, only pulled her over to him but did not kiss her (he was driving after all). The party continued to a roadhouse, probably for more clandestine drinking since they did not eat.[15]

In 1920, Marion Taylor's date still tried to observe the traditional formalities of social exchange. His awkward behavior might have come from an etiquette book or a course on deportment. They even end up visiting in her family parlor, and if he made any advances for sex play, she did not record them. A decade later, all the social niceties seem to have disappeared. Edyth's drunken escort leaves her feeling ill used because he *failed* to attempt any sex play. In both cases, couples go out together in public, with no chaperone. The gender roles, formalized by etiquette in 1920, are still clear, if quite different in 1929. The escorts (the boys) pay, make decisions about recreation, and make advances. The girls respond, but they generally have little power except in the matter of sex play, where they have an ambiguously understood veto.

These elements of dating appear repeatedly, and with some variation describe the entire range of dating behavior. "Attended a high school dance with Frank Howard," Dorothy Smith wrote in 1924. "Sherwin Brown took Harriet. It was fun—both were good dancers & I felt like dancing. . . . We buzzed over to Natick for a hot dog & nearly rattled the poor Ford to death." Here we see the group setting—two couples attending a school-sponsored dance, but then leaving on their own for a joy ride or possibly in search of an ice cream parlor. Automobiles often played a supporting role, as it did for the couples in figure 2.1. Adele Siegel, in 1931, went to a public dance hall with her date, "and we went for a ride afterwards. He behaved." Date destinations included roadhouses and ice cream parlors, along with movies, dance halls, amusement parks, all often with some drinking mixed in. But the social center of dating in the 1920s was the dance floor.[16]

**FIGURE 2.1** A double date in 1920s.
*Source*: Michael Ballew collection.

## Social Performance on the Dance Floor

Dances and dancing had become popular in the United States before World War I, and much of adolescent social life both in cities and in the country took place on and around dance floors. Although an urban movement beginning about 1910 in New York City, open admission dancing spread through the country, even penetrating into rural areas. City girls like Edyth Weiner and Adele

Siegel often wrote about dances in their diaries. But Gladys Hasty in Maine also recalled dancing a tango with a cousin during the summer before her freshman year in college. Even on the Great Plains, dances provided much of the social life for young people like Ann Marie Low. A writer in 1918 lamented, even as he foresaw, the trend toward youthful dancing: "The dance seems to be attracting young people more and more strongly every year," wrote M. V. O'Shea. "And once a youth comes under the influence of the dance, he never knows when to stop." His warning came far too late.[17]

At dances, boys and girls performed not just the dance steps they had learned, but also the gendered rituals of conviviality. Couples arrived together, and left together, but they spent little time dancing together. Most girls craved the kind of experience that Nancy Hale had at age 14: "[A]fter I first got a partner, which was right off, I had a wonderful time. I had a different partner for every dance, and was cut in on two or three times every dance." The practice of cutting in made a girl's popularity public knowledge. A girl who danced more than once with the boy who brought her seemed pitiable. As on any date, a boring or rude dance partner could turn the evening into a struggle, but at a dance the personal agony had to be endured in public. After the dance, groups of boys and girls often went out. Older youth and young adults might have cars available to them, and they frequently gave rides to friends. They might go to eat or in search of drink, but they might just go driving, "gadding about" as one rural young woman put it, and end up at someone's house sitting on the front porch.[18]

## The "Meaning" of the Date

Although not actually on dates, girls spent a lot of time considering what their dates meant. This could apply to a single date, as when Dorothy Smith judged Frank Howard "about the drollest fellow I know" or Gordon van Kirk "a stupid talker." But girls believed that dating held meanings about themselves. Edyth Weiner, already "boy crazy" (in her own judgment) at fourteen, gave as much attention to the social discourse of dating as any culture critic might have, but for Edyth the meanings were personal. After finishing a magazine article on "Dates," she recorded that among its "other truths, it said that if it gets around that a girl is unpopular, she might just as well move to another state or enter an old ladies' home!" Popularity, the boy's or girl's standing with his or her peers, matched the individual's success in dating. When sociologist Willard Waller described the rating and dating complex at Penn State in the mid-1930s, he noted that a college woman's popularity depended on having weekly (or more than weekly) dates with a new escort for each date. Going more than once with the same fraternity boy could mean that one had no other options. Beth Twiggar summarized her social goals: "to be popular, to go out, to dance, to know boys and boys and boys."[19] Edyth Weiner and Beth Twiggar, as young teenagers, already understood the social landscape of high school.

Yvonne Blue offers an important contrast to Beth and Edyth. Yvonne, who turned 13 in 1924, grew up in a comfortable Chicago neighborhood in an upper-middle-class family. Her teenage years featured an extended girlhood, with close relations with her parents, siblings, and other girls. The first boy she mentions is named Elliott, someone her friend Thekla liked. Thekla, who seems more like Edyth Weiner than Yvonne, disappears from Yvonne's diaries when they begin attending different schools, then reappears three years later. "She's pretty," writes Yvonne, "but awfully loud and boy-crazy." But boy craziness seemingly paid off for Thekla. The next winter she happened to be on her way to school at the same time as Yvonne, and the two walked part of the way together. "She walked to school with me and millions of boys yelled 'Hi Teddy!' at her as she skipped along while I walked at her side in torments of self-consciousness."[20] Even though her experience differed from Thekla's (and Edyth's), she understood the terms of heterosexual popularity that Thekla had achieved.

Adele Siegel offers another guide to 1920s adolescence. She seems to have achieved the kind of popularity that Edyth craved. At 16, she recorded going to a Halloween dance. "I danced with every boy there, almost." She made it back home after two in the morning. Three days later another boy took her to see the Marx Brothers in *Monkey Business*. But her date obviously had such a crush on Adele that "all he could do was look at me." Later that same year she made a list in her diary of *"Boys in love with me."* She included the hapless lad who had taken her to the movie, and several others. "I don't encourage any of them," she wrote. In a separate list she evaluated 16 boys she had spent time with, almost all of them 16 to 18 years old. She included remarks on how she felt about the boy, what kind of company he provided, and how well they kissed. Adele took a matter-of-fact attitude toward her social success: "I should have as much fun as possible with all the boys I like, flirt just a bit, and 'neck' only with a boy I really care for."[21]

Nancy Hale, who as we saw earlier had such success at her first dance in 1922, also seems to have gone through her high school years as a social success. She kept a separate book of her "beaux," from 1923 to 1927, with 72 entries in all. She did not evaluate these boys and young men based on their suitability as life partners, but rated their social skills, and also their likelihood of necking. This list, like Adele's, emphasized the social role of dating.[22] Dates provided a public performance of one's success or failure in the social hothouse of high school or college. When young people began to pair up and remain satisfied with a single partner, they had already moved to the horizon of youth and begun to prepare for adulthood.

## Petting and Sex Play

A writer in *Parents* recalled the kissing games she played in her pre–World War I childhood: "Post Office, and Clap in, Clap Out, and Spin the Platter, and For-feit." A generation later Adele Siegel had a list of similar games that she and friends played at one of her parties, including forfeits but also "Advertisements," "Initials," and hide-and-seek in the dark.[23] But these ritualized forms of sex play, typically within the home and with adults nearby, seemed to have little relation to the new practices of the twentieth century. The goal of the date had always been to give young people independence of adult supervision, to escape both cramped living quarters and the ever-present relatives on the other side of the room or, at best, in the next room. This independence was mainly to allow for sex play.

By the 1920s adolescents expected "[k]issing, petting, and other tentative excursions into sex experience," as juvenile court judge Ben Lindsey wrote of a "sweet-faced" teenaged girl. Fiction of the period both popularized and exploited the theme of a new, wilder youth. Patricia Fentriss, the 18-year-old daughter of an upper-middle-class family in Warner Fabian's novel *Flaming Youth* (1923), admits that she has been an enthusiastic "necker ever since—since I began to be grown up. Most girls are." Robert Carr's *The Rampant Age* (1928) featured small-town Paul Benton, who begins dating as a high school freshman. Paul watched his friend Hungry on their double dates "in an effort to perfect his own necking technique."[24]

The terms *petting* and *necking* had already entered the American vocabulary by 1920 and quickly replaced *spooning* as terms for caressing or kissing. Petting had assumed many meanings. It could refer to a boy and girl kissing on the mouth for the first time. Or, it might mean a "human clinging-vine lolly-popping over [another] specimen of the genus homo." Although couples sought privacy for sex play, the marker of the private for youth in the early twentieth century was not necessarily shared solitude but freedom from adult supervision. Double dating was probably almost as common as solitary couples alone. Even group settings could be "private." Psychologist Lorinne Pruette reported arriving at a party in an artist's studio where a "few hardy youths were hanging about a punch bowl. . . . The rest of the crowd were out, huddled two by two in big chairs. Some of them were in a heavy clinch."[25] Even in groups of their peers, couples felt much the same freedom to pet that they did when alone.

For middle-class youth, the casual acceptance of heterosexual caresses sig-naled a new, and permanent, shift in adolescence. Lorinne Pruette believed that much of the practice of petting came from "herd instinct"—"youth is under a sort of compulsion to be wild and free." But even though it is tempting to explain the popularity of petting as a straightforward shift toward sexual libera-tion, the greater physical expressiveness of modern youth had complex roots. The practice was motivated by some combination of sexual excitement, curios-ity, social conformity, and status seeking, and the sexual excitement may have been the least important element for many. Warner Fabian captured the ambigu-ity of petting in the coming-of-age tale of Patricia Fentriss. One of the nonenti-ties who became briefly involved with Pat made advances after a brief chat with her: "In [his] inured mind there was no room for surmise. To him this was all formula . . ." Later in the book, when Pat is asked why she necks she answers, "'I don't know. The boys sort of expect it. . . . And it's—it's fun, in a way.'"[26]

The fictional Pat's ambivalence about necking reflects the findings of social science. A mid-1920s interview of college women asked when they had begun "keeping company" and when they began "spooning" or petting. Most of the women recalled having permission to go with boys by age 16. Almost all (92 percent) of the women admitted to petting, with ages for starting ranging from 12 to 25, and the median between 16 and 17. The motivation for spooning varied among the women, and for each woman different reasons applied depending on the situation. (The investigator noted that some women checked several of the boxes.) The most common motivation, accepted by half of respondents, was "infatuation." But 40 percent marked "curiosity," and another 30 percent "because others did it."[27]

Private reflections from girls in the period revealed the same range of expectations and conformity. We have seen already that Edyth Weiner took for granted that her date should pet with her, as the other couples on their after-dance drive were doing. She could hardly have felt "infatuated" with her drunken escort. When Nancy Hale made her list of 72 male acquaintances, she noted of several that they were petters. She must have known this from her own experience, but she does not rate any of the boys on their petting abilities. Adele Siegel, on the other hand, noted boys whose kisses left her feeling dull and those she found thrilling. Beth Twiggar, about the same age as Edyth, seems to have taken some physical intimacy for granted when on dates, and worried when none was offered. At the end of one quiet week she complained, "I wanta be necked!"[28]

Marion Taylor, after her disastrous first date, slowly began to find boys more and more exciting. "I am learning to 'jolly' and 'small talk,' to 'flirt' in an embryonic, amateurish sort of way!" she wrote in her college diary. She also took for granted petting, "crude, primitive love-making," as she called it. Six weeks later she wrote about her "suppressed excitement" that Gerald should take her out, "put his arm around me again, and look at me with that certain look in his eyes." But she knew that this had little to do with affection, "but a longing for the sheer physical excitement, and the intoxicating knowledge that one is admired and desired."[29]

One group of social researchers who talked to high school students about petting found that almost two-thirds of the girls (and more than half of the boys) petted "in order to be popular." Petting, in other words, just like dancing, served as part of the social performance of dating. Although expected, the amount of petting depended on negotiations between the partners. As Zelda Fitzgerald proclaimed in a 1922 magazine article that "'boys *do* dance most with the girls they kiss most.'" But every decision about sex play carried more ambivalence, more risk for girls than for boys. Petting too freely carried consequences. The boys at her school began to talk about Beth Twiggar's easy reputation. "I am hurt, battered, wholly crushed," she wrote when she learned of it. One of the respondents to a survey of high school youth opined that "The girl who permits liberties is certainly popular with boys, but her popularity never lasts very long with any one boy." One girl summed up her solution to the dilemma of petting: "I always let every boy kiss me the first time he meets me, but I always tell him it's against my wishes." Nancy Hale took repeated vows not to be "a common little petter, who bushwhacks with any and every boy." But she also recognized that "every time I say 'yes' it makes it that much harder to say 'no.' At any rate, I must try horribly hard to say 'no' from now on—*even if it means losing some popularity.*"[30]

## From Sex Play to Sex

Adult authorities spent a lot of time and ink during the 1920s considering the question of petting. Making love, which had formerly meant the flirtatious talk that could lead to the whispered exchanges of courtship, took on the meaning of exchanged caresses in the back seats of automobiles. *The Sex Life of Youth*, the YMCA's guide for parents and children, offered calm advice about petting (that earned it a reputation as a guide for petters) but also warned that the practice needed levelheaded control. Petting, of course, worked against levelheadedness: "The sex organs become tumescent, the blood is withdrawn from the brain centers which control purposeful action and the lovers in a measure 'lose their heads,' which is normal to proper intercourse." In discussing the sexualization of early-twentieth-century society, sociologist Ernest Groves worried that young people might find the shift from friendship to a sexual relationship too rapid, that "without warning" a young person might suddenly "feel the strength of a sex drive that is both physical and psychic."[31] Since the 1920s the question has remained open whether petting indicated not just the acceptance of heterosexual sex play but also an emerging acceptance of early intercourse. The commonsense answer has always been "Of course it did—how could it not?" But the evidence remains ambiguous.

For many older youth and young adults, petting became foreplay. Even so, the testimony of middle-class diarists usually demonstrates restraint rather than abandon. Martha Lavell, already in college, was shocked when her friend Janet told her that "she didn't believe that it is possible in this age to ever find a man (whom you'd care to marry) who hadn't had intercourse with other women." For some women, engagement became the context for the beginning of inter-course. Others, like Gladys Bell, remained virgins until marriage. Several sur-veys, including psychologist Lewis Terman's work and the sex researches of Alfred Kinsey, show a growing proportion (36 percent in Kinsey, 86 percent in Terman's study) of women coming of age in the 1920s who had sex before marriage. In fact, Kinsey's study found the rate of premarital intercourse more than doubling for women coming of age in the 1920s compared to women only a decade older, the biggest change of sexual behavior between older and younger generations. The impression of many commentators agreed with the research.

V. F. Calverton, an advocate of what he called the "sexual revolution," lauded the sophistication of modern youth to find ways (i.e., birth control) "of tasting joy without its old penalties and pains."[32]

Most research depended on samples of convenience, and even Kinsey's massive study fails to rise to current statistical rigor in the social sciences. Taken together, however, these studies along with personal accounts point in the same direction, toward a growing openness to sexual experience among American women. Because women typically underreport sexual experiences that are disapproved within the double standard of morality, the growing number who reported pre-marital intercourse suggests an even larger wave of sexual experimentation. The Kinsey study also revealed that middle-class men coming of age in the twentieth century began to shift their early sexual experience from lower-class women (often prostitutes) to their social peers.[33]

From our vantage almost a century later, we see petting as foreplay. But for the 1920s, the rituals of heterosexual conviviality also provided new forms of control, or perhaps management, for some of the real problems of adolescent sexuality. Dating in high school and college meant seeing many new partners. These escorts would have been relatively casual acquaintances, certainly not the kind for whom girls would risk pregnancy or a venereal infection. Also, as we saw above, petting often took place in semipublic places or even among groups of couples. Both the casualness of the date, and its group setting, would have made intercourse unlikely. Premarital sex in the period mainly meant just that, sex with someone you planned to marry. So, for instance, when Adele Siegel wrote about making love with her boyfriend in college, this was the man she would later marry. A study from the 1930s noted that women who can easily fend off the temptation of sex while dating found that they had fewer resources to resist once they made an emotional commitment.[34] For middle-class (and probably for most working-class) youth in the 1920s sexual intercourse meant what it had in most times and places—the end of youth and the beginning of adult responsibilities.

## Crushes

New companions, as much as dating and petting, shaped adolescent sexuality in the 1920s. Whether we take fictional teenagers as our guides or the diary entries of contemporary adolescents, we quickly learn that adolescents in the 1920s entered a world of new desires and new sexual practices. But the wider social reality of high school meant that not only did boys and girls find themselves in the company of strangers of the opposite sex—almost everyone was a stranger. Extended education also extended the social possibilities for girls and boys. At dances and on dates, girls and boys found that they could play together. But the girls still mainly made friends with girls, boys with boys. American youth in the 1920s managed the physical and social awkwardness of high school by relying on their same-sex friends.

Homosociality—a term not invented until the mid-1970s and referring to both close, same-sex friendships and networks of same-sex friends—became an important subject for psychologists and social scientists early in the twentieth century. Sex-segregated institutions had attracted attention for fostering friendships and even intense love relationships that had some of the hallmarks of the recently minted category "homosexuality." But it was one thing when this behavior appeared in prisons or even reformatories, quite another when it turned up at summer camps for children or in women's colleges. And, still another thing entirely, and in many ways far more surprising, when these passionate relationships persisted in coeducational high schools.[35]

Marion Taylor, growing up in California, hero-worshiped her English teacher, whom she called "Miss Green" in her diary. She idealized her looks and her personality, sent her notes and matched her mood to the attention she received (or did not receive) from Miss Green. This interest lasted through her junior high years, 1914 to 1916. She would later have crushes on other teachers: "I adore first one and then another but it sure is strong while it lasts. I just can't think of anything else when I'm in love, and I love so hard it hurts."[36]

Marion also had friends her own age, but only later, in college, did she experience a peer relationship that gave her the same feelings that she had for her teachers. "I just love her to distraction," she wrote. Marion's "crush" is noteworthy only because she attended the coeducational University of California, Los Angeles. At women's colleges across the country, crushes or "smashing" became well-established phenomena early in the century as part of the experience of young college women. Passionate friendships were, if anything, more common among younger adolescents. Yvonne Blue wanted to make "blood sister" pacts with her friends, and she had the same yearning for her friend Bobbie that might now figure into a teenage heterosexual romance. Separated from Bobbie for weeks during a summer vacation in 1926, Yvonne was thrilled when Bobbie made a surprise visit with her family. "I dragged Bobbie back in the dining room, where we fell on each others' necks and almost wept. We both felt awfully trembly and shaky." Beth Twiggar, 11 years after Marion and on the other side of the continent, expressed her strongest affection for her friend in terms very similar to Marion's: "I love that girl. . . . Nothing makes me happier than when I have her approval. Nothing is so delightful as to be alone in her presence."[37]

The emerging field of expertise in adolescent development included both boys and girls when discussing the "crush" and "hero worship." Crushes typically took place among peers and might be a secret on one side, though they tended to be reciprocal. Hero worship usually involved a young person's admiration for an older adolescent or adult, and typically would not be reciprocal. The literature assumed that adolescence began for all children with a transitory period of homosexuality. Paul Benton, in Robert Carr's novel, took for granted that he had to join one of the young men's cliques in his small town. His first action on being allowed to wear long pants is to try to fit in with the boys who "hang around" at the pool hall. Sociologist Jeffrey Dennis uses a variety of sources to demonstrate that, until World War II, boys typically interpreted an interest in girls as girlish. Although this applied less to older boys, during high school the typical relations for most boys were with other boys. In films, boys related to other individual boys and ran in gangs or groups. "[I]n fact," writes Dennis, "the intensity, intimacy, exclusivity, and permanence of these partnerships resemble nothing in mass culture so much as adult heterosexual romances."[38]

Homosocial relations could help in uncovering the erotic, in particular making the "solitary vice" often not so solitary. A study from early in the 1920s, in North Carolina, showed that the great majority of boys, whether in high school or working in the mills, masturbated. In response to what led to the practice, "boys' talk" and "boys' example" were the most common replies. School allowed boys to share methods. At one school they masturbated at their desks so frequently that teachers called it the "pocket habit." In another district the superintendent ordered that boys' pockets be sewn up. A contemporary study of young women found fewer who admitted to masturbating, and a lower proportion who had developed the practice with friends. Still, about 40 percent of women interviewed who had begun the practice in childhood recalled that it had been suggested by others.[39]

By the 1920s, experts in child development viewed the achievement of heterosexuality as a crisis and treated homosocial or seemingly homosexual relations among young adolescents as normal. Psychologists advised that the strong friendships boys and girls formed with members of their own sex should be seen as way stations on the journey toward heterosexuality. They warned teachers and camp counselors against encouraging hero worship and offered reassurance to parents about youthful friendships. Apparently this had some effect. Anne McKay recalled that when her friend Ellie, in the 1940s, asked her mother what a lesbian was, the mothers of the two girls had a discussion that resulted in a little talk from Anne's mother who reassured her that this kind of thing was perfectly normal, "the old 'Going Through a stage [sic]' routine," wrote Anne. According to the advice literature, as long as attachment to same-sex partners did not continue too long, these would serve to foster normal (i.e., heterosexual) tendencies.[40]

Homosociality fits poorly with popular memory of the 1920s, the decade of flaming heterosexuality. At the time, apart from experts who studied youth culture, the intensity of same-sex relationships attracted relatively little attention. But within the mixed setting of the public junior and senior high schools, boys and girls lived in separate worlds. One bemused high school boy in 1928 wrote that girls "walk down the corridors all twined together like a figure eight." Psychologists like Leta Hollingsworth assumed the years following puberty gave youth their best opportunity to "to develop an unhampered, unabashed, unafraid, undisgusted attitude toward contact with the opposite sex."[41] She obviously assumed that most people arrive at puberty with an attitude toward the opposite sex that is hampered, abashed, afraid, and disgusted.

Becoming heterosexual required a lot of help. Individual best friends and groups of same sex peers supported one another as they struggled to understand and embrace the transition. The North Carolina study found that most boys learned about "sex matters" from other boys. Dates frequently began in groups, and the double date seemed far more common than the lone couple. On the double date, Geoffrey Gorer noted, the deeper emotional bond is between the two friends of the same sex who arranged the date. Robert Carr's Paul Benton begins his dating experience with a double date, and learned the skills of flirting, petting, and dancing either on double dates or with the encouragement of other boys. Yvonne Blue (shown in figure 2.2) and her friend Bobbie discussed every sighting of Yvonne's boy crush, Lorence O'Hara, and tried to understand his nature without ever talking to him. Fourteen-year-old Edyth Weiner talked to her friend Barbara about her crushes on various boys, and also spent time

**FIGURE 2.2** Yvonne Blue, no date (probably late 1920s).

*Source*: Schlesinger Library, Radcliffe Institute, Harvard University, Cambridge, MA.

between classes (perhaps even during class time!) talking about the boys she liked. Groups of students gathered at ice cream parlors after school or after movies. "You meet everyone you know, there," wrote Edyth Weiner. Informal parties might include only single sex groups for games, bridge, and gossip, though these could easily turn into mixed groups. Clubs, or the sororities and fraternities that survived in some high schools into the 1920s, could organize social events and, to some extent, the social lives of members by arranging for escorts. A group could determine how well one did in the dating game. Edyth Weiner was certain that she would do better with boys if she were "in with a popular crowd of girls."[42]

While success in the peer world of the high school could seem more important than anything, only a narrow minority attained it. Success meant becoming popular, which in turn meant attracting dates. But dating did not preclude strong attachments to same sex peers, and dating did not exclude boys or girls from their same-sex groups. The homosocial relations in the adolescent world that formed in the first third of the twentieth century provided a familiar environment for youth confronting the confusion of high school and the rapid changes in their social world and within themselves. Close friends provided the emotional support that the much shallower world of dating would never provide. Also, boys and girls, in groups or with close friends of the same gender, could work out the mysteries of the strange people on the other side of the gender divide. "Girls talk to chums they can trust about a boy they like but criticize the same boy to the crowd to hide their interest."[43] Homosocial relations did not necessarily have greater importance than heterosexual conviviality. Rather, the two existed together. Boy and girl craziness existed within the homosocial environment. Homosociality made heterosexual conviviality possible.

## Homosexuality

The strong friendships that provided adolescents shelter from the confusion of their dawning sexuality may have also given some comfort for other teenagers whose desires never matched those of their peers. The autobiography of "Diana Frederics" traces her growing recognition of lesbian desire during her high school years. Even her modest success with an attractive older man, Gil, left her unsatisfied. But during her senior year she began a friendship with Ruth, a girl in her class. They soon become inseparable, and as time passes her feelings for Ruth grow stronger. After a friend's Christmas party they share the same bed, and Ruth's casual good-night embrace filled Diana with desire. She later recalled, "My longing for Ruth was the most exquisite pain I had ever known." Soon, however, she stumbled on some contemporary literature on lesbianism that convinced her of the abnormality of her feelings. She began to retreat from her usual life in high school and even to avoid Ruth. When she confessed to her brother, a medical student, he responded using the best insights of the psychology of the time: "I was the victim of a school-girl crush," he told her, "that crushes were common at my age . . . But there was nothing abnormal about it. I would outgrow it." When she managed to convince him it was not only a crush, he shared with her work by Havelock Ellis, which allowed her to see homosexuality in a different light.[44]

Diana's experience provides a clue to the ambivalent comfort of homosociality for homosexual youth. In some cases, homosocial friendships might have given girls and boys opportunities to experience sexual relations with same-gender peers. This may have been the case for Yvonne Blue, who pursued a lesbian relation in college without much apparent inner conflict.[45] In general, the homosocial networks probably made "passing" easier—boys or girls with crushes on other boys and girls would not have seemed unusual, especially in the early teen years.

Passing may have been easier for girls than boys. Even if casual sexual exploration for boys might include homosexual acts, gendered norms of behavior became fairly clear and demanding by the teenage years. Cornelius Utz, born in 1909, recalled that even though he felt desire for some of his high school companions, he never dared let this be known for fear of being labeled a "sissy." "To be a good, sturdy, non-sissy guy, you had to be interested in sports like football and basketball." He only found the possibility of having a homosexual relationship when he went to college, where one of his professors introduced him to gay sex. Interviews of homosexual college men who sought counseling showed that many of them had clearly understood their homoerotic desires as adolescents but kept them secret. Of one man the case study reported, "He first noticed that he was unlike other boys during high school, when he realized that his feelings about girls were vastly different from theirs." Like Cornelius Utz, most of the young men interviewed only found sexual or love relations when they went to college.[46]

For most older teenagers, especially those who did not go to college, heterosexual relations assumed more and more interest, time, and commitment, usually leading to courtship. Gay youth, however, would have faced greater difficulties as they grew older. Life in one of the large cities could allow a youth or young adult to find a gay subculture. For most adolescent Americans, however, homosexuality was easy to hide but difficult to live.

## Coercive Sex

Petting became an expected part of the date, a ritual of sex play for the couple. Still, girls could often set their own limits. At a friend's party, Adele Siegel's date "wouldn't behave. I slapped his face hard, and he was very respectful and gentlemanly the rest of the evening." She also recorded that "Johnny Duncan fell in love with me. He tried to get me to let him kiss me, but I wouldn't let him . . ." In some cases, men wanted more than a kiss. Beth Twiggar wrote of one date during which she resisted her escort's suggestion that they "go the limit.'"[47] These scenes played over again endlessly during the roaring twenties. The dawning assumption that girls possessed sexual desire could also carry with it the belief that girls who did not express their desire misunderstood themselves or resisted their true urges. This could serve as justification for some men to push for sex even when women resisted. In workplaces, too, girls spent time with older boys and men, and during their free time they still had the opportunity for local amusements, sometimes with petting, sometimes with intercourse, as the price.[48]

Novels like *Flaming Youth* and movies like *It* reinforced the image of the flapper, young working women still not ready for marriage but possibly ready for some sexual adventure. The nineteenth-century narrative of sexual purity seemed no longer to apply to young women in the twentieth century, and seemingly gave greater power to the older male counternarrative that scheming girls would lie about rape for their own purposes. A 1928 guide to sex by psychiatrist William Robinson claimed that only 10 percent of rape charges were true.[49]

Yet even though the flaming youth of the period became more sexually exploratory, expanded schooling may have changed the social structure of coercive sex. As dating in junior high and high school shifted socializing toward couples of approximately the same age, the likelihood of peer-to-peer coercion may have declined. And as more and more girls had the benefit of extended schooling, this removed them from sexual predation by older coworkers and bosses. Of course, once they entered the workforce in their late teens, girls still had to negotiate sex play and sexual favors with older males. They may, however, have entered the workplace with more resources for dealing with sexual demands. The falling age of marriage during the 1920s shows that girls and young women made love and marriage agreements at younger ages. From a twenty-first-century standpoint this does not seem like sexual liberation, but for the youth of the 1920s this at least offered greater economic safety and social acceptability.

College, of course, complicated the model described earlier. Girls in college almost inevitably had more experiences with older men. Consider Yvonne Blue. As we saw, Yvonne was a late bloomer in the adolescent world of heterosexual play. In college she became interested in boys and balanced her studies with time for friends and dates. Petting went with dating, something she enjoyed but still chided herself for. During her senior year she wrote, "I know that if Helen or Olive or Adele—or anybody here—had looked in Bill's car Saturday night their opinion of me would change a lot & I wouldn't blame them." Later that same year she went with her friend Lillian to the home of an artist who had an interesting social circle and sponsored wild parties. Yvonne met a young man who convinced her to leave with him, and they spent the night together at a hotel, though without having intercourse. Yvonne chastised herself for her foolishness, but a few nights later she returned to the artist's home. Drinking, dancing, and necking with various men ensued, and one of those men almost raped her. Even though Yvonne fended off the advance, she still blamed herself for being a victim of coercion and violence.[50] Her college years exposed her to a wider range of sexual experience, and to the possibility of sexual violence, but she also had greater self-possession than she would have had as a younger adolescent.

## The New Adolescent Sexuality

By the time the stock market collapsed in 1929, "dating"—an "idiosyncratic" and "highly patterned activity" (as Geoffrey Gorer described it) had spread across the United States.[51] In cities and most small towns, people from their early teen years to their early twenties went on dates, often with other couples. High school students added school activities to their dating, but both middle-class and working-class youth escaped adult supervision by going to movies and dance halls or just "gadding about." Sex play almost always followed the date. During the 1920s the middle-class peer group judged as a success someone whose dating was varied and episodic. Adolescents wanted new partners for every date, a pattern that some college fraternities formalized. The sex play remained exploratory and typically ended short of intercourse precisely because of the socially promiscuous and episodic nature of dating. Success meant popularity in the peer group. But in addition to being embedded in a peer group usually defined by where one went to school and even the grade in school, adolescents in the 1920s moved into the world of heterosexual adventure with close same-gender friendships and with homosocial networks that provided support, encouragement, and most of the deepest emotional relationships for early-twentieth-century adolescents.

The key element of this pattern—teenagers socializing without adults—remained a permanent feature of adolescent sexuality. But American youth arriving at high school after 1930 began to alter and abandon many of the most recognizable features of dating. The dating culture of the 1920s—the most distinctive sexuality of American youth—would survive only one generation.

## Notes

1. Geoffrey Gorer, *The American People: A Study in National Character* (New York: W. W. Norton, 1948), 109, 110. Gorer's work, although from the late 1940s, describes dating in its classical form. He apparently based his "anthropological" report not on field work but on sociology from the previous decade, particularly Willard Waller.
2. Mabel Craig Stillman, "Practical Talks for Parents and Teachers," *Journal of Genetic Psychology* 29, no. 1 (March 1922): 41; and Kathleen W. Jones, *Taming the Troublesome Child: American Families, Child Guidance, and the Limits of Psychiatric Authority* (Cambridge, MA: Harvard University Press, 1999), 139 and chap. 5 generally.
3. Susan J. Matt, *Keeping Up with the Joneses: Envy in American Consumer Society, 1890–1930* (Philadelphia: University of Pennsylvania, 2003), 153; Paula Fass, *The Damned and the Beautiful: American Youth in the 1920's* (Oxford: Oxford University Press, 1979), 54–57, and chap. 2; and Steven Mintz, *Huck's Raft: A History of American Childhood* (Cambridge, MA: Belknap, 2006), 216; for a discussion of the new importance of youth of American life, Gilman Ostrander, *American Civilization in the First Machine Age: 1890–1940* (New York: HarperCollins, 1972).

4. Jones, *Troublesome Child*, 131. Robert S. Lynd and Helen Merrell Lynd, *Middletown: A Study in American Culture* (New York: Harcourt, Brace and Co., 1929), 183, 187; David Nasaw, *Schooled to Order: A Social History of Public Schooling in the United States* (New York: Oxford University Press, 1979), 163; Jeffery Dennis, *We Boys Together: Teenagers in Love Before Girl-Craziness* (Nashville, TN: Vanderbilt University Press, 2007), 4; and U.S. Department of Commerce, Bureau of Foreign and Domestic Commerce, *Statistical Abstract of the United States* (Washington, DC: Government Printing Office, 1930), 108.

5. Beth Twiggar Goff, "The Papers of Beth Twiggar Goff," Diaries, Schlesinger Library, Radcliffe Institute, Harvard University, Cambridge, MA, n.d., 1:1, 2/19/28; 2/25/28; Yvonne Skinner, "Papers of Yvonne Blue Skinner," n.d., MC459 M-26, Schlesinger Library, Radcliffe Institute for Advanced Study, Harvard University, April 4, 1926; July 1, August 4, and February 4, 1927, quoted in John C. Spurlock and Cynthia A. Magistro, *New and Improved: The Transformation of American Women's Emotional Culture* (New York: New York University Press, 1998), 40; and Joan Jacobs Brumberg, *The Body Project: An Intimate History of American Girls* (New York: Vintage Books, 1998), 100–107.

6. Irving King, *The High School Age* (Indianapolis, IN: Bobbs Merrill, 1914), 28; Robert Carr, *The Rampant Age* (Garden City, NY: Doubleday, Doran and Co., 1928), 38; and Sanford M. Dornbusch, J. Merrill Carlsmith, Ruth T. Gross, John A. Martin, Dennis Jennings, Anne Rosenberg, and Paula Duke, "Sexual Development, Age, and Dating: A Comparison of Biological and Social Influences upon One Set of Behaviors," *Child Development* 52, no. 1 (March 1981): 179–185.

7. Stillman, "Practical Talks for Parents and Teachers," 24; Mintz, *Huck's Raft*, 222; and Jeffrey P. Moran, *Teaching Sex: The Shaping of Adolescence in the 20th Century* (Cambridge, MA: Harvard University Press, 2002), 106–107, 111.

8. Gorer, *American People*, 109–110.

9. Sarah Gamble, "Sarah Merry (Bradley) Gamble Papers," Diary 1912, Schlesinger, 3/18/12, 8:163.

10. John Modell, *Into One's Own: From Youth to Adulthood in the United States, 1920–1975* (Berkeley: University of California Press, 1991), 89; and John Modell, "Dating Becomes the Way of American Youth," in *Essays on the Family and Historical Change*, ed. David Levine, Leslie Page Moch, Louise A. Tilly, John Modell, and Elizabeth Pleck (College Station: Texas A&M Press, 1983), 107. Elizabeth Clement has traced this shift from working-class treating being seen as a close approach to prostitution to its becoming mainstream heterosexuality. Elizabeth Clement, *Love for Sale: Courting, Treating, and Prostitution in New York City, 1900–1945* (Chapel Hill: University of North Carolina Press, 2006).

11. Modell, "Dating Becomes the Way of American Youth," 109.

12. Nicholas L. Syrett, *The Company He Keeps: A History of White College Fraternities, Gender and American Culture* (Chapel Hill: University of North Carolina Press, 2009), 186, 221, http://reeveslib.setonhill.edu:2174/ehost/pdfviewer/pdfviewer?vid=3&sid=bf6349a5–31ae-4ae0-bc7a-568914cbe464%40sessionmgr110&hid=123; Helen Lefkowitz Horowitz, *Campus Life: Undergraduate Cultures from the End of the Eighteenth Century to the Present* (New York: A. A. Knopf, 1987), 124, 127, 208; and Fass, *Damned and Beautiful*, chap. 6.

13. Modell, *Into One's Own*, 72–73; M. V. O'Shea, *The Trend of the Teens* (Chicago: Frederick J. Drake, 1920), 105; and Oliver M. Butterfield, *Love Problems of Adolescence* (New York: Teacher's College, 1939), 34.

14. Marion Taylor, "The Papers of Dorothy Sherman Pencharz," Diaries, Schlesinger Library, Radcliffe Institute, Harvard University, Cambridge, MA, 1:14, 6/19/20.

15. Edyth Weiner First, "The Papers of Edyth Weiner First," Diary, Schlesinger Library, Radcliffe Institute, Harvard University, Cambridge, MA, 1929, 2/17/29.

16. Dorothy Smith Dushkin, "The Papers of Dorothy Smith Dushkin", n.d., Sophia Smith Collection, 3:1, 6/20/24; and Adele Siegel Rosenfeld, "The Papers of Adele Siegel Rosenfeld," Diaries, Schlesinger Library, Radcliffe Institute, Harvard University, Cambridge, MA, 1:11/6/31.

17. Lois Banner, *American Beauty* (Chicago: University of Chicago Press, 1984), 176; Modell, *Into One's Own*, 71–72; Gladys Hasty Carroll, *To Remember Forever: The Journal of a College Girl, 1922–1923* (Boston: Little, Brown, 1963), 36–37; and Ann Marie Low, *Dust Bowl Diary* (Lincoln: University of Nebraska, 1984), 121.

18. Modell, *Into One's Own*, 104; Nancy Hale, "Papers of Nancy Hale," n.d., 13A, Sophia Smith Collection, 2/21/1922; and Penrod Papers, 9/16/21.

19. Dushkin Papers, 3:1, 8/21/24; First Papers, 4/4/29, 2/21/29, 5/11/29; Willard Waller, "The Rating and Dating Complex," *American Sociological Review* 2 (October 1937): 727–734; Goff papers, quoted in Spurlock and Magistro, *New and Improved*, 40, and also a discussion of Marion Taylor and Dorothy Smith's ambivalence about men.

20. Yvonne Skinner, "Papers of Yvonne Blue Skinner" [hereafter YBS Papers], n.d., MC459 M-26, Schlesinger Library, Radcliffe Institute for Advanced Study, Harvard University, reel 1; May 10, 1924; May 14, 1924; and October 11, 1924.

21. Rosenfeld Papers, 10/30/31, 11/2/31, 1: page for 7/6 but dated 8/1/31.

22. Hale papers, "Beaux book."

23. Izola Forrester, "When a Girl Gets Boy Crazy," *Parents* (March 1929), 18; Rosenfeld Papers, 6/13/31; Ann Marie Kordas, "Girl Troubles: Female Adolescent Sexuality in the United States, 1850–1950" (PhD diss., Temple University, 2002), 59–60; and Rosenfeld papers, June 13, 1931.

24. Ben B. Lindsey and Wainwright Evans, *The Revolt of Modern Youth* (New York: Boni and Liveright, 1925), 25–26; Warner Fabian, *Flaming Youth* (New York: Boni and Liveright, 1923), 99–100; and Carr, *Rampant Age*, 87. According to Wikipedia, Carr was only 17 when he wrote this novel! So, that adds a layer of credibility to it as a testimony to youthful social lives.

25. Joseph Kett, *Rites of Passage: Adolescence in America, 1790 to the Present* (New York: Basic Books, 1977), 261; the terms *petting* and *necking* were seemingly interchangeable in 1920s, with *petting* more common; Malcolm Cowley, *Exile's Return: A Literary Odyssey of the 1920s* (New York: Viking, 1934), 22; Arthur Dean, "A Survey on Petting," *Journal of Education* 10 (1929): 414; and Lorinne Pruette, "The Revolt of the Virgins," in *Our Neurotic Age: A Consultation*, ed. Samuel D. Schmalhausen (New York: Farrar & Rinehart, 1932), 578.

26. Eddy Sherwood, *Sex and Youth* (New York: Doubleday, Doran and Co., 1929), 54; Pruette, "Revolt," 579; Fabian, *Flaming Youth*, 60, 100. Peter Laipson shows that marital advice literature had begun to encourage foreplay by the 1920s; Peter Laipson, "'Kiss without Shame, for She Desires It': Sexual Foreplay in American Marital Advice Literature, 1900–1925," *Journal of Social History* 29 (March 1996): 507–525, http://www.thefreelibrary.com/%22Kiss+without+shame,+for+she+desires+it%22:+sexual+foreplay+in+American+ . . . -a018498206. Pamela Haag, "In Search of 'The Real Thing': Ideologies of Love, Modern Romance, and Women's Sexual Subjectivity in the United States, 1920–40," *Journal of the History of Sexuality* 2 (1992): 547–577.

27. G. F. Smith, "Certain Aspects of the Sex Life of the Adolescent Girl," *Journal of Applied Psychology* 8, no. 3 (September 1924): 347–349. Dean, "A Survey on Petting," 414.

28. Quoted in Spurlock and Magistro, *New and Improved*, 42.

29. Pencharz Papers, 1:14, 1/9/25, and 1:4. 2/21/24.

30. Zelda Fitzgerald, *The Collected Writings of Zelda Fitzgerald* (Tuscaloosa: University of Alabama Press, 1997), 391; Dean, "Survey on Petting," 414; Hale Papers, "Beaux Book" and Oct. 25, 1924, and January 7, 1925; Rosenfeld Papers, 1:12/4/31; Goff papers, v. 22, quoted in Spurlock and Magistro, *New and Improved*, 43.

31. Max J. Exner, *The Question of Petting* (New York: Association Press, 1926), 65; and Ernest Groves, "Sex Psychology of the Unmarried Adult," in *The Sex Life of the Unmarried Adult: An Inquiry into and an Interpretation of Current Sex Practices* (New York: Vanguard, 1934), 105.

32. Lavell Papers, 2: 9/22/30; Penrod Papers, April 1925; Terman is cited in Kett, *Rites of Passage*, 261; Alfred Kinsey and Institute for Sex Research, *Sexual Behavior in the Human Female* (Bloomington: Indiana University Press, 1998), 298–299; G. V. Hamilton, *A Research in Marriage* (New York: Medical Research Press, 1929), 346; V. F. Calverton, *The Bankruptcy of Marriage* (New York: Macauley, 1928), 124. Calverton, of course, also referred to married couples as well as the unmarried.

33. Kinsey and Institute for Sex Research, *Sexual Behavior*, 411–413. Kinsey attributed the decline in the resort to prostitutes as resulting from education campaigns associating prostitution with venereal disease and to criminalization of prostitution.

34. Rosenfeld Papers, April 17, 1936; and Dorothy Dunbar Bromley and Florence Haxton Britten, *Youth and Sex: A Study of 1300 College Students* (New York: Harper and Brothers, 1938), 60.

35. Jessie Bernard, "Homosociality and Female Depression," *Journal of Social Issues* 32 (1976): 213–235. Jean Lipman-Blumen, "Toward a Homosocial Theory of Sex Roles: An Explanation of the Sex Segregation of Social Institutions," *Signs* 1, no. 3 (Spring 1976): 15–31.

36. Pencharz Papers, April 1919: 1:10, 15; Ada Hart Arlitt, *Adolescent Psychology* (New York: American Book Co., 1933), 43; and John C. Spurlock, "From Reassurance to Irrelevance: Adolescent Psychology and Homosexuality in America," *History of Psychology* 5 (February 2002): 38–51.

37. Pencharz Papers, 1:14, 1/4/21; Nancy Sahli, "Smashing: Women's Relationships before the Fall," *Chrysalis* 8 (Summer 1979); YBS, diary for 1923 and August 4, 1926; Beth Twiggar quoted in Spurlock and Magistro, *New and Improved*, 47; Katherine Bement Davis, *Factors in the Sex Life of Twenty-two Hundred Women* (New York: Harper & Bros, 1929), 247–249; and Phyllis Blanchard and Carolyn Manassas, *New Girls for Old* (New York: Macauley, 1930), 99. Katherine Bement Davis's study of sexuality, published in 1929, identified 183 homosexuals in her sample of 1,000 college-educated women, but more than 50 percent of these women reported intense emotional relations with other women. Some women had viewed the relations as sexual, others had not. About half of these intense relations had begun before college; Katherine Bement Davis, *A Study of Certain Auto-erotic Practices: Based on Replies of 2,255 Women to Questionnaires Prepared by the Bureau of Social Hygiene with the Advice of a Cooperating Committee* (New York: National Committee for Social Hygiene, 1925), 247–249. Although Davis's sample has no claim on either representativeness or randomness, it is highly suggestive. Blanchard and Manassas also found crushes found common and widespread.

38. Carr, *Rampant Age*, 23; Dennis, *We Boys*, 12; and Spurlock, "Reassurance."

39. Walter L. Hughes, "Sex Experiences of Boyhood," *Journal of Social Hygiene* 12 (1926): 262–266; Stillman, "Practical Talks," 24; Carr, *Rampant Age*, 23; Davis, *A Study of Certain Auto-erotic Practices*, 12.

40. Spurlock, "Reassurance"; quote from Susan Maria Ferentinos, "An Unpredictable Age: Sex, Consumption, and the Emergence of the American Teenager, 1900–1950" (PhD diss., Indiana University, 2005), 157, http://wwwlib.umi.com/dissertations/fullcit/3204295.

41. Quote from Papers of Ruth Raymond, box 1, volume 24, March 30, 1928, quoted in Spurlock and Magistro, *New and Improved*, 46; and Leta Hollingworth, *The Psychology of the Adolescent* (New York: D. Appleton, 1928), 117.

42. Walter L. Hughes, "Sex Experiences of Boyhood," *Journal of Social Hygiene* 12 (1926): 265; Carr, *Rampant Age*, 87–89, 146; YBS, October 23, 1926; First papers, Diary,

January 1, February 10 and 23, 1929, March 6 and 15, 1929, December 16, 1929; and Gorer, *American People*, 118.

43. Frances Bruce Strain, *The Normal Sex Interests of Children: From Infancy to Childhood* (New York: Appleton-Century-Crofts, 1948), 58.

44. Diana Frederics [pseud.], *Diana: A Strange Autobiography* (New York: Dial, 1939), 17–19, 20–23, 26–27.

45. YBS, January 24, 1928.

46. Martin W. Peck, "The Sex Life of College Men," *The Journal of Nervous and Mental Disease* 61, no. 1 (January 1925): 35; Vern Bullough and Bonnie Bullough, "Lesbianism in the 1920s and 1930s: A Newfound Study," *Signs* 2 (1977): 895–907; George Chauncey, *Gay New York* (New York: Basic Books, 1994); and Will Fellows, ed., *Farm Boys: Lives of Gay Men from the Rural Midwest* (Madison,: University of Wisconsin Press, 1996), 40–41.

47. Rosenfeld Papers, 1: 12/4/31; and Goff Papers, 1:3v, 4/19/28.

48. Pamela Haag, *Consent: Sexual Rights and the Transformation of American Liberalism* (Ithaca, NY: Cornell University Press, 1999), 121–142; and Haag, "The Real Thing," 547–577.

49. Estelle B. Freedman, *Redefining Rape: Sexual Violence in the Era of Suffrage and Segregation* (Cambridge, MA: Harvard University Press, 2013), 147–167.

50. YBS Papers, 8/31/31, December 18 and 24, 1931.

51. Gorer, *American People*, 110.

# 3

# COMPANIONATE SEXUALITY

The public and promiscuously heterosocial world of dating, in which young couples went out for a night of dancing, ice cream cones, and petting, has a firm place in our collective memory of the early-twentieth-century youth culture. Removed from its urban origins, where it existed in the penumbra of sexual negotiation and prostitution, dating became a sanitized, usable past, a convenient prop for making invidious comparisons with an imagined present of oversexed youth. The date, in fact, claimed such a powerful place in the public imagination that it lived on as a model for youthful sexuality long after it had all but disappeared.

The Roaring Twenties, and dating with it, was swallowed by the Great Depression. After 1929, as unemployment soared, even those families with a working breadwinner struggled to cover all the necessities of life. The discretionary income needed to support the dating culture disappeared. When both employment and income recovered during the 1940s, the emergency of the war years shaped the lives of older youth and young adults. But by the 1940s heterosexual conviviality had already taken a new form.

After the passage of several decades, steady dating or "going steady" coexists with dating as a natural corollary. The rituals of going steady, "pinning" (the boy giving the girl some token of his commitment) and the earnest monogamy of mid-century high school students, may seem overly precious to us in the opening years of the new century. But, even though the terms *steady* (as in the person one has the relationship with) and *going steady* have dropped out of use, the "going steady complex" (as sociologists called it) imposed a structure on adolescent sexuality beginning in the 1930s that continues, in some form, to the present. Every element of adolescent sexuality, from declining age of marriage, declining age of first pregnancy, and rising rates of premarital sex, worked within the context of the steady system and were accelerated by it. If we want to assign a single cause to the lower age at which teenagers, especially girls, became sexually active in the late twentieth century, then "the pill," World War II, and the sexual openness of the 1960s all have less claim on our attention than does the shift from the ephemeral dalliance relationships of dating to the long-term involvement of going steady.

## "He's Always Bothering Me. Well, He's Not Bad."

We can gain a sense of the shift in adolescent socializing through the diaries of April Bennett, which open almost exactly 30 years after Yvonne Blue's began. In 1951, April was a 13-year-old, growing up on her family's farm, near Versailles, Indiana. Diaries with extended entries, especially when kept over long periods, contain as much (and often more) emotional turmoil as personal triumph. April's writing will contain turmoil in abundance, including her doubts about her mental health in later years (probably inspired by her college psychology course). But in most respects, her diaries reveal a girl and a young woman who had good relations with her parents, especially with her mother with whom she talks openly about her self-doubts and boy problems. April goes to many movies, attends church, and participates in 4-H. As we would expect from a high school girl in the Hoosier state, she goes to a lot of basketball games.[1]

And then there are the boys. Talk about boys appears frequently in the diaries from her junior high years onward, though until high school most of the talk deals with boys at a distance. For instance, in a 1952 entry she feels very "mixed up" because she does not like any of the boys in her class. They seem too "premature," although she also wishes "some nice handsome boy would like me." Later that spring she expressed her confusion about popularity and her "brooding" over not having a boy take her out. In ninth grade she has what seems an almost too typical early teen experience. Her friend Janet reveals that there is a boy who has a crush on April. A few days later the same boy pulls a chair from under her in biology class. He then very gallantly "asked to help me up as if I was hurt. Janet was right when she said he had a crush on me. It shows all over. He's always bothering me. Well, he's not bad."[2]

Through the rest of the high school diaries, the topic of boys reappears frequently. "Oh glorious! Glorious!!" she exclaims in March 1954. Eugene had walked her to the library, and two weeks later she writes, "Everything is wonderful. . . ." She felt she was on the verge of beginning her "teen-age dating years." Yet every passage of relief, joy, and triumph is matched by several of doubt, frustration, and despair. Boys do not seem to care for her because of her reserve, her self-confidence, her sophistication. Another self-assessment a few months later reads, "April Bennett who is 16 & a junior [at Versailles High School] who is a bit stuck up, & who dresses dramatically, who longs so terribly for dates . . ."[3]

For April, as for Yvonne Blue, relations with boys and young men became easier, although also more complicated, after she began college. Although there are gaps in her diary keeping, by her second year at Indiana University, April has apparently had a romance with a student named Ron. After a gap in her diary writing, she begins writing again in February 1957 about a new love interest, Dan. April's reflections in her diary show that both in terms of physical intimacy and life commitments, the stakes are much higher with Dan. "We both desire the other so much that our dates become a matter of keeping our sense and not going on as we both want to." "Kiss me, damn it!" he tells her when she sits down in his car on one of their dates. "I *liked* being commanded," she wrote.[4]

Her struggle with sexual desire was only part of April's emotional turmoil. Dan, a few years older, already works full-time, and in fact, his work takes him away from time to time. Also, Dan is Catholic and she is Baptist. This religious difference complicated the relationship far too much. During her final years at college April and Dan try to make things work but cannot. He has to go away to work. She dates other men. Finally, in October 1959 they split up. But the emotional cost of both her loss of Dan, and the struggle with her physical desire, seemingly affected her mental health. She wrote of a nervous breakdown and feeling that she might have another. One night after finals she felt dead inside, and spent three hours crying "alone, hysterical." Also, that December she spends a night with a man she had little emotional interest in. And that is where the diaries end.[5]

April Bennett's adolescence resembles Yvonne Blue's in many details. During their high school years, both girls became fascinated with boys. We saw Yvonne's interest in Lorence O'Brien take hold and linger even after he leaves her high school. For April, there are specific boys, like the joker who pulled the chair from under her and, later, Eugene, and then there are "boys." Like Yvonne, April has doubts about her attractiveness for boys. By the 1920s the term *boy craziness* had become common, and popular magazine articles instructed parents on the proper approach to help their girls out of it.[6] For April, the craze seems to have taken hold much earlier than it did for Yvonne. Like Edyth Weiner, she worried about how she looked and whether she would ever have the right personality to attract the boys around her. April's mother took boy craziness for granted, and in her talks with April tried to help her deal with her attraction to boys rather than attempt to talk her out of it.

Yet it is not the boy talk in April's dairy that most distinguishes it from Yvonne's, but the relative absence of girl talk—and, for that matter, of girls. Yvonne had at least two deep friendships with girls that she considered profoundly important and that she discussed at length. In addition, she had a network of girlfriends whose company made up most of her social life. Even after she went to college and began to date boys she had a long-term crush on bohemian Lucille. As we saw, most girls attending high school in the 1920s seem to have had a special "someone," a peer, an older girl, or a female teacher. Same-sex friendships remained important to girls in the generation that follows, but take up less of their emotional time and energy. When April uses the term *crush* in her diary she refers to Kenton's feelings about her. This first possibility of a boyfriend appeared for April in her early teen years, a time when girls in the 1920s would have still spent most of their spare moments hero-worshipping camp counselors or older peers. Among 1950s adolescents, the crush had been heterosexualized.

Both Yvonne and April become popular with boys in college, and they record remarks repeated to them about how attractive their male peers found them. Still, the contrasts are clear. We see Yvonne dating more or less wildly—drinking, riding in cars, and apparently going out with a variety of college boys and older men. She treats these excursions as "dalliance relations," fun for an evening but only important when consumed wholesale. April refers to dates, yet her college diary concerns mainly one man, Dan, whom she dates consistently for at least two years. With this long-term relationship came the possibility of deeper physical intimacy. In the last chapter, Yvonne found herself in strange, perhaps drunken, situations where she almost lost her virginity to men she hardly knew. April may have felt as much emotional caution and conflict over the possibility of intercourse, but that possibility seemed only to center on Dan, at least until they broke up. In the single generation between Yvonne and April, boys and girls replaced episodic excursions into the society of the opposite sex with longer, more comprehensive relationships. They moved from playing together to playing house together.

## Dating and Social Environment

These points of contrast in the biographies of two middle-class girls a generation apart point toward profound shifts in the social organization of sexuality. Even at its height in the late 1920s, dating functioned more like a fad—a fashion that everyone wanted to copy—and in its classic form probably never matched the lived experience of a majority of high school or even college students. Still, most adolescents understood themselves as living in a social world dominated by dating, either participating or else being left out of it. A generation later, dating had become a marginal activity. The other element of middle-class adolescence, the passionate friendships with others of the same gender, had faded away. Instead, high school and college youth formed long-term, committed heterosexual relationships, and when these ended they moved on to other long-term relations. By exploring these shifts we can better understand the direction that adolescent sexuality would take from the 1930s until late in the century.[7]

Dating would continue into the 1940s, but it flourished only in special social settings. When sociologist Willard Waller in 1937 gave a name, an explanation, and a seemingly indelible image to the "rating and dating complex," he made the point that what he called the "dalliance relationships" or "pure competition" that prevailed at "X university" (Penn State) existed in a social hothouse, where

fraternities and sororities dominated the social life of students and males outnumbered females six to one. In his article, Waller did not make clear what style
of conviviality prevailed among the students passed over for fraternity membership. He noted, however, that students at other colleges had quite different
"complexes." In one, girls are advised that they can "shop around" early in the
term, but by November "they should settle down and date someone steadily."
A professor at another college chaperoning a fraternity dance in 1935 worried
that one of the boys was "stuck" with a girl the entire evening. He asked one
of the boy's fraternity brothers to help out by cutting in, as was the custom in
colleges in the 1920s (and still was at Penn State). "The young man looked at me
wide-eyed and replied, 'Oh no! That's Fred's girl.'" Sociologist Michael Gordon
has shown that relations between boys and girls varied depending on where one
lived, from the early twentieth century onward. By the 1930s, dating and its
status system competed with other forms of youthful play.[8]

Late in the century sociologists claimed that populations in which women
outnumber men tend to favor Waller's dalliance relationships, or short-term
mating strategies to use the more recent term.[9] But Waller's study at Penn State
suggests a different conclusion: dating, or other dalliance relations, requires some
gender imbalance, whether in favor of male or female youth. Early-twentieth-
century high schools provided just such a setting. Even in the mid-1920s, girls
still formed a majority of teenagers attending high school, and a large majority
of those who finished. In the classic form of dating, girls competed for status
by dating many different, high-status boys. But the frequent changes of dating
partners also meant that more girls had opportunities for dates. On the boys'
side, the availability of so many girls, and the wide opportunity for some sex
play, must have made the expense of dating seem worthwhile. In the Greek
system at Penn State during Waller's study, brothers far outnumbered sisters.
The skewed sex ratio in favor of men made access to women both a sign and a
perquisite of status.

During the war years, the shift in sex ratios became far more volatile. In
addition, the transience of military personnel and the movement of many civil-
ians to take new work created opportunities rare in peacetime. One teenager,
already working at a defense plant after he left high school each day, recalled
dancing at a bar with an older, married woman whose husband was away in
the military. At the end of the dance they kissed, and she began to French kiss,
the first time for him.[10] The United Service Organizations (USO) attempted
to domesticate heterosexual relations. From 89 clubs in 1941, the USO grew to
3,035 by 1944, serving as many as 1 million people each day. This extraordinary
public/private partnership stands as perhaps the United States' most extensive
organization for sexual service, though without sex. Rather than chase pickups
or waste their leave at bars or brothels, servicemen were urged to go to USO
clubs to spend time with respectable girls and young ladies. Soldiers and sailors
could talk to and touch (while dancing) the USO hostesses, but rules in almost

all the clubs forbade hostesses from leaving with the servicemen. The Chicago USO made clear that "slipping out on a private date [meant] slipping out of the USO forever."[11]

Yet even though the USO ruled out dating, the "ritualized heterosexual courtship practices" on display at the clubs resembled dating from an earlier generation. The skewed gender ratio at the clubs, typically three military men to one hostess, created an environment hospitable to dating, though without rating. Every hostess could be the popular girl at the school dance, changing partners every dance as servicemen waited in stag lines for their turn at some closer contact with a girl. Senior hostesses chaperoned the club dances, like the faculty at high school dances or even parents providing young people space in a much-extended parlor. At the rare USO clubs that permitted dating, these excursions were usually to the home of a senior hostess and were carefully chaperoned. The practice of conviviality at these events would have seemed familiar to the generation of the senior hostesses, and they also matched the kind of advice that adult authorities offered concerning adolescent dating.[12]

The example of Freda Mae Rustemeyer, born in 1924, shows that the war emergency and the USO revived something of the traditional date. Freda Mae worked for the Red Cross during the war. She went out frequently, often to USO dances, and she dated many different men. In February 1943 she wrote, "I am going with Charles tonite [sic]. I don't know why I do. Just can't turn down a good show I guess." In early spring two soldiers call her after a "dry spell," and she had yet another date with a soldier she met while roller-skating. Socializing among shifting groups of soldiers and sailors, and young women moving around the country for work, almost inevitably led to episodic or "dalliance" relations in which men and women exploited one another for thrills. Like Waller's Greek brothers and sisters, youth in the war years could dispense with the pretense of deep emotional involvement. With the USO sponsoring dances and other social events, young men and women could meet to make dates for movies, drinks, and joyriding.[13]

Another special circumstance that might have allowed dating to survive in some times and places was the availability of spare cash. If movies and joyriding required little prior knowledge, they both cost something. And weekly dates, which formally included clothing, admission, and transportation costs, taxed the budgets of even middle-class youth. In the Depression years the relatively affluent middle-class students in fraternities and sororities could still afford the costs of weekly dates. Some of those costs were underwritten by the university in the form of dances and athletic events. The war also provided some money for young adults to spend on their social lives.[14]

Dating had always worked like a game with clear winners and losers. Except in special circumstances of relative prosperity and unbalanced sex ratios, there were far more losers than winners. The "stag lines and the cutting in and the multiple dates," one observer recalled, "meant that a popular girl had a very good time . . . But the majority of girls were not popular. They dreaded being wall flowers."[15] Successful girls had the attention of many boys, and successful boys had dates with the most attractive girls. But British anthropologist Geoffrey Gorer judged that only the most popular girls had any hope of this kind of regard: "the rest having to be content with a steady boy friend, or even the companionship of a fellow unfortunate." A sociologist found that students in the high school he studied "deride the steady daters as 'sappy,' 'mooney,' 'sleepy,' 'in love,' or 'dopey.'" In the game of dating, going steady marked one as a loser.[16]

## Decline of Dating

The Depression years would change both the economic and the demographic environment for American youth. We noticed above that dating flourished in settings with unbalanced sex ratios. With the 1930s, the youth included in the peer culture would grow dramatically as more working-class and rural youth entered and remained in high school. The economic crisis of the Depression prompted many school boards and state legislatures to raise to 16 the minimum age for leaving school. There were wide differences from region to region, and between white and black youth. But, for the United States as a whole, by 1934 two-thirds of 14- to 17-year-olds attended high school. The number who graduated doubled from 1924 to 1934. The most dramatic gains were in rural high school attendance. In 1930 of 14- to 17-year-olds, 58 percent of urban and 39.5 percent of rural youth attended high school. In 1934 this had risen to 67.9 percent urban and 60.5 percent rural.[17]

More boys went to high school after 1930, but they had fewer resources, especially cash. This brought different expectations for both conviviality and sex play. Urban working-class youth had originated many of the practices associated with dating. But in earlier decades, these youth worked. The Depression made employment far scarcer, tipping the balance toward high school attendance for many working-class youth. Journalist Caroline Bird noted that the Depression made a deep impression on the social lives of youth. "Boys and girls had time on their hands, but they had no money for the clothes, the Cokes, the movies, and the carfare that go with even a modest scale of sin." One study estimated that the average cost of a date in the early 1940s was $2.35, at a time when even a middle-class teenagers' allowance might be a dollar a week. A working-class young man in a small town in Illinois in the 1940s responded to questions about his social life. "'Hell, how can I date? I'm broke. . . . I only make a dollar a week at the junkyard and dates cost money!'"[18]

Ready money was not the only thing in short supply for Depression-era youth. Dating, even the improvised sort that flourished in the wartime crisis, still required what Eva Illouz calls "cultural capital": "surplus income and time to invest in leisure pursuits" plus the expertise (usually associated with middle-class status) "for each type of leisure consumed." Boys successful at dating had not only the ability to dress well, but they also had to be tidy, friendly, and verbally effective—they had to have a "line" that girls would find entertaining. But even the skills of meeting other young people, simple conversation, and the basic social niceties might be beyond the reach of some youth. A study form the 1940s found that many young people "do not know how to meet people socially." Shy boys would have a hard time asking a girl out, let alone carrying on a conversation on a date. Prudence, a high school senior in Connecticut, complained that "some of the high school boys act so childish when you go out for a date." She thought that "the fellows ought to know how to act."[19]

For those youth without the resources that made membership in the Greek system at Penn State possible, the constraints brought by the Depression would have readily tipped the balance in favor of fewer dates. At the same time, the more even sex ratio at the high school level would have eliminated the bargaining advantage of boys in general. Perhaps this applied initially to older students, who may have shifted to courtship rather than dalliance-style dating as their high school years moved toward a close. But the preference for going steady slowly became more general. Except for the most popular students in high school, steady dating appealed more and more to both boys and girls.

## Going Steady

By the 1950s, going steady became a social standard, an expectation of peers and even of parents. Junior high and high school students began dating for many reasons. Like April Bennett, they may have wanted to begin an active social life. Others admitted that they felt pressure to find a dating partner because everyone else seemed to be doing it. Participation in the social activities at high school required a date. "Date security" made steadily dating a single person attractive to many young people. "Each partner [in a steady couple] knows that the other can be counted on for the coming high-school dance or the next football game." As one student explained, "[Y]ou either went steady, or you never went." Status shifted away from the dating model, where the goal was many dates with many partners. Girls who went steady with the "right" boy could gain "a sense of achievement" among their peers.[20]

Although not poetic, the definition provided from a study of the "going steady complex" in the 1950s can help us understand the system in general terms. The students that sociologist Robert Herman had questioned led him to characterize going steady "as a relationship between dating partners which survives through time long enough to permit and encourage group awareness and sanction." How long a time? The couple could agree to go steady somewhere between three and six dates, although this probably varied depending on the setting. The college freshmen in Herman's study reflected on their high school experiences, where 77 percent had already gone steady at least once. A later study that directly surveyed high school students found three-fourths of girls and more than half of boys in 11th and 12th grades had gone steady. More than a fourth of the boys and almost half of the girls who went steady did so for a year or longer. These couples not only went to movies and dances together—the steady relationship included a much wider range of activities than dating, from walking together to school to studying together. About a third each of boys and girls reported spending four or more evenings a week with their steady partner.[21]

Going steady may seem at first glance antisocial, especially in contrast to the profligate conviviality of 1920s dating. The authors of a guide to psychology for teachers noted, "Anyone attending a high school dance or a dance at a teenagers' club will see fifteen- and sixteen-year old couples arrive together, refuse to dance with anyone but their own dates, and leave together." Yet the "going steady complex" operated with the active collusion of the entire student body of a middle school, high school, or college. A sex education book from the YWCA noted that "[s]ome high schools and colleges are so tightly organized on a steady-couples basis that a solitary boy or girl feels left out of most of the social activities." The clearest example of the strength of the social rules and norms surrounding the steady system was the relative inviolability of the relationship. "The ring and/or bracelet are universal symbols of going steady," a columnist wrote in the 1950s. One of the fads of the decade was the dog collar. When a girl wore one on her ankle it meant she "has her fellow." Of course, the sexist implications of this fad received no attention at the time. Even as late as the 1980s researchers found that the public announcement of the steady relationship "frequently takes the form of the exchange of gifts, such as articles of clothing (team jackets) or jewelry (class rings), the symbolic significance of which is widely known in the local adolescent culture."[22]

These various charms gave a physical form to social information. Everyone at school knew who the established couples were. Twelve-year-old Ruth Teischmann, feeling, as adolescents often do, like the perpetual outsider, wrote in her late 1950s dairy, "I really wish David—or Louis—would like me. They're *so* handsome and popular too! But Louis has Tina and David has Roslyn . . ." Sanctions, usually loss of reputation or status, existed for those who ignored the rules: "A boy today who seeks to make friends with a girl somebody else brings to a dance is known as a 'bird-dog' . . ." Even at one 1940s high school where dating was still generally accepted, the "hands-off" policy of the steady system was respected.[23] Among boys, physical violence could result from trespassing the boundaries of steady relations. Girls might resort to violence too; however, as we will see in the following, girls more readily relied on social sanctions.

## Variation and Convergence

By the early 1940s the term *teenager* came to stand in for terms such as *adolescence* or *youth* in most popular discussions of American adolescence. This recognized the continuing shift toward a national youth culture. Of course, social trends never work evenly. The meaning, and consequences, of steady dating divided along class lines and differed by location. Those who had plans of going on to college might go steady in high school, but treat the relation more lightly. As Waller noted, for a college man, "a love affair which led to immediate marriage would be tragic because of the havoc it would create in his scheme of life." But working-class students without prospect of further education more often treated high school steady relations as the first step in courtship leading to marriage. In Elmtown, a small city in Illinois (mainly white, working and middle class) in the 1940s, going steady applied more to teenagers out of high school than those who continued in high school. Another study in a Michigan suburb in the early 1940s found that only about a fourth of senior girls were currently going steady, mainly with boys and young men out of high school. The majority of students there said they disapproved of going steady.[24]

Parents could also make a difference in adolescent standards. Middle-class parents, like their adolescent children, shared a media-driven national culture. Experts such as Frances Strain and Max Exner often addressed parents in their books, as did the advice columns in *Parents* magazine, which began publishing in 1926. One common theme in the literature was the anxiety parents felt over the social lives of their growing children. According to this advice literature, parents should plan parties for their teenage children and urge them to socialize with peers. A 15-year-old who complained in a letter to an advice column that his mother wanted him to go to more parties found no comfort—the advice columnist sided with his mother.[25]

Parents in the Deep South of the 1940s still expected to influence, if not control, their children's social lives, especially the female children. They checked up on the boys who asked to take their daughters to social events. Social scientists found, however, that daughters "may go about with boys who are disapproved of by their parents, if they wish to risk defiance of conventional parent-child relation . . ." Even some northern parents still had a strong say in their children's social lives. In one northern urban high school where going steady was expected among the urban youth, the rural teenagers who attended appeared to accept the standards set by their parents "even when these conflicted with the codes and standards of their urban schoolmates." They were more likely to disapprove of both frequent dating *and* going steady, as well as kissing, dancing, and smoking.[26]

We would expect a social trend, the transition from dating to going steady, to proceed unevenly, and to differ greatly from place to place. For an individual in this period, this large-scale change in social structure would have seemed to be just life. Consider Helen Harmon, 14 in 1936, and absorbed in her hero worship for one of her teachers. She lived comfortably in a homosocial world that fit seamlessly with her all-girls school in Brookline, Pennsylvania. Even three years later, she still frequently mentioned her teacher crush, saw her every Wednesday, and confessed, "I am as crazy about her as ever." But Helen's persistent hero worship must have set her apart from her age peers. She wrote that her mother had begun to worry, "wondering why I'm so different from other girls." At about the same time her mother also began to worry about Helen's brother, Dan, though for different reasons. "She's so darn afraid of him getting girl crazy and sophisticated—my heavens, he'll be in the 7th grade—I hope she won't get him out of it." From Helen's point of view, a stronger interest in the other sex might have been good for her. Perhaps because of going to a girls' school "I didn't grow up as soon as I should have."[27] Both her homosociality and the "girl craziness" that Helen noted in the world around her places her within the dating cultural complex. Or, at least, that is the conclusion at first glance.

By the fall of 1939 Helen had moved to Philadelphia to study at the School of Industrial Arts. She still had a hard time imagining any future that would include a man. But that changed rapidly. In October 1940, at age 18, she went on her first date, one set up by a friend. In December she began a romance that continued for several months, with an older man named Ernest. She soon felt lost when he did not call on the weekend: "When it gets near the week-end I jump every time the telephone rings. I never think of doing things anymore but what I think of doing them with him; little things like sledding, taking a walk, or learning a new song." Having a man had undermined her sense of isolation. "Once you have been taken out to dinner, to the movies, played with, and kissed, you find it hard to do without such things." Helen went from early-twentieth-century homosociality to mid-twentieth-century style going steady with no intermediate stage. The romance with Ernest ended soon after the preceding diary entry but left Helen interested in dating. She records several dates in the subsequent pages of her diary. Just two years later she eloped to South Carolina to marry, over the fierce objections of her mother.[28]

A few years later, and in a public school setting, going steady would have appeared much more like a natural development. Mary Cantwell grew up in Bristol, Rhode Island, and entered high school about the same time that Helen Harmon married. She recalled her affection for one boy, Norman. But she seems to have spent her high school years in the late 1940s going out as frequently with girls as with Norman. Petting, by her testimony, was confined to good-night kisses after the junior prom. "In three years at Colt High I was kissed by three boys," she recalled.[29]

The differences among distinct groups of American youth were real, yet so was the trend toward convergence. As high school attendance became more common, the cultures within high schools also became more similar. Advertisers from the mid-1930s tended to treat young people as a homogeneous market. Even though this strategy ignored poorer adolescents, it reinforced the development of a national youth. Teenagers themselves often copied the lifestyles of peers in other places or cultures. White youth often adopted dances from black youth, like the Lindy Hoppers in figure 3.1. One study of 1950s' Buffalo noted "a certain middle-class admiration for, and emulation of, working-class

**FIGURE 3.1** Unidentified couple, probably Lindy Hoppers, dancing at an unidentified nightspot, 1930s.

*Source*: Photographs and Prints Division, Schomburg Center for Research in Black Culture, The New York Public Library, Astor, Lenox, and Tilden Foundations.

and black subcultures."[30] Historian Susan Cahn has shown that in the South of the 1940s "new high school rites, and consuming interest in dating, couples, romance, and marriage created the elements of a romantic heterosexual culture." Just like northern youth, southern adolescents elaborated a "school-based culture" that fostered romantic companionship. Even white and black subcultures tended to become more similar through the 1940s. One sociologist wrote that "[i]n general, sex attitudes of rural Negro youth and those of white youth appear to be rapidly approaching each other." Especially among upper-class black girls, sexual standards became more restrictive as those of white youth became more permissive.[31]

One of the central rituals of high school heterosexuality was the annual prom. Although school-sponsored dances played an important role in dating, the prom became the most important event in the high school social year. By the 1950s even southern high schools commonly held proms, which became ever more elaborate, including elections of prom queens. Decades after her junior prom, June Goyne recalled it as the high point of her relationship with her boyfriend: "I felt like a princess, wearing a borrowed black taffeta gown with bare shoulders, and wide straps, fitted waist and tiny pink trim at the pockets."[32] Mary Cantwell described in detail the rituals of her Bristol high school prom. To prepare for her own entrance, Mary spent the afternoon at her mother's hairdresser. Finally, coiffed and ready, she waited with family members. "The boy entered, a white box from Kinder's in his hand and I would slide the corsage . . . onto my wrist. Then down the stairs and out to somebody's father's car." Once at the auditorium, friends and family members of couples "lined the marble entranceway to watch them promenading toward the massive mahogany door." The popularity of proms grew during the same years that going steady became the normal organization for the sexuality of high school and college students.[33]

## Opposition to Going Steady

From the early twenty-first century, our look back at going steady in the middle of the last century is shaped by an idyllic narrative from movies and television programs. The period stands in for an age of innocence as an easy foil for the popular narrative of sexual revolution and excess of the late twentieth century. But as historian Beth Bailey has shown, going steady called out persistent, intense opposition from adult authorities. As early as 1926, at the height of the dating fad, a social hygiene educator advised in a YMCA pamphlet that "young people should have many companionships among the opposite sex rather than . . . confine themselves too closely to single friendships." The problem, according to Max Exner, was that too much time spent with one companion would raise the possibility "of being swayed by a blind, muddling infatuation—often mistaken for love." This could only handicap a boy or girl "in the most vital of all life's choices—the choice of a mate." A generation later a YWCA pamphlet advised that unless you are considering marriage, "there is no sense in depriving yourself of dates with other boys" or to expect any boy to date only you. These warnings from experts, then passed on by parents and teachers, had some impact. Students in a suburban high school near Detroit in the early 1940s told interviewers that confining themselves to steady couples "was unwise when they were young because it lessened their chance to become acquainted with others."[34]

The danger of limiting one's circle of friends, of gaining too little knowledge of the opposite sex and so failing to make the right choice, would appear in expert advice repeatedly in the 1940s and continue into the 1950s, even when the "going steady complex" had become the established norm. A Child Study Association pamphlet in 1954 treated going steady and dating as parallel systems, both equally available to adolescents, and advised that teenagers take the time to know lots of different people of the other sex. A 1956 YWCA publication included a chapter on "going steady" that gave it its due as a means of economizing and of attaining some "social security" but still concluded that a steady would "reduce your opportunities for knowing other congenial people whom you might enjoy."[35] In 1951 Coronet life education produced a film for high school students that shows Marie and Jeff who have drifted into going steady after going out together for too long. They both find that they have fewer opportunities for dates with other classmates. "How did I get into this, anyway?" Jeff wonders. "Going steady! That makes it sound so exclusive." When he discusses this with his parents, they give him conditional encouragement. "You've played the field for two or three years, Jeff," his mother says, thus offering general advice to the teenagers watching the film. "Now you begin to settle on one girl." And later, "You'll probably go steady with two or three girls."[36]

Although reasonable on the surface, the argument for dating—a wider acquaintance and so a wider mate selection—looks shallow on closer inspection. How could the dalliance relationship of dating provide the basis for finding true love, as so many experts claimed? The couple spent only an evening together, often at formal affairs. At the dances, the popular couples spent their time dancing with partners other than their dates. In fact, as we noted earlier, dating always worked best for students who were highly regarded among their peers, usually those with more resources, both cultural capital and spending money. At the Detroit-area high school mentioned previously where steady dating had not taken hold, popular girls resisted going steady since "this limited their chances for dating some boys."[37]

One of the distinctions we noted earlier between middle-class and working-class adolescents was that working-class sex play turned into steady dating and courtship earlier, sometimes many years earlier. This provides an insight into the resistance to going steady. The middle-class authors of advice literature wrote for an audience that either accepted or respected middle-class values. Dating—with its formal clothing and expenses—became a middle class fad in the 1920s and later worked as a class boundary marker. Experts were advising young people to maintain class standards, to refuse their creeping assimilation to lower-class practices. This meant putting off courtship and marriage until later, until after college or a career had been established. To do this this, they needed to go on dates with lots of different people.

## The Sex in Adolescent Sexuality

This also meant they should keep petting with people they barely knew. As historian Susan Ferentinos has shown, by the 1940s petting had become accepted not only by teenagers but also by many experts. In contrast to young people whose parents were foreign born, American parents believed that dating and the caresses involved allowed young people to move out of the protective embrace of the family toward independence. "Better have adolescent petters now," one article stated, "than miserably neurotic failures in marriage later!"[38] Middle-class dating norms in some ways gave a place to physical desires, but also contained them. The single evening that a girl spent with a boy, even with the expectation of some physical closeness, may have given the couple enough time to perform coitus but limited the time available for the negotiation that typically preceded it.

But going steady gave the couple plenty of time. "It is not difficult for the normal American girl to resist the advances of a casual date whom she scarcely knows," wrote a family sociologist. "The real problem arises when a girl gets to know a boy well, becomes fond of him, perhaps thinks she is in love with him." Even in the late 1950s adult chaperones at high school dances in Levittown, New Jersey, tried to convince strangers to dance with one another, "to get everyone on the floor and to discourage intimate dancing among couples." Students attending the dances protested this interference, and older students simply refused to go to school-sponsored dances. For steady couples, petting became heavier. Alice Denham recalled her 1940s high school years. She remained a "technical virgin," but she and her steady boyfriend explored one another's bodies, including not only fondling but also mutual masturbation. She believed that her experience was typical, although perhaps made easier because her boyfriend had a car. "People spent a lot of time in the woods," she told an interviewer, "and they would come out with briars sticking to their clothes."[39]

No wonder Catholic leaders deemed that "going steady is a proximate occasion of sin—a situation from which sin will almost inevitably result." The practice was prohibited at the parochial schools in some dioceses. In Newark, New Jersey, the pastor of St. Michael R.C. High School mandated that "any student found dating one person to the exclusion of all others would be immediately expelled from school, with no hope of reinstatement." Leaders in other churches also opposed going steady, as did a range of authorities in other fields. One expert rephrased the theological formula of "occasion of sin" as "biology plus propinquity equals intimacy." A YWCA sex educator warned that couples going steady "begin habits of necking and petting that bring them to a high point of sexual excitement." They may work themselves up so much they cannot control it.[40] Many girls assumed that going steady gave petting greater respectability— "they engaged in extensive physical love making activities '*only with a steady, not with just any boy that came along.*'" Elmtown's teachers believed that going steady could lead couples to behaviors that were "too intimate." Even popular singer Pat

Boone told teenagers that the danger of going steady came when it seemed like more than an "April love" and the couple rushed "into the behavior patterns of a much later stage."[41]

*How Much Affection*, a McGraw-Hill film textbook supplement from 1958, took on the issue of sex and the steady couple. As the drama opens Mary returns home from a late-night date with Jeff, visibly upset. She admits to her mother that she and Jeff almost went too far. Like all parents in these films, her mother is both understanding and wise: "All at once you can find yourself in a situation where your physical urges fight against reason." She advises Mary to slow down the petting when she and Jeff are alone to allow her reason a chance to lead her to the right decision. A little later in the film, Mary's reason is fortified when she overhears fellow classmates talking about Eileen, who became pregnant and had to leave school. She has the baby, now, and the father—another former classmate—is working to support them, giving up all hope of ever going to law school.[42]

Although it seems quaint now, the film raised real issues for mid-century adolescents. Family sociologist E. E. LeMasters made explicit the issue for middle-class youth who went steady: "It seems that sexual conquest with a 'nice' girl is a matter of gradual involvement: each night, each week, each month, the relationship becomes a little more intimate, until finally the possibilities are more or less exhausted."[43] This middle-class expert view, of course, still contained the naïve assumption that "nice" girls were only accessories after the fact of male persuasion. But sex fascinated girls as well as boys. Adele Monagan was 15 in 1945, growing up in New York City. Her conservative father warned her away from books on the Index, prohibited by the Catholic Church, and objected to her having a compact for her birthday because he "thinks it's disgraceful for a girl of fifteen to wear powder." Adele was alive to ideas about sexuality. She had already had her first date, a blind date with a boy going into the navy. She recalled the talk of boys while having a soda as "worse than I had thought," but later noted that when two of her girlfriends came to see her their talk of religion eventually "turned to the absorbing topic of sex. [They] explained to me what fuck means." On another occasion she talked to friends about marriage and having children. Her friends thought "marital relations" were "disgusting but I don't know."[44]

The thought of "marital relations" for middle-class girls mixed fear of life-altering consequences with the allure of exciting experiences. Even if they slowed down the petting, as Mary's mother counseled, they often participated with an interest equal to boys in sexual exploration, crossing boundaries toward what seemed like adult secrets. June Goyne, the same age as Adele Monagan, lived a world away in small-town, Protestant central Pennsylvania. Even so, her memoir shows that she and her best friend June Colyer had already discussed sex in their early teens. June began to date Norman Gressens in ninth grade, and recalled dancing with him at Candyland, the local soda shop. In tenth grade they began to use their relationship to explore some of the possibilities of desire, moving "very slowly, and progressed only to very firm, close-mouthed kisses, and some fully clothed sexual body moves."[45]

These personal writings suggest that religious leaders and social experts were right when they claimed that going steady led to broken rules about sex, or, put another way, that middle-class girls would not follow the roles prescribed for middle-class girls. A working-class girl early in the century told social workers that "when a girl gets a 'steady,' there's only one way to have him and to keep him . . ."[46] As the century proceeded, that formula seems to have held for more and more youth. Going steady made chastity until marriage less likely. For instance, in "Elmtown," in the early 1940s, dating practices for the majority in high school still resembled the 1920s, at least for middle-class and higher status groups. But, of the teenagers still in high school, "8 student couples date steady. Three of the 8 admit having sex relations, and 3 others were alleged by other students to have done so. The other two were not innocent of suspicion." The Elmtown evidence emphasizes the class basis for steady dating. Steady daters tended to be older than those who dated in the classic style, and they tended to be lower-class students. The large majority (70 percent) of steady couples included a partner who was out of high school, either a graduate or a dropout. Of these "mixed" couples, 29 of 38 admitted "'very confidentially' they were having sex relations." And the sexually active steady couples came mainly from the two lowest social classes in Elmtown.[47] The Elmtown evidence suggests that going steady, with its challenge to chastity, spread from working-class youth to the middle class.

While steady dating had more popularity among lower-class students in Elmtown, for lower-class youth out of school steady dating was the dominant practice. The couples that formed tended to have the features of steady couples, even if the relation lasted only a short time. In contrast to Mary in the family life movie is the story of another Mary, an Elmtown girl who left school as a sophomore and dated a young man in his 20s. "Mary and the boy petted heavily and, in her own words, she 'held him off for weeks.'" Then one Saturday night they went out, drank a lot, then drove somewhere and parked. She had decided that he "could have it." Eventually they drifted apart. "After her first experience Mary said . . . she had 'at least four dates' before she became intimate with a boy." In her own way, Mary was like the higher social class girls in high school who "played the field" in the dating game. But for most of the lower-class youth in the study, going steady quickly turned into the first stage of courtship. Or, it might even be thought of as the first stage of marriage, because it typically included at least the presumption of monogamy along with sexual relations. Of the youth who married in the lower classes, 55 percent had children within eight months after marriage.

Elmtown's lower-class students and dropouts had already established the dating patterns that would become typical for American youth in the coming decade. Steady dating—monogamy or serial monogamy—became the accepted norm for adolescents during the 1940s. And so did sex with the steady partner. A wide range of "sexual bookkeeping" (to use John Gagnon's phrase) has consistently shown rising rates of premarital sex for girls beginning in the 1940s. While wartime mobilization helped break down some conventions regarding female chastity, the trend did not reverse with the passing of the wartime emergency and demobilization. Rather, it accelerated. Historian Alan Petigny rightly points to statistics on illegitimacy and premarital pregnancy as reliable markers of sexual behavior. From 1940, children born to unwed mothers rose steadily, with hardly a plateau, until about 1994. Of course, use of birth control, spontaneous miscarriage, secret births and adoptions, and abortion would have masked the prevalence of teenage sex revealed in illegitimacy statistics, as would the traditional "solution" for white girls suggested in the comic book cover in figure 3.2. "I can't think of a girl who got pregnant in my high school who didn't get married," recalled an adult in the 1990s. Legitimate births to teenage mothers rose far more rapidly than illegitimate, peaking in 1957. Even though sex before marriage remained a formal taboo among middle-class youth, going steady provided a kind of marriage that legitimated the more intense intimacy of the couple.[48]

The relationship between going steady and intercourse is clear but not simple. Both gender and class complicated the picture. We have already seen that middle-class boys and young men took advantage of lower class girls and women. A 1951 study of youth on college campuses across the country seemingly corroborated this with its finding that 66 percent of male students, but only 25 percent of female students admitted to intercourse. This may also have reflected underreporting by the females and overreporting by the males. Another, more intensive study of college youth showed that for males, number of people dated in a single month correlated with greater likelihood of intercourse. But for females, this correlation reversed. College girls who dated only one boy had the most dates *and* had the highest likelihood of having had intercourse.[49] The greater intimacy of the steady relation led to greater intimacy, QED.

As a recent study shows, girls in the 1950s were bombarded with messages to channel their energy and exploration into teenaged "sexual etiquette" that would control their spontaneity. Yet for girls and young women at the time, going steady may have allowed them to set their own terms for sexual experience. Girls were still subjected to coercion to have sex. A high proportion of college women in the 1950s who had sexual experience had it either while inebriated or because of some kind of coercion (20 and 10 percent, respectively, in one study). Date rape, even for middle-class girls, remained a possibility. But girls who had steady boyfriends had some sense of what they could expect in "parking situations" after a party or a school dance. In fact, steady dating for girls provided an added meaning of date security—they could negotiate the pace and to some extent the terms of sexual experience.[50]

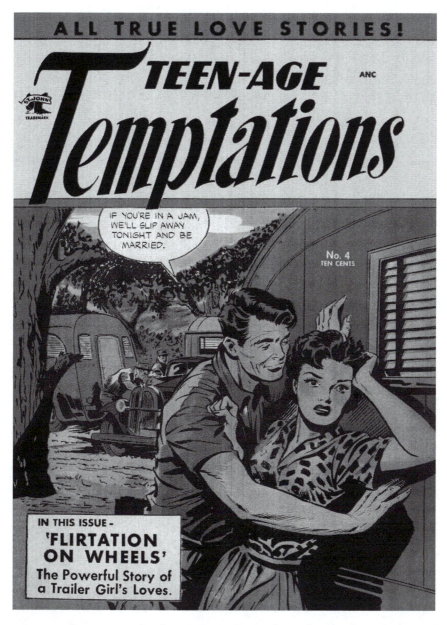

**FIGURE 3.2** Pregnancy and early marriage, often in that order, was the experience of many teenaged girls in the 1950s.

*Source*: Cover, *Teenage Temptations*, no. 4 (October 1953).

## The Attenuation of Homosociality

Intense friendships, homosocial groups, and early adolescent same-sex relations became less important during the Depression years and after. This development was closely linked to changes in heterosexual conviviality. The "going steady complex" came to dominate high school social life, for those who participated and for those who did not. American adolescents, from the 1930s onward, became more heterosexual, whether they wanted to or not.

Even a casual familiarity with adolescents in high school reveals the importance of friendships and group identities. An early 1940s study near Detroit found high school boys and girls alike identifying with "a group or crowd to run around with." In 1950s Buffalo, adolescents divided into gender-segregated groups, each with clothing styles that demonstrated group membership. For boys, the "subculture found expression in the cult of the automobile, the wrestling mania of the late 1950s, school athletics, and other examples of the 'American tough.'" Girls often studied together, spent hours discussing fashion and accessories, and arranged slumber parties. In Levittown in the same decade, a sociologist reported that "[m]ost teenagers do not even date; their social life takes place in groups." A study of an Italian neighborhood in early 1940s Boston featured a range of homosocial cliques or gangs. In midwestern Elmtown, cliques dominated the social life of high school youth: "You go into the hall, or the commons room . . . and you will find the same kids together day after day," one teacher told the sociologists. "Walk up Freedom Street at noon, or in the evening, and you'll see them again."[51]

Within the dating complex, individuals passed most of their time with the group and often enough the group set the terms for becoming involved with opposite-gendered groups. In the Boston study, the Norton group made a collective decision to begin socializing with a female group, the Aphrodites. Or, consider the working-class dropouts, boys and young men in midwestern Elmtown who spent hours "in restless, random movement from one public place to another" searching for girls to go riding with them. "When some girls willing to go for a ride are found the group usually heads into the country. . . . If the weather permits, they park along a country road where they pet with varying degrees of intensity." For students still in school in Elmtown, cliques prevailed: "The first date is often a cooperative enterprise which involves the members of two cliques of the opposite sex." In Highland Park, near Detroit, teenagers typically found dates through friends.[52] The two couples in figure 3.3 seem on the verge of moving from same-sex friendships to heterosexual dating.

But even as homosocial groups and same-sex friends continued to play vital roles in the lives of American youth, socializing with others across the gender divide became more and more of an individual adventure. As noted earlier, the diary of April Bennett says far less about girls and girlfriends than it does about boys and boyfriends. On Boston's Italian street corners, when individual Nortons

**FIGURE 3.3** Moving from same-sex to mixed-sex socializing often proceeded slowly. Boys and girls, Caldwell, Idaho, 1941.

*Source*: Library of Congress Prints and Photographs Division, Washington, DC.

began to pair up with Aphrodites, both groups became less cohesive and tensions rose. Even in Elmtown, still tightly controlled by cliques and disparaging of steady relationships, when couples began to go steady "they separate themselves from their fellow students, lose interest in normal clique activity, the school and the opposite sex except the boy or girl friend." Some evidence suggests that the loss of their same-sex reference groups was more dramatic for girls than for boys. In Highland Park, near Detroit, both boys and girls primarily socialized in same-sex groups. But, while a fourth of boys said they were equally comfortable with boys and girls, none said he preferred the company of girls. Half of girls, however, said they were equally comfortable with boys and girls, and a few even preferred boys. "Boys are easier. I don't trust other girls too much," one girl told the interviewer. Another one said, "I'm more at ease with boys. You can joke with them but with girls you have to be very careful."[53]

## From the Crush to Going Steady

Dating in the 1920s did not destroy or supersede the importance of girls' relationships with other girls. Rather, parallel systems of relationships coexisted. Heterosocial relations revolved around dating; homosocial relations revolved around the crush. The date often occurred in groups, with couples using a school or community activity as their reason for going out. Dates were transitory, and were valued in bulk. The crush, on the other hand, more closely resembled romantic love. The couple had time only for each other, and even though they might display their affection openly, they sought time alone. Crushes, sometimes called grand passions, were stable and characterized by much deeper feelings than those accorded to dates.

Girls who kept diaries often spent pages and pages trying to understand the strange ways of boys. Even so, the diaries of the 1920s make clear that crushes still played a major role in the lives of many adolescent girls. By the 1930s crushes tended to lose space in girls' diaries, and by the 1950s and 1960s diaries seldom give hints of close same-sex friendships. The most fascinating game in town in the 1920s is the only game by the 1950s. Why the fascination with boys? Why the greater status for dates than for crushes? Probably relationships with girls came much more easily, while the opposite sex seemed incomprehensible. Fascination grew out of the need for close study. Status probably had a similar origin. With a persistent shortage of boys into the 1920s, dates may have been prized because of their relative scarcity. Also, friendships with girls would have begun much earlier for girls; dating was part of the transition to adolescence, and so an exciting new experience. And, because frequency and variety were the measures of popularity in the dating complex, status would be accorded based on more or less public behaviors. Beth Twiggar, a jazz-age teenager, responded to both the attraction of boys and status consciousness when she broke off an arranged meeting with her girlfriend Gretta in order to have a date with a boy. She clearly understood why Gretta would be angry, but she believed that in a similar situation, Gretta would have done the same thing.[54]

High-status behavior does not necessarily drive away lesser-status behavior. In the 1920s, as we have seen, the dating system coexisted with the crush with little apparent conflict, even of the cognitive kind, among those who participated in both at the same time. By at least the mid-1930s, however, the dating system itself began to lose importance. Going steady became more popular and involved more serious emotional commitment. The steady couple mimicked, in many ways, an engaged couple, giving high school socializing more of the attributes of early courtship that the dating system never possessed.[55]

Except in being heterosexual, steadies also resembled the passionate, mutual crushes of an earlier period. Like the crush, the steady relationship was comparatively long term. Steadies expected commitment from one another. The status of each of the members of the steady couple tended to be equal. Compared to dating, going steady carried relatively deep emotional attachment. Just as in the homosocial crush, steadies could engage in a romantic relationship, with courtship, mutual acceptance, and merging of identities. And, just like the homosocial crush, going steady took up much more time than dating. Couples not only went out to dances and sporting events; they also studied together, traveled to and from school together, even walked together between classes. By the 1950s it was not the girl crushes who were holding one another's arms in the school hallways; it was the steady couples. About a third each of boys and girls in one study reported spending four or more nights a week with their steady partner. With so much time spent with the steady, girls had less time for their girlfriends, boys less time for their pals.[56]

## Companionate Marriage

During the decades when going steady grew into the accepted norm for adolescent heterosexual conviviality, the practice seemed strange enough that observers and social scientists looked for comparisons to describe it. An early sociological study, for instance, assimilated going steady to broader courtship practices: "in some situations going steady seemed to resemble descriptions of engagement as it is usually interpreted as being marriage oriented, while in other situations going steady seemed to have the characteristics of a dalliance relationship practiced as an end it itself." By the late 1950s Charles Cole, described going steady in ways that would be familiar to readers in the early twenty-first century. "At the start, it means merely a monogamous social arrangement, but it is likely to move on to a point where the couple gets 'pinned.'" This could mean simply that the couple liked one another and planned to go steady indefinitely. But it could go further: "To be seriously pinned means 'engaged to be engaged' or perhaps even 'engaged' preparatory to getting a ring, securing parental approval, and clearing up other details." Because pinning could resemble "the betrothal of earlier times, it is frequently quite ceremonious." Friends might throw a party where the girl appears with the boy's frat pin for the first time.[57]

That going steady could become a kind of engagement is hardly surprising. The Anne Welles character in the movie *Valley of the Dolls* recalled her high school sweetheart as the movie opened: "The day Willy pinned me he said we were engaged to be engaged." Yet even going steady briefly, when the relation seemed more like the "dalliance" relations of dating, could give the couple the time together and the confidence in one another to bring them closer both socially and physically than dating would have. A *Maclean's* article in 1959 described steady couples "as inseparable as a husband and wife and their union is regarded as inviolable by their contemporaries."[58] In fact, American youth in the decades from the Depression into the postwar era elaborated a sexuality that had all of the features of companionate marriage.

In 1924 authors in *Social Hygiene* suggested the term *companionate marriage* "to describe a union in which spouses intentionally controlled their fertility and embraced a modern egalitarian ideal." The term came into general use by the late 1920s thanks to the work of Judge Ben Lindsey and was adopted by sociologists such as Ernest Burgess as the century advanced. The concept marked an extraordinary shift in American culture, offering marriage as an end in itself, apart from family. Companionate marriages would allow the couple to develop warmer personal relations and to enjoy sex without the responsibilities of child raising. As such, companionate marriage might seem more selfish than the traditional, family-oriented marriage. But as the birth rate declined (generally, but especially for middle-class white couples), marriage for companionship could seem like a worthy goal. The term acquired related but less neutral meanings from Judge Lindsey's book on youth and marriage. Lindsey advocated that divorce laws be eased, to allow young, childless couples to escape marriages that proved unworkable. Moralists attacked Lindsey and his books, claiming that he advocated trial marriage.[59]

Taken together, all of these meanings applied to going steady; going steady was companionate marriage without marriage. Young people came together in relatively serious, monogamous relations so they could make the most of the social opportunities available in their schools and communities and save some money. Adolescents, as older children themselves, could hardly regard child-bearing as desirable. The couple could develop the "pure relationship" that had only the relation itself, and its benefits to the two people, as the goal of being together.[60] They could also far more easily enjoy physical intimacy, and more and more often this led to intercourse. The rituals and social sanctions surrounding the steady couple further legitimated their relation. As we saw earlier, many observers equated pinning with engagement, and the elaborate proms matched the glamor of weddings. And "divorce"—breaking up—although emotionally painful, was still relatively easy, common, and even expected, whether due to personal incompatibility or some violation of the monogamous understanding.

American adolescents adopted a companionate conviviality at a time when the companionate ideal was becoming pervasive in American culture. Movies probably made companionate marriage seem like the ideal relationship. One study from the 1920s found that average attendance at movies for both boys and girls was more than four times per week. Although the industry tried to provide adolescent characters such as Andy Hardy and Betsy Booth, American teenagers identified more powerfully with the adult characters. Social scientists in Middletown (Muncie, Indiana) reported that "adolescent Middletown goes to school to, as well as enjoying, the movies." "Man! that Lauren Bacall," Adele Monagan wrote in her diary in 1945. "She is really torrid. . . . The way she talks, lights a cigarette, moves her hips, or kisses are really something to watch. And I'll bet every girl in the audience (including me) would love to be able to imitate her." A 17-year-old girl told the social scientist who interviewed her, "I learned something about the art of lovemaking, and that bad and pretty girls are usually more attractive to men than intelligent and studious girls." The same report noted that "some young men" took their dates to "passionate motion pictures as a means of inducing a greater attitude of receptiveness."[61] Criticism of sexual content in American movies came from so many quarters by the early 1930s that industry leaders developed a voluntary code, known as the Hays Code, that pledged, in part, not to undermine the institution of marriage.

The social scientists and church leaders who worried about the influence of movies on American youth failed to notice that movies had consistently shifted with the culture toward a view of marriage as the ideal setting for adult fulfillment. An early version of the companionate ideal appeared in 1920, a Cecil B. DeMille production *Why Change Your Wife?* When Gloria Swanson's husband abandons her for someone who is sexually more alluring and fun, she realizes her mistake in preferring sad music and reserved ways. To win her husband back, she adopts what she had scorned as her husband's "oriental ideas," learns to dance, and buys dresses meant to attract attention: "Make them sleeveless," she tells the dressmaker, "backless, transparent, indecent. Go the limit." One of the most successful films of 1934 was *It Happened One Night*, with Clark Gable escorting married heiress Claudette Colbert back to her father and her husband. He teaches her how to make do with the limited means of ordinary people. They chastely sleep on either side of a hanging blanket, the "wall of Jericho" that Gable puts between their beds. But audiences loved the chemistry that the two characters expressed in their snappy exchanges. After Colbert successfully gets them a ride from a passing car by showing off her leg, Gable gripes, "Why didn't you take off all your clothes? You could have stopped forty cars." She responds in one beat, "I'll remember that when we need forty cars." In the end, of course, love conquers the huge class distance between Gable and Colbert. Their trial marriage ends with real marriage.[62]

Another version of the companionate marriage also appeared in 1934, with William Powell and Myrna Loy as Nick and Nora Charles in *The Thin Man*, the beginning of a Thin Man franchise that would extend into the 1940s and later become a TV series. The crime-solving couple lived in luxury in their New York apartment, where they enjoyed a child-free life full of martinis and witty repartee. "You got types?" Nora asks Nick after he has mentioned a "pretty girl." "Only you darling. Lanky brunettes with wicked jaws."[63] Marital disputes only required a quick wit. Companionate marriage—whether trial marriage or marriage for companionship, sex, and luxury—looked like fun in the movies. As American teenagers shifted their sex play toward longer term and more intimate relations they could draw on the wider culture for both models and validation of a companionate ideal. No wonder the critics of going steady had so little effect on the actual practice of American youth.

## Marginalization

Even in the 1950s, when going steady had become a social norm, only a minority went steady at any given time. In one survey of high school students, for instance, a large majority of girls had gone steady by 11th and 12th grade, but some of these steady relations only lasted a short time. Another study of college students in the late 1940s into the 1950s found 25 percent and 36 percent, respectively, of male and female students going steady exclusively. The preferred status of going steady was available to most high school students, but the group of steady couples changed constantly, with a substantial minority going steady for a year or more. And, of course, there were gradations in the relation: dating someone more or less informally and casually, dating someone more than others but not considering him or her a steady, dating someone steadily but without an understanding, "'deciding to go steady,' 'being asked to go steady,' and 'officially going steady.'"[64]

But even if, at a given moment in time, only a minority of couples were genuine steadies, all other practices came to be measured by the companionate standard. Robert Herman found in the early 1950s that the most popular students in high school went steady. Just as rating of dates made evident the winners and losers of the game, going steady distinguished those worthy of couplehood from all others. A sizable minority of 20 percent or more seems never to have gone steady in high school.[65] These might have been late bloomers, like April Bennett, girls and boys who yearned for steady partners but did not find them until later in life. Or, this group may have included those who had other interests—girls and boys who wanted to continue their close relationships with same-gender peers.

Many children still began their discovery of sexual selves with peers of their own gender. A 1940s study of boys in Indiana found about 38% of the sample had engaged in some form of homoerotic play during what the author termed preadolescence. During the teenage years, to age 17, about 30 percent of the boys had some experience (mainly mutual masturbation) with another boy. The Indiana study, inspired by the work of Alfred Kinsey, dealt with acts and not desires. One case study reported on a boy who, still quite young, had developed a homosexual relation with another boy that had continued for three years. "The boys were bringing each other to climax three or four times each week," the author noted, "and had employed several techniques." Ronald Knight, who grew up in rural Mississippi, recalls sex play—"cornholing"—with other boys while away from adults. As they grew older, many of his friends gave up this kind of play, although he knew of at least five actively gay adolescents.[66]

One study of college youth in the early 1950s found that a significant portion of both men and women admitted to homosexual "inclinations" (22 and 13 percent, respectively) and to some experience (12 and 6.4 percent, respectively). For most of these, the experience came in the teenage years or before. This study, along with the more imposing Kinsey study, demonstrates that young Americans experienced and acted on homoerotic desire in large numbers.[67] Until at least the 1930s both boys and girls, especially in the younger teen years, took advantage of homosocial networks and special friendships that could serve as a haven for homosexual youth and an environment for exploring desire. Dating, with its emphasis on dalliance and social capital, could extend all the way beyond high school into college or early adulthood. The "lovemaking" (usually meaning caresses) in parked cars might be as much a result of social expectations as of desire, even among youth who were heterosexual. Those who did not date could simply claim not to be girl or boy crazy, an attitude that would have found ready social support among adults and even some peers.

But by the 1940s, dating began earlier for most teens—around 14—and going steady followed within a year or so. Prescriptive heterosexual norms became harder to avoid. For an adolescent with gender confusion or homoerotic desire, the intense emotional and physical commitments of going steady would have been hard to feign. Adolescents, especially boys, who failed to conform to gender norms quickly became the targets of exclusion and bullying. Rickie Leigh Smith, born in 1939 in rural Mississippi, was very feminine from an early age. He secretly cross-dressed but had no help from his social world to understand his transgendered longings: "My self-image, my self-esteem was so low by the time I reached my teens, it couldn't have been much worse. I knew nothing, zero, nothing, about sexual matters. I didn't know why I had these feelings. I was made to feel bad about them. So, it was all very negative."[68] This lack of clear guidance for those who believed themselves outside the heterosexual norm came through clearly in a letter to Alfred Kinsey in 1954: "Is it possible for a person to be male and female at the same time? I am a girl, 20 years old, and I love another girl very much and she also loves me; and I know that that isn't right."[69] Like many of the men and women who wrote to Kinsey, this correspondent wanted to know how to understand her desire, how to find a way to live her life in spite of the social constraints she faced.

Some individuals found they could lead a life that gave full play to homosexual desire or even transgendered feelings. Young men and women in the nation's large cities could find queer communities, and during World War II, the mobilization of millions of men and women meant that far more young people found themselves in sexually charged and nontraditional situations. Alan Berube has chronicled the wartime experience of gay men and women during the war. "With less supervision than their parents had provided at home and with more money than many had seen during the depression, young gay GIs enjoyed a new freedom, looking for each other and a good time." For young men and women just out of high school and mobilized from small towns and rural areas, the military emergency may have given them their first experience of gay life and perhaps even of gay sex.[70]

Outside of urban areas, however, adolescents had to struggle as much with issues of identity as of desire. Even boys who might have had some opportunities for sex play in adolescence had to negotiate their place within the peer group. Harry Beckner, a teenager in the late 1940s in Nebraska, recalled, "In high school you had to fit the mode or you were queer, so I played the straight line. But I wasn't interested in girls." "I dated in high school," recalled Jim Cross, the same age as Harry but in Iowa. "But I never went out with high school sweethearts with the idea of going to bed with them. I always thought it was gross." The idea was always to fit in with gendered expectations. James Heckman, a Hoosier like April Bennett although a few years younger, asked a girl to prom one year "because we got to double with her best friend's boyfriend. I was just in a fog that he and I would be sitting at the same table the whole evening." In the rural South, as in the Midwest, even the boys who shared sex play might turn on a fellow student who seemed too effeminate. "The worst thing you could be called in high school was a homo," according to Dennis Lindholm.[71]

## Double Standards and Class

Going steady also fostered another kind of marginalization. The double standard always placed greater burdens on the reputations of girls than boys. If girls crossed a certain line in sexual matters, they lost status among their girlfriends and perhaps with boys. The difficulty of maintaining a good reputation for middle-class girls became greater as the line became blurrier. Petting could be fun and healthy, even according to adult specialists. A YMCA educator wrote in 1926 that the "greater freedom in sex-social relations of young people . . . may serve to give a degree of wholesome release to sex." But "the question of petting" came down to how much was wholesome and when did it become too much. A *Parents* article from the mid-1930s made clear that a line existed without giving much valuable guidance on where to find it: "I have yet to find a boy who does not frankly state that 'a heavy petter' is an epithet he would object to having applied to his sister or his sweetheart."[72]

High school students had a precise understanding of the power of reputation, though the sanctions applied only to girls. According to a high school boy quoted in another *Parents* article from the 1940s, "[t]he girls who fooled around a lot and date with practically any fellow who comes along are pretty apt to have their names thrown around like a wet ball on a slippery field." An interviewer in the late 1940s quoted a high school senior: "What do the boys do if a girl every time she goes out kisses a boy on the first date? Of course, the boys talk among each other—but where's the girl left?" "I never go parking," said a girl at the same high school. "To have someone come and say, 'Oh, that Kathryn'—I'd hate to get, I mean, I'm afraid of getting a bad reputation." The double standard persisted in college, and perhaps became more rigid as marriage became more of a possibility. "Most college men expect a certain amount of familiarity from the girls they date," wrote an advice manual for girls heading to college. But "most older men, seeking wives, want girls that other men can't touch." The double standard was clear—the line was not.[73]

The question of petting, even if still a concern for adult caretakers and experts in the 1940s, must have already moved into the category of quaint for most adolescents. A girl who had intercourse, however, had to negotiate shifting markers of reputation dictated by the double standard. For middle-class girls, intercourse (if it became known) still meant loss of status. In Elmtown they could be assigned to the group known as "grubbies." "We're hated by the other girls because we've broken the taboo," one of the girls in this group said. Working-class girls had different boundaries to negotiate. High school dropouts in 1940s Elmtown often had several boyfriends before marriage. But no girl could risk "becoming known as 'free and easy with the boys,' 'common property,' 'a little chippy,' or 'a home-wrecker.' If it becomes known generally among the girls and older women that a girl is 'loose,' she is gossiped about, ridiculed, perhaps ostracized."[74]

Girls whose sex lives became a matter of gossip were assigned a marginal status. This may have become more common by the 1930s. In Robert Carr's novel of the 1920s, his protagonist finds himself driving at night with Gertrude, an attractive girl, and an aggressive one, too. She suggests they park, then almost literally throws herself at him in a scene of reversed-gender ravishment. For the first of several times in the novel, Paul Arnold is drawn toward a desire he knows will compromise his morals. Like Tom Jones, he manages throughout to maintain his virtue. But when Paul tells his friend Buck that he drove "Dirty Gertie" home, Buck assumes they had sex.[75] Gertrude may be an entirely fictional character, but she shows part of the development of the role of the girl who could use sex appeal outside of the limits set in the adolescent social world. In her brief appearance in the novel, Gertrude does not suffer shunning. But she remains popular only with boys who themselves have no concern for reputation.

Roughly 20 years later, the sociologists studying Elmtown wrote of another girl who managed a similar kind of transgression, apparently to her own advantage: "This girl has mastered the glamour role in the culture; she knows how to groom herself so that she is sought after by the boys. To be seen with her adds to a boy's prestige in the elite peer group; to have a date with her is 'something.' She pets with her dates discreetly—never goes too far, just far enough to make them come back again." She only dated high-status boys. Among the girls, she is known as a "date stealer," and her female peers regularly exclude her from their parties: "The girls gossip about her 'boldness,' but she successfully violates the rules and still maintains her prestige with the boys." One example can hardly explain a trend, but this one is suggestive, especially juxtaposed with Gertrude. Elmtown, like Paul Carr's Westfield of the 1920s, still maintained a dating culture.[76] The Elmtown girl seemingly had little concern over her reputation among the other girls. With the boys, her discretion enabled her to attract high-status dates.

These examples reveal several key themes related to sexual reputation. First, no surprise, the issue existed only for girls and women. Although as far back as the nineteenth century, women's rights advocates, radical marriage reformers, health crusaders, and evangelicals had called for a sexual morality that applied equally to men and women, the double standard remained the assumption of most Americans. Second, reputation meant everything. Adolescents in Elmtown "have long since learned they can commit wrongs with impunity if they 'keep their mouths shut.'" The gossip of peers, whatever the motivation and whatever its basis, became the ingredient that tainted sexual reputation. During their interviews in Elmtown, sociologist August Hollingshead and his wife heard rumors "about a particular girl who was reputed to be 'putting it out' to her friends." Also, some socializing was "tabooed" for reasons of group identity.[77] A lower-class girl could earn a reputation as promiscuous just by going out with boys from other towns. Finally, the sexual outlaws were ostracized, pushed to the social margins. Although the narrative seems to flow from loss of reputation to marginal existence—either in a despised social group or without any clear social group at all—the process may as easily have run the other way.

The boundary that divided the sexually acceptable from others was, at least in part, a class line. Working-class youth in Elmtown, especially those who dropped out of high school, dated more and married younger than adolescents in high school. Dropout recreation featured pickup dates, riding in cars, and petting. A handbook for teachers on adolescent psychology, apparently basing its insights on the work of Kinsey, took for granted a gaping divide in the sexual standards of middle-class and lower-class youth. Among lower-class boys kissing or petting could seem "silly or even perverse. . . . A lower-class boy of fourteen or fifteen who has not had complete 'sexual experience' is a rarity. . . . Lower-class girls quite naturally drift into 'sexual experiences' as did their mothers and older sisters." Recent studies have often noted that class can define reputation. Simply based on their style of clothing, working-class girls can be labeled as promiscuous by their more middle-class peers.[78]

Although the handbook cited earlier seemingly draws the divide between class standards in such sweeping terms as to make them into caricatures, the portrait mixed both popular perceptions and social science. Studies of working-class African American youth during the 1930s and 1940s, for instance, showed that these adolescents became sexually active, and also became parents and often married, at much younger ages than middle-class youth, black or white. These youth often had few prospects for continued schooling, so the shortened route to adulthood—work and marriage—was the only one available. In the Ozarks, young people married young, and there was little surprise at the early arrival of the first child.[79]

Among middle-class black youth, on the other hand, sexual standards resembled those among middle-class whites. Hattie Cochran's teenage years during the Depression in Cleveland appear to have little to distinguish them from a white youth in the same years and social class. She has many friends over to her house, goes to movies and sports events. She especially enjoyed her summers at a church camp in Pennsylvania in 1931 and 1932. She has little to say about worship services but notes time spent with other young people. We "had a gang of fun" she wrote about one outing with another girl and two boys. During her second summer at camp she met her future husband, Rufus Hunter, who took her for a ride in a roadster. Researchers in the Deep South noted that "more rigid moral standards are applied to girls whom middle-class boys expect to marry." They quoted one 17-year-old boy, "A bad girl is anybody's girl." In the early 1950s a survey found that half of black college women reported they were virgins.[80]

Whether the youth were black or white, attitudes toward sexual practices followed different social expectations.

Of course, the double standard meant that middle-class boys (and men) could take advantage of the difference in class attitudes. Even in the early 1940s in "Elmtown," in 82 percent of known intercourse cases, the girls were in a lower social class than were the boys. A study of college students at a large Midwestern university found that the "tendency of males to descend the social ladder for dating companions seems to be motivated to a considerable extent by a desire to find willing sexual partners." The male college students stated the double sexual and class standard bluntly: "It is all right for a boy to go as far as he wants, but not with the girl he is to marry or with a girl in his own class." Another student said that when it came to lower-class "pick-ups," "[t]here's no point [in] considering anything other than going as far as you can with them." One young man, who apparently held to some kind of single standard of sexual morality, also took for granted the class divide when he told the interviewer that the reason he did not have sexual intercourse was that he didn't "date cheap sluts."[81]

Although the double standard worked mainly to the benefit of boys, enforcement came mainly from girls. "Girls never treat each other very well," recalled Phyllis Chesler. Although a top student at her New York high school in the 1950s, Phyllis was called a tramp and was shunned by many of the girls in her class. She never had intercourse in high school, but because she had larger breasts than other girls, many of them claimed that she was sexually promiscuous. By the 1950s, girls had become far more stringent guardians of the boundaries set by steady relations. The line was not whether a girl had sex—"all my friends, with only a few exceptions, were fucking people," Louise Desalvo said of her Massachusetts high school. "What distinguished the 'sluts' from the rest of the girls was that we were not in monogamous sexual relationships. The other girls were with one guy at a time, wearing his sweater or his ring. The slut never wore a guy's sweater or ring." Because she and her friend Liz remained independent (and Liz actively sought other girls' boyfriends) they became targets for name-calling and ostracism: "the two of us were a real threat to the prevailing idea of heterosexual monogamy. It wasn't that we were fucking when nobody else was . . ."[82]

The class and gender-bound assumptions about proper behavior, morality, and reputation provided the strands of the role of the slut. Their peers assumed that the girl in the slut role had no sexual boundaries and would agree to intimacy with any boy. Even so, only high-status boys seemed to be prey for her wiles. In a world where boys and girls had long-term, emotionally intense relations (all finely tuned to status), a girl who could use the lure of easy intercourse to draw the attention of boys away from their steadies threatened the status of individual girls and the entire system of companionate relationships. Movies of the early 1960s such as *Beach Blanket Bingo* and *Gidget Goes Hawaiian* made humor out the idea of the sexually unfettered steady-wrecker. But on high school or college campuses, the girls assigned the role of the slut had to live with the persistent hostility of their female peers and an ambiguous, exploitive attitude from male peers.

## Incest and Abuse

Most Americans reacted with shock at reports of incest and other sexual abuses of the young. But the social science of the period from the Depression into the 1960s seemed intent on lowering the concern over these issues, portraying the problem as statistically insignificant and, in most cases, innocuous. Historian Rachel Devlin has noted the distance between public and judicial abhorrence of incest, on one hand, and "equanimity" with which "criminologists, anthropologists and psychoanalysts" of the period discussed father–daughter incest.[83]

*Peyton Place*, the mid-1950s novel of passion and hypocrisy in a New England town, provided postwar adolescents and adults the kind of titillation and insight that a later generation took from movies such as *M*A*S*H* or books such as *The Rape of the A*P*E*. The core of one of the plots concerns an incest rape of a high school girl by her brutal father. The book's best-selling status in both 1956 and 1957 showed that Americans were ready to be horrified by such stories, along with the sexual initiations and abortions that author Grace Metalious served up. The movie version (1957) by contrast downplayed the incest, turning the father into a stepparent. Abortion also disappeared from the movie, as did many of the colorful, sexually transgressive characters in the book. Adult sexual abuse of children seemed too volatile a topic to be allowed out of the covers of a book that included passages that a *Catholic World* reviewer deemed "unmitigated pornography."[84]

If a large reading public could still be shocked by stories of incest, it did so in spite of the labors of social scientists and psychologists. In the mid-1930s a study of rape cases devoted an entire chapter to incest. In a table on the sexual initiations of girls, friends and acquaintances make up the largest group, with smaller contributions from fathers, stepfathers, uncles, brothers, and "mother's friend." Yet this work, like a similar volume dealing with delinquent women seemed to confine rape and abuse to low-income families with flawed family structures, often with alcohol abuse playing a key role. The Kinsey study of women, published in 1953, seemingly worked against this portrait. It reported that 24 percent of white women had some sexual contact, as children, with adult men. Yet the statistics themselves leave the reader with the impression that most girl victims had only to deal with strange men showing off their genitals and then perhaps some fondling. A book-length study of incest in the 1950s noted that if criminal prosecutions were used as a guide, incest only affected one or two persons in a million.[85]

While the incidence of coercive sexual contact for the general population remained unclear, social scientists and psychologists sought to shape its meaning. Rachel Devlin has shown that the psychoanalytic frame used to study sexual contact with adults, and incest in particular, portrayed the girls involved as acting out an Oedipal wish. More damaging than the involvement with fathers was the overbearing mother who might extinguish the child's sexuality. At least as early as the 1930s, case studies gave children roles not as victims but as active participants in incest: "The most remarkable feature presented by these children who have experienced sexual relations with adults was that they showed less evidence of fear, anxiety, guilt or psychic trauma than might be expected," wrote researchers in 1937. They continued later, in an astonishing passage, stating that these children "do not deserve completely the cloak of innocence with which they have been endowed" and that the "excuses of fear of physical harm or the enticement of gifts" were obvious rationalizations and secondary reasons. "Even in the cases in which physical force may have been applied by the adult, this did not wholly account for the frequent repetition of the practice." This same set of attitudes—that the experience itself was more or less benign and that the children actively participated—continued to thrive in the 1950s. One study opened with the rhetorical question, "Do some children participate with the adult offender in initiating or maintaining a sexual relationship with him?" The writer's answer, "yes," led to the label "participant victim."[86]

The attitudes of specialists and experts probably shaped the empirical investigations of incest and rape into the 1960s. As one consequence of this view of childhood sexuality, the impact of all types of sexual violence becomes a matter of speculation. If later investigations, including retrospective assessments of adult-child sexual acts, give us any clear picture, it is of a continued, relatively large (10–20 percent, more in some studies) of women whom we would consider victims of incest or statutory rape. If so, this must have played a role in the social organization of adolescent sexuality. Even if only a minority of girls had experienced this kind of sexual violence, this might help explain the rigidity of the peer rules related to going steady. Girls may have seen the settled nature of a steady relation as a haven from a chaotic home life or from a deeply felt trauma. Or, perhaps, some of these girls responded by acting out. One extended study of incest discussed the reactions of girls who were victims of incest. In many cases, the girls became very promiscuous because of their experience. Many "required psychiatric attention as a result of the traumatic incest affair. Others became very shy of men, since they never had a male companion until postadolescence."[87] Incest and rape would shape adolescent sexuality without ever becoming visible to it.

By the 1950s the "going steady complex" of companionate pseudo-marriages settled into its most ritualized form. The subsequent half-century would seemingly undermine it, with sexual upheavals and moral panics. But adolescent sexuality from early and mid-twentieth century contrast more sharply with one another than do mid-century and the early-twenty-first sexuality. Rather than boys or young men calling on girls in their family parlors, or urban working youth seeking some amusement in public places with sex play as an expected ingredient, by mid-century most youth attended high school and participated to some extent in long-term relationships that looked more like trial marriages than dates. In the opening decades of the twentieth century most youth passed their time with members of their own gender, and the calling or dating served as short excursions into a heterosocial world. By mid-century, boys and girls spent a growing portion of their free time with someone of the opposite sex. The decades beginning with the 1960s would complicate this heterosexualized world, but in many respects leave in place the fundamental changes of the early century.

## Notes

1. April Bennett [pseud.], "The Papers of April Bennett," Diaries, Schlesinger Library, Radcliffe Institute, Harvard University, Cambridge, MA, n.d. (hereafter, Bennett papers).
2. Bennett papers, February 13, April 12, and April 26, 1952, and January 29 and February 3, 1953.
3. Bennett papers, March 1 and 15, April 9, June 15, and October 5, 1954, and March 3, 1954.
4. Bennett papers, April 12 and 13, 1957.
5. Bennett papers, June 6, 1959; the note on being hysterical is dated December 21, 1959, but I am not sure of the actual date.
6. Izola Forrester, "When a Girl Gets Boy Crazy," *Parents* (March 1929), 18–19, 72.
7. Paula Fass, *The Damned and the Beautiful: American Youth in the 1920's* (New York: Oxford University Press, 1979), 127–131; her discussion deals with college youth, although the operation of fads could be seen in all age groups; the general concept of a youth- and fad-driven culture comes from Gilman Ostrander, *American Civilization in the First Machine Age: 1890–1940* (New York: HarperCollins, 1972).
8. Willard Waller, "The Rating and Dating Complex" *American Sociological Review* 2 (October 1937): 727–734; Charles W. Cole, "American Youth Goes Monogamous," *Harper's Magazine* (March 1957), 29; and Michael Gordon, "Was Waller Ever Right? The Rating and Dating Complex Reconsidered," *Journal of Marriage and Family* 43 (February 1981): 67–76.
9. David P. Schmitt, "Short- and Long-Term Mating Strategies: Additional Evolutionary Systems Relevant to Adolescent Sexuality," in *Romance and Sex in Adolescence and Emerging Adulthood: Risks and Opportunities*, ed. Ann C. Crouter and Alan Booth (Mahwah, NJ: Lawrence Erlbaum Associates, 2006), 41–47.
10. Audio Smut, "I Didn't Know What a French Kiss Was," *Cowbird*, September 26, 2014, http://cowbird.com/story/100549/I_Didnt_Know_What_A_French_Kiss_Was/.
11. Meghan K. Winchell, *Good Girls, Good Food, Good Fun: The Story of USO Hostesses during World War II* (Chapel Hill: University of North Carolina Press, 2008), 2, 5–6, 107, 112, 120.
12. Winchell, *Good Girls*, 117–118, 135–136, 159.
13. Freda Mae De Pillis, "The Papers of Freda Mae (Rustemeyer) De Pillis," Diaries, Schlesinger Library, Radcliffe Institute, Harvard University, Cambridge, MA, February 3, 1943, and March 31 and August 31, 1943; and Marilyn E. Hegarty, *Victory Girls, Khaki-Wackies, and Patriotutes: The Regulation of Female Sexuality during World War II* (New York: New York University Press, 2010), 87.
14. As late as the 1950s, only 18 percent of 20- to 24-year-olds in the United States had completed one or more years of college. U.S. Department of Commerce, Bureau of Census, *Statistical Abstract of the United States* (Washington, DC: Government Printing Office, 1952), 112.

15. Cole, "Youth Goes Monogamous," 22.

16. Geoffrey Gorer, *The American People: A Study in National Character* (New York: W. W. Norton, 1948), 112; and August B. Hollingshead, *Elmtown's Youth* (New York: John Wiley and Sons, 1949), 175.

17. Steven Mintz, *Huck's Raft: A History of American Childhood* (Cambridge, MA: Belknap, 2006), 239; Bruce L. Melvin and Elna N. Smith, *Rural Youth: Their Situation and Prospects* (Washington, DC: Government Printing Office, 1938), 51; and Fass, *Damned and Beautiful*, 211.

18. Caroline Bird, *The Invisible Scar* (New York: David McKay, 1966), 284; Wolford, "Dating Behavior," 202; and Hollingshead, *Elmtown's Youth*, 171.

19. Eva Illouz, *Consuming the Romantic Utopia: Love and the Cultural Contradictions of Capitalism* (Berkeley: University of California Press, 1997), 71. J. Roy Leevy, "Social Competence of High-School Youth" *School Review* 51 (June 1943): 346; Gorer, *American People*, 115; and Adna Marion LeCount, "A Study of Certain Boy-Girl Relationships in a Group of High School Seniors," (EdD project, Teachers College, Columbia University, 1950), 95, 175–176, 275.

20. John R. Crist, "High School Dating as a Behavior System," *Marriage and Family Living* 15 (February 1953): 26; Cole, "Youth Goes Monogamous," 33; Robert D. Herman, "The Going Steady Complex," *Marriage and Family Living* 17 (February 1955), 39–40; Glenn Myers Blair and R. Stewart Jones, *Psychology of Adolescence for Teachers* (London: Macmillan, 1964), 80–81; and Wolford, "The Dating Behavior," 172.

21. Herman, "Going Steady Complex," 36, 37; Cole, "Youth Goes Monogamous," 29; and Thomas Poffenberger, "Three Papers on Going Steady," *The Family Life Coordinator* 13 (January 1964): 7–13.

22. Blair and Jones, *Psychology of Adolescence*, 80–81; Evenlyn Mills Duvall, *Facts of Life and Love for Teen-agers* (New York: Association Press, 1956), 341; Elizabeth Pope, "Is Going Steady Going Sexy?" *McCall's* (May 1957), 41; and Michael Gordon and Randi L. Miller, "Going Steady in the 1980s: Exclusive Relationships in Six Connecticut High Schools," *Sociology & Social Research* 68, no. 4 (July 1984): 464. The example of the dog collar comes from http://easydreamer.blogspot.com/2009/06/paws-off-shes-taken.html.

23. Ruth Teischmann, "The Papers of Ruth Teischmann," Diary, Schlesinger Library, Radcliffe Institute, Harvard University, Cambridge, MA, October 29, 1959; Cole, "Youth Goes Monogamous," 30; and Wolford, "Dating Behavior," 172.

24. Ferentinos, "An Unpredictable Age," 47; Waller, "Rating and Dating," 729; Herman, "Going Steady Complex," 38; Wolford, "Dating Behavior," 170–171; and Hollingshead, *Elmtown's Youth*, 175.

25. Hollingshead, *Elmtown's Youth*, 175; and Ferentinos, "An Unpredictable Age," 142.

26. Allison Davis, Burleigh Gardner, and Mary R. Gardner, *Deep South: A Social Anthropological Study of Caste and Class* (Chicago: University of Chicago, 1941), 105–106; and Crist, "High School Dating," 27.

27. Helen Harmon Weis, "Helen Harmon Weis Papers," Schlesinger Library, Radcliffe Institute, Harvard University, Cambridge, MA, July 28, 1939, and August 30, 1939.

28. Weis Papers, February 12, 1941, and November 30, 1941.

29. Mary Cantwell, *American Girl: Scenes from a Small-Town Childhood* (New York: Random House, 1992), 185.

30. Ferentinos, "An Unpredictable Age," 134; William Graebner, *Coming of Age in Buffalo: Youth and Authority in the Postwar Era* (Philadelphia: Temple University Press, 1994), 15.

31. Susan K. Cahn, *Sexual Reckonings: Southern Girls in a Troubling Age* (Cambridge, MA: Harvard University Press, 2007), 215–216; and Davis et al., *Deep South*, 232.

32. June Goyne Corotto, "I Remember," 1984, A/C 822, Schlesinger Library, Radcliffe Institute, Harvard University, Cambridge, MA, 25.

33. Cantwell, *American Girlhood*, 183; and Cahn, *Sexual Reckonings*, 217–218.

34. Beth Bailey, *From Front Porch to Back Seat: Courtship in Twentieth-Century America*, John Hopkins Paperbacks ed. (Baltimore: Johns Hopkins University Press, 1989), 50–55; Max J. Exner, *The Question of Petting* (New York: Association Press, 1926), 5–6; Esther Emerson Sweeney, *Dates and Dating* (New York: The Woman's Press, 1948), 24; and Wolford, "Dating Behavior," 171.
35. Child Study Association of America, *What to Tell Your Children about Sex* (New York: Permabooks, 1954), 105–106; and Evelyn Mills Duvall, *Facts of Life and Love for Teenagers*, new rev. ed. (New York: Association Press, 1956), 339–346.
36. Judson T. Landis, consultant; Coronet Films; http://www.youtube.com/watch?v=LWQ9eSyLeRU; also see Marion O. Lerrigo and Helen Southard, *What's Happening to Me? Sex Education for the Teen-ager* (New York: E. P. Dutton, 1955).
37. Wolford, "Dating Behavior," 172. For a recent assessment of going steady, Sue Shellenbarger, "The Case for Going Steady: Studies Say Teen Dating Habits Affect Marriage Skills," *Wall Street Journal—Eastern Edition* 246, no. 48 (2005): D1.
38. Ferentinos, "An Unpredictable Age," 142–143.
39. E. E. LeMasters, *Modern Courtship and Marriage* (New York: Macmillan, 1957), 110; Herbert J. Gans, *The Levittowners: Ways of Life and Politics in a New Suburban Community* (New York: Pantheon Books, 1967), 207; and Leora Tanenbaum, *Slut! Growing Up with a Bad Reputation* (New York: Perennial, 2000), 82.
40. Pope, "Steady Going Sexy"; The Reverend James A. Carey, "What Happened When My School Banned Going Steady," *McCall's* (June 1963), 69; and Poffenberg, "Three Papers," 7; also see Andrew M. Greeley, *Strangers in the House: Catholic Youth in America* (New York: Sheed and Ward, 1961), 104–111; and Duvall, and *Facts of Life*, 349. A friend of mine, who grew up attending to Catholic schools in the 1950s and early 1960s, recalls that going steady was taught to be a mortal sin.
41. Winston Ehrmann, *Premarital Dating Behavior* (New York: Henry Holt, 1959), 141; Hollingshead, *Elmtown's Youth*, 175; and Pat Boone, *'Twixt Twelve and Twenty* (Englewood Cliffs, NJ: Prentice Hall, 1958), 63.
42. "How Much Affection?" http://www.youtube.com/watch?v=J3_hkgu6MGc&feature=fvw) Adrian Perez Melgosa, whose field is cinema studies and comparative literature, noted several features of this film. The protagonist looks more like a young adult than a girl. And the short film took on many elements of the film noir, for instance, opening at night, city scenes, and automobiles.
43. LeMasters, *Modern Courtship*, 139.
44. Adele Fasick, "The Papers of Adele (Mongan) Fasick," Diary, 1945, Schlesinger Library, Radcliffe Institute, Harvard University, Cambridge, MA, March 11 and 18, February 23, and April 9.
45. Carotto papers, "I Remember," 12.
46. Hollingshead, *Elmtown's Youth*, 176.
47. Ibid., 314–315, 322.
48. John Gagnon in Gregory Baum and John Coleman, eds., *The Sexual Revolution* (Edinburgh: T&T Clark, 1984); Alan Petigny, "Illegitimacy, Postwar Psychology, and the Reperiodization of the Sexual Revolution," *Journal of Social History* 38, no. 1 (Fall 2004): 63–79; also see Alan Petigny, *The Permissive Society: America, 1941–1965* (New York: Cambridge University Press, 2009); Lillian B Rubin, *Erotic Wars: What Happened to the Sexual Revolution?* (New York: HarperPerennial, 1991), 44–45; and Ehrmann, *Premarital Dating*, 142.
49. Gilbert Youth Research, "How Wild Are College Students?" *Pageant* (November 1951), 15; and Ehrmann, *Premarital Dating*, 130–131.
50. Wini Breines, *Young, White, and Miserable: Growing Up Female in the Fifties* (Chicago: University of Chicago Press, 2001), 113; Gilbert Youth Research, "How Wild?" 17; "Kinsey Era Correspondence Collection," Letters, Kinsey Institute for Research in Sex, Gender, and Reproduction, 1939–1959. Kinsey Institute for Research in Sex,

Gender, and Reproduction; Marilyn Braner; Svend Riemer, "Courtship for Security," *Sociology and Social Research* 45 (July 1961): 423–424.

51. Wolford, "Dating Behavior," 73; Graebner, *Coming of Age*, 69; William Whyte, *Street Corner Society: The Social Structure of an Italian Slum*, 4th ed. (Chicago: University of Chicago Press, 1993); and Hollingshead, *Elmtown's Youth*, 151.

52. Whyte, *Street Corner*, 25–28; Hollingshead, *Elmtown's Youth*, 165, 298–299; and Wolford, "Dating Behavior," 167–169.

53. Whyte, *Street Corner*, 25–28; Hollingshead, *Elmtown's Youth*, 165, 298–299; and Wolford, "Dating Behavior," 167–169.

54. Beth Twiggar Goff, "The Papers of Beth Twiggar Goff," Diaries, Schlesinger Library, Radcliffe Institute, Harvard University, Cambridge, MA, n.d., quoted in John C. Spurlock and Cynthia A. Magistro, *New and Improved: The Transformation of American Women's Emotional Culture* (New York: New York University, 1998), 43.

55. Poffenberger, "Three Papers," 7–13.

56. Mary Chadwick, *Adolescent Girlhood* (New York: John Day, 1933), 243, compared crush relationships to heterosexual romance; Poffenberg, "Three Papers," 8; and Herman, "Going Steady Complex," 37.

57. See Waller, "Rating and Dating." Herman, "Going Steady Complex," 38; and Cole, "Youth Goes Monogamous," 31.

58. Mark Robson, *Valley of the Dolls* (Red Lion, 1968); and Pope, "Steady Going Sexy?"

59. This paragraph opens with a quote from a recent review of the idea that serves as a valuable guide to the development of the concept: Rebecca L. Davis, "'Not Marriage at All, but Simple Harlotry': The Companionate Marriage Controversy," *Journal of American History* 94, no. 4 (March 1, 2008): 1137–1163, quote from 1140; Ben B. Lindsey and Wainwright Evans, *Companionate Marriage* (New York: Arno, 1972); and Ben B. Lindsey and Wainwright Evans, *The Revolt of Modern Youth* (New York: Boni and Liveright, 1925); Ernest Burgess and Harey Locke, *The Family, from Institution to Companionship* (New York: Van Nostrand Reinhold, 1945); and Andrew Cherlin, "The Deinstitutionalization of American Marriage," *Journal of Marriage and Family* 66 (November 2004): 848–861, traces the decline of the traditional marriage model.

60. David R. Shumway, *Modern Love: Romance, Intimacy, and the Marriage Crisis* (New York: New York University Press, 2003), 139; and Wolford, "Dating Behavior," 172.

61. Clarence Arthur Perry, *The Attitude of High School Students toward Motion Pictures* (New York: National Board of Review of Motion Pictures, 1924), 14; Kelly Schrum, *Some Wore Bobby Sox: The Emergence of Teenage Girls' Culture, 1920–1945* (New York: Palgrave MacMillan, 2004), 134, 137; Robert Lynd and Helen Merell Lynd, *Middletown in Transition: A Study in Cultural Conflicts* (New York: Harcourt Brace Jovanovich, 1985), 262; Fasick papers, February 23, 1945; Alice Miller Mitchell, *Children and Movies* (Chicago: University of Chicago Press, 1929), 4–5; and Herbert Blumer, *Movies and Conduct* (New York: Macmillan, 1933), 154.

62. William DeMille, *Why Change Your Wife?* (Famous Players Lasky, 1920); and Frank Capra, *It Happened One Night* (Columbia Pictures Corporation, 1934).

63. W.S. Van Dyke, *The Thin Man* (Metro Goldwyn Mayer, 1934).

64. Poffenberger, "Three Papers," 8; Ehrmann, *Premarital Dating*, 132–133, 162; and Herman, "Going Steady Complex," 162.

65. Herman, "Going Steady Complex," 37.

66. Glen V. Ramsey, *Factors in the Sex Life of 291 Boys* (n.p: n.d., 1950), 83–87; and John Howard, *Men Like That: A Southern Queer History* (Chicago: University of Chicago Press, 1999), 18.

67. Gilbert Youth, "How Wild?" 18.

68. Howard, *Men Like That*, 21–22.

69. Kinsey-era correspondence, L.A., July 1954.

70. Allan Berube, *Coming Out under Fire: The History of Gay Men and Women in World War II* (New York: Free Press, 1990), 98.

71. Will Fellows, ed. *Farm Boys: Lives of Gay Men from the Rural Midwest* (Madison: University of Wisconsin Press, 1996), 72, 81, 89, 97; and Howard, *Men Like That*, 59.

72. Exner, *Question of Petting*, 8; and Francis Bradshaw, "Sex Problems of the Teens," *Parents* (August 1935): 34.

73. Dorothy Anderson, "What about Petting?" *Parents* (August 1943): 42; and Elizabeth Eldridge, *Co-Etiquette: Poise and Popularity for Every Girl* (Philadelphia: Blakiston Co., 1936), 177. LeCount, "Certain Boy-Girl Relationships," 96, 209.

74. Ehrmann, *Premarital Dating*, 108–109, 142; and Hollingshead, *Elmtown's Youth*, 164, 314.

75. Robert Carr, *The Rampant Age* (Garden City, NY: Doubleday, Doran and Co., 1928), 42, 69–72.

76. Hollingshead, *Elmtown's Youth*, 235–236.

77. Ibid., 176, 214, 316.

78. Ibid., 299; and Blair and Jones, *Psychology of Adolescence*, 22–23; on the stereotyping of working-class girls, see Tanenbaum, *Slut!*

79. Vance Randolph, *The Ozarks: An American Survival of Primitive Society* (New York: Vanguard, 1931), 56.

80. Wilma King, *African American Childhoods: Historical Perspectives from Slavery to Civil Rights* (New York: Palgrave Macmillan, 2005), 108–116; Milton A. Smith, "How Moral Are our Coeds?," *Ebony*, July 1952; and Charles S. Johnson, *Growing Up in the Black Belt: Negro Youth in the Rural South* (New York: Schocken, 1941), 295.

81. Hollingshead, *Elmtown's Youth*, 177; and Ehrmann, *Premarital Dating*, 155, 166–167.

82. Tanenbaum, *Slut!*, 52–56, 72, 74. Harold E. Jones, "Physical Maturing among Girls as Related to Behavior," in *The Course of Human Development*, ed. Mary Cover Jones, Nancy Bayley, Jean Walker Macfarlane, Marjorie Pyles Honzik (Waltham, MA: Xerox College, 1971), 257–259, found that girls who physically mature late are most frequently the most popular in their classes.

83. Rachel Devlin, "'Acting Out the Oedipal Wish': Father-Daughter Incest and the Sexuality of Adolescent Girls in the United States, 1941–1965," *Journal of Social History* 38 (Spring 2005): 610.

84. Grace Metalious, *Peyton Place* (New York: Dell, 1964); and n.a., "Peyton Place," *Catholic World* (November 1956): 152. I discuss the place of *Peyton Place* in the development of post war sexuality in "*Peyton Place* and the Boundaries of Sexual discourse in 1950s U.S.A.," in *On the Borders of Convention*, ed. Aleksandra Nikčević Batrićević and Marija Knežević (Newcastle upon Tyne, UK: Cambridge Scholar's Press, 2010), 183–190.

85. Jacob A. Goldberg and Rosamond Goldberg, *Girls on City Streets: A Study of 1400 Cases of Rape* (New York: American Social Hygiene Association, 1935), 294–295; Sheldon Glueck and Eleanor Glueck, *Five Hundred Delinquent Women* (New York: Alfred A. Knopf, 1934), 118–119; and Kirson Weinberg, *Incest Behavior* (New York: Citadel Press, 1955), 39.

86. Devlin, "Acting Out," 609–633; L. Bender and A. Blau, "The Reaction of Children to Sexual Relations with Adults," *American Journal of Orthopsychiatry* 7 (1937): 510, 514; and Joseph Weiss, Estelle Rogers, Miriam R. Darwin, and Charles E. Dutton, "A Study of Girl Sex Victims," *Psychiatric Quarterly* 29, no. 1 (1955): 1.

87. Weinberg, *Incest Behavior*, 147–152.

# 4

# THE SEXUAL EVOLUTION

"The sixties" have come to stand for a period of transformation—political turmoil and shifting alignments, cultural upheaval, and sexual revolution. The most common narrative of twentieth-century sexuality places the decades of the sixties and seventies as a crucial period of rapid and fundamental change. With our longer-range view, however, we can give a better accounting of the shifts in adolescent sexuality for this era. The most important developments for young heterosexuals in this period were a greater willingness to discuss sex openly, an earlier age at first intercourse for girls, and the rapid acceptance of oral–genital sex. Changing behavior moved in parallel to a decades-long shift toward a single standard of sexual morality in which girls and young women, just like boys and young men, could choose sex before marriage without loss of reputation. The new standard that America's youth adopted was fundamentally a female standard, of permissiveness with affection. But, although diminished, the double standard persisted.

From the vantage of half a century, the period seems less revolutionary and more like a consolidation and extension of the sexual system that began during the Depression. Teenagers began dating in middle school or early in high school. They left their single-sex groups for mixed groups about the same time, and a majority dated steadily. As the term *going steady* disappeared, the more general term *relationship* became the common, and apparently permanent, term for couples who felt affection and some commitment to one another. Even with these changes, formal events, like the high school prom and the dance pictured in figure 4.1, continued to play important roles in the social lives of American youth. And the way most young people became sexually active, continued to look much the same as it had for at least a decade before the beginning of Eisenhower's administration.

**FIGURE 4.1** Formal dancing remained an important part of college life in the postwar period. Students at the Christmas dance, Seton Hill University, 1950s.

*Source*: Seton Hill University archives.

## Two Girls, a 1,000 Miles Apart

Two girls who grew up a thousand miles apart give us two tours of post-1950s adolescence. Linda Prentiss grew up near Des Moines, Rachel Rafael in New York City. Both girls came from middle-class families, and both expected to go on to college and pursue careers. But during their early teenage years, they struggled with the far more pressing issues of becoming American adolescents. "They say 'teen-age society is confusing," wrote Linda near the end of eighth grade; then she continued, writing, "[S]o far it sure has been!" She admonished the Linda of the future—"remember how it feels to be 13. Sometimes wonderful, sometimes horrid, sometimes neither." During one of her disagreements with her parents Rachel wrote, "My parents almost *live* by Freud; I suppose they have not reached the part where I began. Adolescents have varied emotions . . .," she observed dryly. Not surprisingly for girls born after the early twentieth century, weight and appearance issues provoked a lot of anxiety. "Another pretty item: I am gaining weight!" wrote 13-year-old Linda. "STOP EATING!! If I don't watch out, I'll be enormous." Rachel dreamed at 14 of having "blond hair, a beautiful face, a very thin and graceful figure." For both girls, appearance issues became critical to their sense of self.[1]

Even more than concerns about appearance, references to boys multiplied in the pages of the two girls' diaries. Rachel described talking with her friend Rochelle, who she thought of as boy crazy, like Yvonne Blue's friend Thekla:

"Day in, day out, it's the same 4-lettered word—BOYS. It's getting to be revolting." Linda, for her part, might have qualified as boy crazy. She wrote about every change in the attitude of one or another of the boys who were (or might be) interested in her. As an 18-year-old she wondered, "Why should I give a damn about boys! But I do." Their diaries show that both girls gain plenty of attention from boys. Linda began going with boys to movies and local events by the time she entered high school. Rachel began dating more tentatively, wandering around Rockefeller Center on her first date with a boy who was also on his first date.[2]

Inevitably, relationships meant touching. Soon enough, both had to face questions about how much intimacy they would allow. "I am NOW going with Sam. . . . Heaven knows I adore him & will for ages," Linda reported during the fall of her freshman year in high school. But she also quickly learned from a friend that in addition to his plans to become a minister; Sam "said he'd like to kiss me. Gosh, the very thought makes me melt. Would I let him? Probably. I don't see anything wrong with it." She must have resisted this pull, however, because she reported her first kiss almost a year later.[3] Rachel also found that boys wanted to kiss her and, like good girls all over the country, put on the brakes. On her second date she wards off a good-night kiss. She wonders about her response—"everyone, it seems, has kissed someone"—but felt she was not yet ready for an exchange of affections. But two weeks later, at the end of a date, she is trapped: "I aimed for his cheek—but he intercepted me with his lips."[4]

Deeper involvement with the boys in their lives meant that the girls had to confront difficult issues, both emotional and physical. Linda had a particularly difficult senior prom: "I didn't have a glorious time," she admitted. She had broken off with one boy and gone to prom with another, although she still wanted to be with the first boy.[5] Both girls had also confronted issues of growing physical intimacy with the boys in their lives. During her senior year, the boy who had taken Rachel out on the first date called to ask her out again. Later, apparently suffering a guilty conscience, he confessed, "[T]he only reason I wanted to see you again was because I wanted to use you sexually. I can't do that to you.—(or rather he wouldn't be able to)." But, a few months later, with another boy, Rachel discovered heavy petting. Uncomfortable at first, she learns to enjoy it as they continue.[6]

At last, both girls found themselves with boys they felt deep affection for. In the summer before she left for college, Linda had again begun to go out with Dave, the boy she had wanted to go to the prom with. After a day at the fair, "we struggled with our senses, and triumphed (?) again . . ." But she yearns for him after he leaves, and then he returns. The language that follows becomes uncharacteristically vague, though she clearly felt they reached some form of consummation.[7] For Rachel, "going all the way" proceeded more deliberately. During a winter internship in her first year at Wellesley she shared a dorm room with a boy she had known since high school. They petted ever more heavily. Finally, looking forward to a life with this young man, Rachel went to see the Wellesley gynecologist to be fitted for a diaphragm. These two girls, both 18 years old, made love for the first time with boys they believed would become their life partners.[8]

## Sexual Evolution

Two white middle-class girls worried about their weight, went out with a few different boys, and fell in love—all these experiences seem unremarkable for adolescent girls, even girls living in different regions of the country. But they lived not only a thousand miles but also 10 years apart. Linda began high school in 1963, the year after Helen Gurley Brown's *Sex and the Single Girl* admitted that young women sought sex outside of marriage and even without the prospect of marriage. By the time Rachel began high school in 1974, the sexual revolution was old news. The Supreme Court had struck down decades-old antipornography laws and even family-friendly theaters could show *I Am Curious (Yellow)*. "Streaking" naked had its fad appearance on college campuses; the Summer of Love and Woodstock had come and gone. The birth control pill was available by prescription only to married women in 1962 but was available to single college coeds by 1972. By that later date pregnant girls (and teachers) no longer had to leave high school. When Linda started high school "making love" still meant making out—kissing and petting. But by the time Rachel began studying algebra, the phrase almost always meant sexual intercourse.[9]

Sexual behavior changed in this period more slowly than we tend to imagine. But if young people began to have a little more sex, they talked about it much, much more. They took their cue from the wider culture. Books and articles from at least the late 1950s declared the beginning of a sexual revolution. By the 1950s, more open and explicit discussions and portrayals of heterosexual eroticism had already become available. *Playboy*, and later *Penthouse*, made erotica somewhat respectable at a time when pornography was becoming more readily available. Television shows like *Rowan and Martin's Laugh-In* began to test the boundaries of sexual innuendo. Magazine editors and movie producers took up the theme of sexual freedom in a variation on the "sex sells" theme— "sexual revolution sells."[10]

Serious discussions also emerged during this period, about sexual agency, coercion, victimization. This is reflected in a note made by Rachel Rafael in 10th grade, in 1975, when she wrote about some boys who had asked girls to go to bed with them. "I don't want to be a 'sex object,' a 'tool,' or a 'plaything,'" she wrote. Both sides of this discussion are revealing. That middle-class 16-year-old boys had started asking girls to have sex appears a more blatant tactic than boys had dared in earlier decades. Rachel, on her part, thinks about this sexual exchange using language drawn from the contemporary women's movement that had begun to identify objectification as an underlying issue for women's lives.[11]

Boys as well as girls had new concerns to confront. Yvonne Blue and Helen Harmon could enjoy extended girlhoods with few distractions from boys. And boys, through the Depression era, had many boys-only activities such as sports or gangs. An outsized interest in girls or boys would still be called "craziness" into the 1940s. By the 1960s the craziness came earlier and was mainly taken for granted. Eliot Margolies, in 1966 Peoria, met Ann at a classmate's Bat Mitzvah. "She pressed close while we slow danced and we made our way to the empty Junior Congregation room where we made out in a pew." Two weeks later he went to meet her again, this time at another party including boys and girls. He did not worry about any harassment from the guys he played basketball with on Saturday morning. Instead, he was excited at the prospect of "more necking and canoodling."[12]

By the 1940s we begin to see parents urging their children to socialize, to participate in the culture of heterosexual play. As we saw, Helen Harmon's mother in the late 1930s worried that she might have made a mistake in sending Helen to an all-girls school because Helen's heterosexual interests had developed so slowly. April Bennett's mother in the 1950s provided support and encouragement for April as she tentatively entered the social world in high school. By the early 1960s some teens felt that parents had become so concerned about their children becoming popular, even in elementary grades that "they push them into dating and sex and wearing bras."[13]

By the middle of the 1960s, however, parents may have justifiably felt like they had little influence in the comparison to the changes in youth culture. As the baby boomers grew into teenagers, the sheer number of Americans going through adolescence was greater from 1960 to 1970 than for the rest of the century before that decade. By the early 1960s, black and white youth joined the civil rights movement, integrating lunch counters and bus lines and, during the Freedom Summer of 1963, registering voters in Mississippi. The antiwar movement that followed drew inspiration and tactics and often recruits from civil rights. Even if only a minority of teenagers and college students participated in these movements, youth generally began to question adult authority. By the mid-1960s, youth, as a group, mattered. Any shift in youthful attitudes toward sex would be an important one for the entire country and for the remainder of the century.

One of the large-scale shifts in American demographics in this period was the end of an almost unbroken decline in the age at marriage. From 1890, the average age for the first marriage of American men was 26.1, for women 22. By 1960 the age for men had dropped to 22.8, and for women to 20.3 with only a slight reversal during the Depression decades. The greater proportion of American youth who attended college by the 1960s undoubtedly explains part of a trend toward later marriage. But as the age at marriage began to slowly rise in the 1960s, this meant longer periods of sex play and going steady for the majority of American teenagers and young adults who participated in both.[14]

By the mid-1960s, college campuses seemed to have become the ground zero of sexual revolution. Beth Bailey's careful study of the changing sexual culture at the University of Kansas traced the shift from the carnivalesque panty raids of the 1950s toward a reorganization of the sexual assumptions of university students, faculty, and administrators. Just one of many fundamental shifts concerned the parietal rules that set curfews and visiting privileges. Many colleges required that dorm doors be left open when members of the opposite sex visited, and three of a couple's four feet had to remain on the floor. By the 1960s these rules already seemed unfair and even sexist. At Harvard a dean complained of rampant infractions of the rules: "Sometimes girls are signed out at midnight on Saturday, and they're still in there . . ." At the University of Kansas, the rules only applied to female students, on the principle, apparently, that if the women were protected the men would behave.[15]

One Harvard graduate from the period recalled the furor over parietal rules. "We just considered it to be an invasion of privacy," he told an interviewer. The double sexual standard, and the implicit double class standard (if the men misbehaved with women off campus, that was not equally of concern) led many deans to reconsider in loco parentis. So many colleges backed away from the rules that by 1966 *Time* magazine declared in loco parentis in rigor mortis. By the mid-1960s, even in conservative Kansas, a student responsibility movement opposed the rules on the basis that women students should be treated like adults. The student organization that set the rules made changes that the administration ultimately ratified. The very term *parietal* fell out of use by the 1970s.[16]

Certainly the discussion of sexual issues became far more common, even if the context of discussion was often a sense of crisis. Yet from the pages of Linda's and Rachel's diaries we see two girls attending to the daily interplay of personal contacts, physical attraction, and social standing. They dated, went steady, considered who they might marry, negotiated physical intimacy—putting it off and slowly accepting it on their own terms. Their adolescent lives resembled one another in most important ways, and also resembled the adolescent experiences of April Bennett, almost exactly ten years older than Linda Prentiss. The changes in lived experience between April Bennett (early 1950s) and Rachel Rafael (early 1970s) seem modest compared to the differences in the experience of Yvonne Blue (late 1920s) and April.

## Still Going Steady

As the 1960s opened, parents, journalists, and academic specialists interested in adolescent sexuality seemed to agree that the major issue confronting youth was the threat posed by going steady. Catholic authorities condemned it as a "moral hazard" and journalist Elizabeth Pope considered investing one's whole social life in a single person a colossal bore. Academic experts and parents reminded young Americans that going steady limited the number of people they would become acquainted with, thereby making the eventual choice of spouse far less informed. Of course, along with the threat of "premature emotional involvement" (as a marriage life teacher put the issues in the 1962 movie *Where the Boys Are*) came the often-unstated opportunity for sex and the problem of unwed pregnancy.[17]

Yet in spite of the resistance of adult authorities, the practice of going steady continued to grow. Studies conducted from the early 1960s to the 1980s showed that majorities of high school students had gone steady by their junior and senior years—sometimes for short periods but sometimes for months or years. And during the decades when the media continually reminded Americans about the sexual revolution they were living through, the practice became more common. One study used samples drawn from coeds at a "large urban university" with surveys conducted in 1958 and 1968. Sixty-eight percent reported having gone steady in 1958, and 77 percent by 1968. The steady complex not only included more adolescents by the later date, but it also seems to have become more intensive. A large, longitudinal study from the Detroit area showed that girls in successive cohorts, from the 1960s into the 1980s, began going steady earlier. The surveys of steady daters in 1958 and 1968 found that college coeds in 1958 could recall or estimate having dated 53 boys; by 1968 that had fallen to 25. The sexual lives of high school and college students became concentrated on fewer people.[18]

Even into the 1980s steady dating dominated high school social life. A study of Connecticut high schools found 81 percent of girls and almost 70 percent of boys had gone steady. Social class as measured by socioeconomic status (SES) or plans for attending college, race, and many other measures made no difference in the likelihood that a boy or girl would go steady. The only variable that indicated a higher proportion of going steady was when dating began—those who began dating earlier began going steady earlier. Dating, beginning at 14 or 15, became steady dating within a year. The authors of the Connecticut study suspected that "going steady has become so central a part of teenage culture that it overrides local variation."[19]

Dating security certainly continued as a primary motivation for the practice of going steady. But it was not only finding a date that mattered. The high school social scene, especially for freshmen, featured a range of difficulties that students had to navigate with limited experience and knowledge. When one group of researchers in 1960 asked high school students about their reasons for going steady, "[w]e [were] referred to security in interpersonal relationships. Boys and girls may want to be sure of a date at all times; they may want to improve their social status, or they may want to know exactly what to expect in the 'parking situation.'"[20] A later study noted that those who were going steady, as well as those who had gone steady, were more likely to spend Saturday night with someone of the opposite sex or with a mixed-sex group than those who had never gone steady. Steady daters were more likely to go to school functions, they gained more status through their participation, and they regularly enjoyed the company of the opposite sex. Going steady helped make sense of a wide range of adolescent issues, and helped to integrate the individual more fully into the life of the high school.[21]

After 1960 the panic over going steady faded quickly. As the news media trumpeted the existence of a sexual revolution, parents and commentators had more disturbing issues to worry about. In the early 1960s new living arrangements on college campuses and the growing counterculture vied for the public's attention. Going steady must have seemed tepid, even safe. At the same time, it may have become less noticeable. The practice lost some of its distinctive character. While gift exchanges still figured in steady-dating arrangements into the 1980s, a study completed in the early 1960s already noted a decline in rituals associated with going steady. But going steady may have become less anxiety provoking simply because it had also become so pervasive. The term itself began to disappear after 1960. Social scientists continued using the term even when high school students had already begun to abandon it. Rachel Rafael, for instance, never refers to a steady. By the 1990s the use of the term in many regions of the country would have seemed quaint, even though high school students still practiced the same kind of serial monogamy described since the 1930s.[22]

## Permissiveness (and Sex) with Affection

In spite of the lurid media attention to "love clubs" and promiscuous sex on college campuses, the sexual organization formerly known as going steady still provided the context for most of the adolescent sex in the United States. Just as they had done in the 1950s, girls were more likely to have sex with the boys they dated steadily. And those girls who went steady more often were more likely to be sexually experienced than those who had fewer steadies. Like Linda and Rachel, girls simply felt more freedom and confidence to agree to more and more physical intimacy with boys whom they knew better and felt closer to. Both girls dated throughout high school. Linda, who dated more often, also had more than one serious high school romance. Rachel dated less, but also seems to have dated steadily with a few boys. That Linda apparently had intercourse earlier than Rachel (though only by about six months) would have been an easy prediction from what we know about the relation of intercourse and steady dating.[23]

Linda Prentiss and Rachel Rafael both took it for granted that powerful emotions and the expectation of commitment went along with physical intimacy. They participated in reshaping the adolescent rationale for sex. The double standard of sexual morality, which gave men freedom to pursue physical intimacy with women while at the same time expecting chastity from the women they planned to marry, had begun to fall apart even before Linda Prentiss entered high school. As a recent graduate of Smith College wrote in 1959, "most girls have only a couple of vague rules of thumb to go by, which they cling to beyond all sense and reason." On one hand, "anything is all right if you're in love," and on the other hand, "a girl must be respected; particularly by the man she wants to marry." This delicate balance "requires constant corroborative discussion while she tries to plumb the depths of a man's intentions." Girls had their own standards for physical intimacy, but they had to avoid violating, when they could not ignore, the double standard.[24]

In 1961 a writer in *Esquire* described what he claimed as a new ethos: "that sex is fine—nay, indispensable—but it has to be validated either by love or by a steady relationship." David Boruff's view was seconded and expanded by journalist Gael Greene from her much more extensive interviews among college coeds all across the country. Engagement or being pinned or going steady or being in love all gave American girls permission to become sexually more intimate. The "mating process," according to sex researchers in 1970, "has become more and more one of exchanging increasing levels of sexual intimacy on the part of the female for increasing emotional commitments on the part of the male." The couple in figure 4.2 seem to demonstrate this new standard. But the shift came about not simply because girls gave up more, but because boys accepted a fundamentally female viewpoint about sex. Gael Greene told an interviewer from the *Harvard Crimson* in 1964 that Radcliffe women were far more "sophisticated" about sex than were Harvard men and that "[w]hen you're in love, it's all right."[25]

Within the steady complex, girls had established the priority of permissiveness with affection over the double standard. Already by the early 1950s the

**FIGURE 4.2** Teenage couple embrace on the bank of the Frio Canyon River, Near Leakey, Texas and San Antonio, May 1973. St. Gil, Marc, 1924–1992, Photographer.

*Source*: National Archives and Records Administration.

difference in male and female standards came through in an intensive study at one Midwestern college. For men, the double standard prevailed. They sought intercourse with lower-class women and considered intercourse with women of their own class—college women—as either unacceptable or unavailable. The college women, however, who had the most serious relationships, were most likely to have had the most sexual experience. For girls and young women, sex play had to be treated more seriously, and it implied that the two individuals were more than just playmates. They were equals.[26]

Perhaps the availability of new roles for women, as companions and sex partners, partially explains the rise of the marriage age. As marriage lost its role as the formal justification for sexual relations, the double standard that had marriage as its rationale, also began to decline. In 1965 and again in 1970, researchers surveyed representative samples of students at a southern university and found that in the short half-decade "there had occurred a great change in the attitudes and public expression" regarding sex. Young women reporting pre-marital intercourse had increased from about 29 to 37 percent. Of course, sexual surveys are notorious for the problematic match between reported and actual behavior. The more startling finding of the survey related to attitudes. In 1965, 70 percent of the college women surveyed believed that pre-marital sex was immoral. Five years later, the proportion holding this same attitude had declined by *half.* The survey's author also noted the shift toward a single standard of sexual morality for men and women. On the issue of promiscuity—was it immoral for women to have sex with many men—the survey found a large drop for men, from 42 to 33 percent of men who said yes, but a far more profound drop among women—from 91 to 54 percent. A gap still divided men and women on the issue, but the trend toward a common view was clear.[27]

By the early 1970s, new sexual standards and behavior had spread among white college students and more generally among working- and middle-class youth. A 1973 survey in Wisconsin sampled not only undergraduate males and females but also a range of people the same age who were not in college. Although the northern study found higher percentages in many categories of sexual experience than the southern one had, the direction of sexual change remained consistent for both studies. Social class did not result in differences in sexual experience. Perhaps the most important finding was that the double standard had weakened. Young men and women reported accepting the same level of intimacy at the same point in the relationship. Even among high school youth the double standard seemed to have less of a hold. A 1974 study of high school-aged youth concluded that "the double standard no longer adequately characterizes the sexual experience of the adolescent." Continuing a trend evident form the 1940s, young males looked to their female peers rather than "bad girls" or lower-class girls as sexual partners.[28] Still, even diminished, the double standard persisted in some form as did a form of the notion of the bad girl—a topic we will explore in the following.

National attitudinal data also point to growing approval of premarital inter-course from the 1960s through the 1970s. National surveys in 1971 and 1976 explored the dating and other sexual behavior of both black and white girls, 15 to 19 years old. Premarital intercourse increased for both groups from 1971 to 1976, with the shifts about the same proportion for both groups, so that by age 19 the total for the sample stood at about 60 percent (56.6 percent for white, 84.2 percent for black 19-year-olds).[29] Questions on attitudes by the mid-1970s showed that a majority of teenage girls believed sex before marriage was a legiti-mate choice. Even those who still believed that sex before marriage was never acceptable knew that some of their friends held the view that it was. "Nothing so undermines a normative prescription as exceptions to it," the authors of one survey noted. They concluded that the norm of premarital chastity "was effec-tively defunct."[30]

Studies of groups differing by race, residence, and SES all point toward a fundamental shift in attitudes. By the early 1970s, men and women, middle class and working class, held views on sex, especially premarital intercourse, that looked more and more similar—the view that an affectionate relationship rather than marriage or engagement justified sex.[31] For April Bennett, spending a night with a man during her college years meant making an exception to a strongly supported social norm. For Linda Prentiss and Rachel Rafael, the norm retained progressively less of its power to shape their decisions. The experiences of Linda and Rachel, and our short survey of empirical evidence, all reveal fundamental shifts in attitudes.

On the other hand, at least until the early 1970s, sexual behavior changed more slowly than attitudes. One sex researcher concluded in 1966 that the most dramatic change had come in "acceptance of premarital coital behavior rather than in increased performance of this behavior."[32] A study that examined the growth of premarital pregnancy and illegitimacy in the United States in light of the falling age at menarche (and with this the lower rates of spontaneous abor-tion) concluded that increased sexual activity accounted for only 11 percent of the growth in premarital pregnancy among white girls, and less than 1 percent for black girls. For those young women not planning to marry, the increase amounted to less than half a percent. Increases in reports of sexual activity may have resulted from the greater freedom that people felt in talking about sex. One survey conducted at 12 colleges at the end of the 1960s found that among women "nearly 60% reported that they were in love with and planning to marry the per-son with whom they first had intercourse." They still placed sex within the con-text of family formation, according to the authors, who concluded that the "romantic ideology is still endemic."[33]

These studies, late in the 1960s or early 1970s, may have missed trends that had only just begun at the end of the 1960s. Both black and white teenagers reported earlier and more premarital intercourse by the mid-1970s. A follow-up study in 1980 of the same southern university mentioned earlier found that reports of intercourse among college women approached what the authors believed was a maximum above which the rates could not rise. Attitudes condemning intercourse, and presumably supporting the double standard, had collapsed, with only 17 percent of college women in 1985 supporting the view that intercourse before marriage was always wrong. Yet these changes in the size of reported behavior followed patterns that had already become clear. Even when a young couple had no intention of marrying, they generally agreed to become physically intimate, and to have intercourse, within what both partners saw as a committed (even if a short-term) relationship.[34]

## Going Very Steady

In his 1961 *Esquire* article David Boruff had identified the term *relationship* as the basic theme of what he already called a sexual revolution. Marriage had become less central to the thinking of many young people in the 1960s. Divorce rates began to rise and the stigma associated with divorce declined. Even engagement lost some of its importance as a transition from singleness to marriage, and no longer served as the only warrant for sexual intimacy. But during the 1960s other kinds of arrangements—relationships—became prominent. Affection, even love, would continue to be viewed as one of life's basic goals, Boruff wrote, but so would sex. And, so would the expectation that whatever the couple did together should serve the mutual good of the couple. With the decline of the double standard, the emergence of the relationship—companionate marriage without marriage and without many of the traditional gendered roles of marriage—can stand as one of the principle shifts for heterosexual couples during this 20-year period of upheaval.[35]

By the end of the 1960s cohabitation had become a common practice among college students. This became widely known in 1968. Linda LeClair, a Barnard student, became a media sensation when her identity was revealed in a *New York Times* article. She had lied to college officials so she could live "off campus," in this case with her boyfriend in his Columbia dorm room. A college judicial hearing followed, and when the administration persisted in attempts to expel LeClair, students circulated a petition and staged protests.[36] LeClair's case brought the practice of cohabitation among college students to public attention. Barnard's president received a flood of letters from around the country, most of them supporting the decision for expulsion and many characterizing LeClair as a "whore" or a moral disgrace. But a year later, when *Fortune* magazine surveyed American youth, the study found that a majority of college students (but only about a third of noncollege youth) would consider living with someone outside of marriage. Later surveys found that from 10 to 33 percent of students went beyond considering it and decided to live together. The portion of students who lived together even part of their four years of college was startling compared to a decade earlier, when couples moved in together only when they became man and wife.[37]

A contemporary account of the new sexuality of the late 1960s noted that one of the most important elements of the new live-in relations among college students was that "young couples are literally and physically together almost all the time."[38] This sounds suspiciously like a high school couple described in the late 1950s to show that going steady was boring as well as wrong. In fact, one researcher called the new phenomenon of cohabiting "going very steady." In a survey at Cornell in 1972, Eleanor Macklin found that 31 percent of her sample had cohabited at some point during their college years. They did not differ from non-cohabiters in religion, parents' education, or other measures of SES. These arrangements were based on strong mutual affection and typically were exclusive relationships. But they were not a form of engagement. Only 10 percent planned to marry. A later, longitudinal study of dating couples in Boston area colleges, found that over four years cohabiting students were no more likely to have married (or to have broken up) than non-cohabiting couples. Cohabiters spent more time together (no surprise), had higher satisfaction with their sex lives, and had greater intimacy, than non-cohabiting couples. And, while 70 percent gave "emotional attachment" as the reason for living together, other reasons included "security, companionship, enjoyment and convenience."[39] This list could have been lifted from earlier studies that explained the motivations for going steady.

The hegemony of the going steady model extends even further. Students in college, still a minority of all youth in their age category, probably were more assimilated to middle-class values than they would have admitted. Almost all would eventually marry. That these adolescents and young adults would transform the high school practice of affectionate, extended, exclusive relationships into a live-in arrangement probably should not surprise us now. But even among young people who consciously rejected middle-class values—hippies and other culture rebels—monogamous relations existed as part of the mix of open, free, and group arrangements. "Acquaintances and friends become fleeting lovers," according to one contemporary description, "strangers meet and become momentary bedmates or soulmates, then dance off again to another partner and another scene." Yet according to the same account, the majority "stay[ed] involved with each other over fair durations of time." Even within the context of a larger revolt against the mores of modern American culture and experimentation with "free love," many in the counterculture claimed to have an "old man" or "old lady" as their primary partner.[40]

As the term *going steady* disappeared in the 1970s, and the practice lost much of its ritual, the social organization of adolescent and young adult sexuality appeared more and more like an elaboration of the going steady complex. The short-term, exclusive relations typical of going steady had become the context for most premarital intercourse by the 1950s, and as going steady became more widely accepted among younger teenagers, so too did "pre-premarital" sex—sex with a partner who you were unlikely to marry. At the other end of the adolescent age spectrum, college-age adolescents and young adults entered long-term relations that often included shared living space. These relationships included not only sex but also growing emotional intimacy. And, like going steady, they were based on some combination of affection, convenience, and security.

## The New Sex in Adolescent Sexuality

During the 1960s, changes became manifest in the sex part of heterosexuality. Masturbation finally became normal. Not in the statistical sense—from the perspective of practice, "self-abuse" had been statistically normal for the entire century, at least. But expert opinion finally agreed to see the practice as benign, and perhaps even valuable. This message slowly made its way through the general population. A mid-1950s "Facts of Life" book by a YWCA educator treated masturbation as normal and drew on other expert opinion to the same effect. By the late 1970s an overview of adolescent sexuality concluded that by age 15 about half of boys and a third of girls masturbated, with rates increasing to 85 and 60 percent, respectively, by age 20.[41] Popular culture by then had already begun to spread the message that "everybody" did it. Treatments of the topic came in widely different forms, including David Reuben's *Everything You Always Wanted to Know about Sex* guide (1969) and Philip Roth's popular novel *Portnoy's Complaint* (1969).

Petting also got heavier. The "American ballet" might include "rubbing and bumping without clothing," mutual masturbation, "dry humping," and an assortment of other sexual exchanges short of intercourse. "It requires skills to satisfy a man and still hold on to your virginity," according to an Ohio State coed in the early 1960s. Sex without intercourse served the goal of "technical virginity"—a term that grew in use and importance from the 1950s into the 1980s.[42] But until the 1970s, sexual researchers assumed that noncommercial heterosexual experience consistently followed a script—almost a checklist—that shaped what a couple did together physically. A prostitute might begin with genital fondling, but the girl next door probably would not. Kissing with the tongue followed kissing only with the lips, and then in turn was followed by the male hand on the female breast, first outside and then inside her clothing. The script carried a gendered rationality of its own, with males acting on females before the reverse, and with physical contact proceeding from the lips downward. Couples did not necessarily go through this sequence each time they became physically intimate, but they typically completed earlier parts of the list before going on to later parts of it.[43]

Of course, each sexual encounter is unique—the timing of what was touched and how it was touched would have varied greatly from couple to couple. In her senior year in high school, 1972, Rachel Rafael traveled to Queens to spend time alone with a boy she had had a romance with at camp the previous summer. They kissed and then petted, going through the motions of intercourse but without ever removing their clothes. The following winter she and the boy she shared dorm space with proceeded to using their hands on each other's genitals before she decided to visit the Wellesley gynecologist for birth control.[44] The ordinary idiom of youth recognized this sexual script in the use of the baseball metaphor of the bases (from kissing to genital fondling) and in the still common terms for sexual caresses, necking (kissing) and petting (fondling). Making love included all of these steps along the way, and of course led to "crossing home plate" or "going all the way." But making love did not necessarily include oral sex. The research literature of the period placed heterosexual cunnilingus and fellatio on the scale as *following* intercourse.[45]

Oral–genital sex (OGS) had a long association with the sex acts provided by prostitutes. Even in the 1950s, heterosexual men and women who practiced this faced misunderstanding and possible legal consequences. In 1950 a man wrote to sex researcher Alfred Kinsey that he could only find sexual satisfaction by kissing his wife's "womb and for her to kiss my penis at the same time." But his wife found this disgusting. Five years later a correspondent who gained pleasure from cunnilingus with his wife wrote, "[M]y wife thinks that I am probably the only man that has such desires, therefore I am either oversexed or queer." One woman who began writing to Kinsey in 1954 revealed, "I have done sex the 'French method,' . . . It is clean, and no worries attached." But she had run afoul of the police in Alaska, where she had been performing as a dancer. She was ultimately convicted under the sodomy law and faced a prison sentence by the time of her last letter to Kinsey in 1957.[46]

Kinsey's survey had found that about equal numbers of college-educated men and women practiced oral sex after marriage. Perhaps husbands who had their first sexual encounters with prostitutes in the decades up to the 1940s had convinced their wives to try this approach to enhance their sex lives. But dating and going steady in the 1950s and 1960s appear to have included little of this surplus sexual intimacy. Ehrmann, in his study of college students from the late 1940s into the 1950s, does not include oral sex on his scale of physical intimacy. Surveys on sexual activity right into the 1970s that documented growing frequencies for petting and intercourse often contained no mention of oral sex acts.[47] These may have seemed too rare for researchers to investigate.

By the late 1960s, however, the script had changed. A 1967 survey at 12 college campuses found that students reported about 30 percent of men and 25 percent of women had experienced oral sex, rates about twice as high as those drawn from the Kinsey studies. The rough equivalence in the proportions of young men and women reporting oral sex tends to support the insight that these acts were exchanged. The survey also found that while those who frequently gave or received oral sex also had frequent coitus, the reverse was not true. Oral sex did not seem to fit either the scripting of intimacy that placed it beyond intercourse, or the view that it was a kind of petting leading to intercourse. Rather, OGS was becoming a separate form of lovemaking, not necessarily linked to intercourse. A 1970s survey at a southern university further supports this shift in sexual experience. Researchers found a rapid increase since 1965 in the number of women who had intercourse—from 29 to 37 percent. As predicted by the scripting of sexual activity, far more co-eds had experienced heavy petting, with the increase greatly outpacing that for intercourse (from 34 to almost 60 percent). But, strikingly, the study reported that 66 percent of males and 54 percent of females had engaged in oral sex. In other words, 17 percent more women admitted to oral sex than to intercourse.[48]

The southern study reveals that a remarkable change in sexual standards had already begun. The author expressed his surprise over the OGS findings as best he could in academic parlance: "In light of the extreme censure in custom, religion, and law for such behavior, it appears that as far as pre-marital petting behavior is concerned, patterns have changed from the traditional Judeo-Christian ethic." We can assume that at least part of the appeal of oral sex was the one given by the Kinsey correspondent, "no worries attached" as far as pregnancy. The culture caught up to the college-age attraction to oral sex in the decade following these studies. Oral sex received enthusiastic and graphic attention in the successful porn film *Deep Throat* (1972) and the best-selling *Joy of Sex* by Alex Comfort (1972). A follow-up study in the 1980s of the same southern university showed that more than 80 percent of males and 74 percent of females had engaged in oral sex. The percentages for women still differed dramatically from the 63 percent who were willing to report they had engaged in intercourse. By 1985 the meaning of oral sex appears to have changed. Oral sex became a valuable tool in maintaining technical virginity as well as a part of sex life enjoyed for its own sake.[49]

## Homosexuality

Compared to the rapid shifts for adolescent heterosexuality in the early decades of the twentieth century, the three decades following World War II appear more of a period of consolidation than of upheaval. For young people whose sexual orientation was homoerotic, however, the same period brought remarkable changes and the promise of more to come. Joan Biren, born in 1944, grew up in suburban Rockville, Maryland. She participated in many school activities and had a lively social life, including attending her senior prom. "I felt different," she told an interviewer in 2004. "You know, kids had pajama parties, slumber parties, you know, and did each other's hair and stuff like that. I didn't want anybody to do my hair. I just wanted to jump into bed with them." She believes now that her mother, on some level, knew that Joan was drawn toward lesbianism, "so she pressured me a lot to go out with boys, almost more than she pressured me to use makeup or anything like that . . . from her, the pressure was to date men, boys and men." For Joan, understanding her own desires came at a cost. While babysitting at the home of a psychiatrist, she read in his library "about how sick it was and I read all the pathology of lesbianism." She refused to admit, even to herself, that she was attracted only to other girls and women.[50]

From high school Joan went on to Mount Holyoke College, where she earned her BA in political science. At Mt. Holyoke, in her sophomore year she finally came out to one other person, her first lesbian partner. "This was coming out into the closet because we couldn't be public." When the interviewer asked Joan if she knew other lesbians, because at that time everyone assumed that women's colleges attracted lesbians, she responded, "We never told anybody and nobody ever told us." In fact, at that time, even at Mount Holyoke, the topic "was very taboo." Later, after a second partner attempted suicide, she went to see the school psychiatrists. "I'm a lesbian," she told him. We can suspect, now, that he had many situations like this and had practiced his response. "Oh, no, you're not. He said, You just think you are. But it's a phase and you'll grow out of it and it's best not to tell anybody. So don't even worry about it."[51]

Holyoke's psychiatrist read from the same books that other developmental psychologists, therapists, and educators used. Boys and girls, even young adults, could be expected to go through a period of strong "hero worship" for older same-sex peers or authority figures and that a "crush" might go on for a time during adolescence. Craig Rodwell, born in the early 1940s, attended a Christian Science school for boys until early adolescence. He recalled the physical play with other boys, and even holding hands and kissing. Teachers may have disapproved, but they accepted this as childish play. "The sexual play accompanying these so-called 'crushes' has nothing whatever to do with homosexuality and should give parents no concern," wrote psychiatrist William Sadler in a 1948 guide. Parents, teachers, and camp counselors were advised to treat these episodes as stepping-stones on the path of normal development—normal, here, meaning heterosexual object craziness. With all the anxiety expressed over dating, going steady, and the ever-present concern about premarital sex, the girlfriend crushes and boy chums may have seemed a great relief to parents.[52]

By the 1960s the expert opinion on the homosexual "phase" was out of step with the times. Textbooks in the 1960s still discussed adolescent "crushes" as same-sex relations, more typical of girls than of boys. But at least by the 1950s, and probably earlier, when adolescents used the term *crush* it carried a clear heterosexual meaning. The social science, as well as the language, of these texts also seemed out of date. Studies from the 1920s still appeared as the basis for generalizations about adolescents in the 1960s. Strong friendships certainly still formed in adolescence, early and late, but, as we have seen, the homosocial underpinnings of adolescent society had attenuated since the 1920s. Studies in the 1950s and later showed dating beginning earlier and that going steady followed hard on the beginning of dating—usually within a year. Going steady emphasized the mixed-sex couple as the model of teenage aspiration, and it existed within a web of mixed-sex social activities. Junior high students already felt pressure from peers and parents to join the heterosocial life of the school. A student who did not date and go steady had to expect a marginal role in the social system of the American high school.

Perhaps the most basic fact of life for the great majority of gay adolescents was "the closet," a term that became widely known and understood by the 1970s. Most gay and lesbian adolescents had to find a way to "pass," to appear "normal." "The sexual information blackout during adolescence, the stigmatized status of the homosexual, and the fears of being different contribute to great pain," wrote child development expert Catherine Chilman in 1978.[53] An American academic who graduated high school in the early 1930s said that he reached his senior year in high school before a teacher explained to him (one-on-one) what homosexuality meant. Craig Rodwell, in the late 1950s, had to rely on his high school's dictionary's definition of *homosexual* to find some purchase for his sense of self. Hiding one's sexual orientation took a heavy toll on adolescents and young adults, and often led to depression and even self-hatred.[54]

By the 1970s, leaving the closet and acknowledging one's gay identity had become far more common. "Figuring out a sexual identity," according to Catherine Chilman, "takes much more careful thought for the homosexual than for the heterosexual." Joan Biren continued her education at Oxford University where she tried to believe what the psychiatrist at Mount Holyoke had told her. She found boyfriends and even had heterosexual intercourse. But after three years at Oxford she returned to the United States more convinced than ever that she was lesbian. She met and became involved with Sharon Deevey: "we finally came out publicly within the Women's Liberation movement . . . I've never gone back since then."[55] For Craig Rodwell, coming out to himself seems to have happened very early. Once he moved to a public school in Chicago, his desires were so at odds with the adolescent world he found himself in that he quickly drew the attention of authorities. At 14 he was arrested in the company of an older man whom he had met casually. His mother managed to keep him from being sent to a reformatory, but Craig had to struggle in high school just to keep going. He met a few other gay boys and men, but his hope for a better life led him to move to New York City's Greenwich Village.[56]

The early experiences of Joan Biren and Craig Rodwell suggest the range of responses that gay adolescents could have to the mismatch of their desires with the cultural messages and social roles available to them in the 1950s, 1960s, and 1970s. Studies of sexuality at the time provide little help in understanding the experience of gay and lesbian youth. Social scientists in the period either turned to adult homosexuals for their surveys and interviews or, if they studied high school and college-aged adolescents, gave virtually all of their attention to the colorful changes in heterosexual attitudes and practices. But some adults could reflect on or recall the sense of isolation during a gay youth. "Anyone who is different has problems," one woman told an interviewer, "especially when you're younger. It's inhibiting. And that inhibits relationships." At the end of the twentieth century a young gay man discussed life stories with older men who had to remain closeted until middle age. "They didn't know what it was like to be with someone. Then, when they [did finally date], they had the same type of problems teenagers have with their first relationships." Adolescent homosexuality had to be put off until a safer time in adulthood.[57]

During the 1960s and 1970s, the visibility, and, to some extent, acceptance, of gay and lesbian adults shifted dramatically. The Mattachine Society, founded in Los Angeles in 1950, would press the cause of wider acceptance of gay lifestyles. In 1956 the Daughters of Bilitis would begin making the same case for lesbians. The studies of sexuality, and especially of homosexuality, in the 1950s and 1960s, ranged from fierce condemnation to open acceptance, but by the 1960s the weight of psychological and sociological studies had shifted in favor of abandoning the deviance idea. In 1973 the American Psychiatric Association removed "homosexuality" from its manual of psychiatric disorders. Even though legislatures in most states made sodomy laws more severe following World War II, in some areas, notably in San Francisco and New York, police slowly dropped the practice of entrapping gay men. In San Francisco, police harassment was largely abandoned. Harassment continued in New York City until 1969 when a routine police raid at the Stonewall Bar provoked a riot and confrontation with the police and city authorities. After Stonewall, more and more gay men and lesbians became unapologetic about their sexual identities. Before 1970, public demonstrations asserting the value of homosexuality—"gay is just as good as straight"—would have been unthinkable. After 1970, gay pride parades became common in large cities.[58]

By the early 1970s gay students and gay student organizations began to gain some recognition on college campuses, even those away from the urban centers on the East and West Coasts. Beth Bailey has chronicled the efforts of gay students at the University of Kansas to create a place for themselves. The administration refused to recognize the Gay Liberation Front as a student organization. But dances scheduled by the group during the 1970s, and open to all sexual interests, gave a core to the gay community there. "In a town without established spaces for gays and lesbians," Bailey writes, "the irregularly scheduled dances were critically important . . . the dances held at the student union throughout the 1970s played a major role in creating and consolidating a gay culture and community in Lawrence." Although sometimes interrupted by antigay rowdies, the dances provided community for gay students and town residents and made gay people more visible and so less ominous in the college town.[59]

Public attitudes lagged behind the gains made in some parts of the country. By the late 1960s conservative movements opposing sex education in public schools began to organize and develop a counternarrative to the sexual changes taking place in the United States. Public opinion surveys showed that most Americans, well into the 1980s, retained negative attitudes toward homosexual practices. Still, the very controversies of the period made some gay and lesbian people recognizable as real people. In 1973 the first reality television program, *An American Family*, was broadcast on PBS featuring the Louds, a California family going through a divorce. Bill and Pat's 20-year-old son, Lance, was openly gay, and his sexuality became a topic of TV talk shows. For countless gay men, Lance Loud became the first openly gay person they had viewed on television. Combined with the burgeoning gay pride movement following Stonewall, the appearance of gay identified men and women in the media meant the opening of a new possibility—gay adolescence.[60]

## Coerced Sex

The baby-boom generation began to come of age in an era of uneven changes in sexual assumptions and practices. For adolescents, premarital and even pre-premarital sex became more common. Most young people knew about birth control even if they did not use it. The overwhelming majority would marry, but cohabitation and even open marriages were well known and more or less openly practiced. Divorce became common. Yet, open homosexuality remained possible in only a few places in the United States and existed in spite of legal prohibitions. And, through the decade of the 1960s, discussions of sexual abuse and incest remained muted.

In the Deep South, the interdict on discussion operated as part of white privilege. Anne Moody, growing up in Mississippi, recalled that in her hometown almost all the young white men had young African American "lovers." These typically were teenaged girls who went to work in white middle-class homes. The white wives of Centreville claimed that these girls seduced their husbands. This convenient narrative supported willful ignorance of systemic coercion and statutory rape.[61]

Until the 1970s, incest seemed to have no place in discussions of sexual danger. Little girls and boys were warned against strangers offering candy, yet it would have seemed perverse to turn suspicion upon those who were, in fact, the most common offenders—employers, fathers, uncles, friends of the family, and other caretakers. Some people could speak the truth, like Anne Moody's transgender friend Lola, whom she met while working in New Orleans: "Stepfathers ain't no damn good," Lola told her in response to Anne's concerns that her own stepfather was becoming more and more attentive. "Once my cousin remarried some no-good man and put him over her teen-age daughter. One day she came home and caught that fucker in bed with her child." In Anne's case, the tension in her own household continued to grow until she was forced to leave and return to her father's home.[62]

To the extent that mental health professionals considered incest, psychoanalytic ideas still held sway. Prepubescent and adolescent girls were seen as struggling to free themselves from pre-Oedipal attachments to their mothers. According to this view, by acting out their desires for union with their fathers, young girls might actually gain greater mental health. Alayne Yates, a pediatrician and psychiatrist, in her 1978 guide for the healthy sexual development of children, warned against continuing ties to mothers. In fact, she considered mother–son incest "malignant." But father–daughter incest she treated as essentially benign. "The girls I have evaluated who were young, uncoerced, and initially pleased with the relationship remain emotionally unscathed, even after protracted incest," she wrote. Not only were they unscathed; they also benefited from the incestuous rape. "They are fully orgasmic, sexually competent, attractive, and sometimes seductive." Girls who entered incestuous relations in adolescence, however, had different responses. According to Yates, it was not the abuse in and of itself that was the problem. Rather, because these girls had already absorbed social standards, they felt guilt about their actions, and this in turn could lead to depression. These girls might become promiscuous or retreat from social life altogether. While statutory rape and incest received at least partial clearance from Dr. Yates, she did warn that parents who gained sexual pleasure from their children might predispose their children to what she considered a real problem—homosexuality.[63]

By the time Yates's work appeared, however, both sexual abuse generally and incest in particular had become far more visible as issues in American society. Driven largely by the women's movement, new views about sexual agency and coercion led to reconsideration of assumptions about incest. More and more women began to talk among themselves and to professionals about sexual abuse. Yates had claimed that when the young, supposedly uncoerced girls who were victims of father–daughter incest "move out into school and community, they swiftly form gratifying liaisons with more appropriate males." Two physicians, Judith Herman and Lisa Hirschman, found very different "liaisons" in the lives of incest victims. "Their experience with their fathers had taught them that sex was the one sure way of getting attention," wrote Herman and Hirschman. "The incest experience had left them feeling that they were good for little else besides sex. The result was often a series of brief, unsatisfying sexual relationships." One-third had periods of sexual promiscuity, and many "oscillated between periods of compulsive sexual activity and periods of asceticism and abstinence." Rather than breaking their attachment to mothers, the incest caused these girls to identify more fully with their powerless mothers and to despise themselves, their mothers, and by extension all women. One victim, for instance, wrote of her stepfather's attempted rape of her in sixth grade and the distance this brought into the relation with her mother.[64]

Within the hothouse atmosphere of the American high school, girls carrying the burden of early sexual abuse may have found their difficulties aggravated. Girls who acted out by becoming sexually available to boys might have gained a certain popularity among their male peers but also probably earned the contempt of these same boys. Among girls, of course, the promiscuous girls threatened the closed social system of the steady relationship. And, while promiscuity might in itself not condemn a girl among her female peers, the incest victim probably labored under the handicap of having few female allies. As Herman and Hirschman noted, "[t]he incest victims' hostility to women generally prevented the development of supportive female friendships. Women were seen as potential rivals who would betray their friends for a man, as vicious gossips, or simply as empty, inadequate people who had nothing to offer." These girls could sometimes fall into, even accept, the social role of the "slut." Their troubled past taught them that sex could bring them attention and some measure of regard. The bad reputation could readily fit with their own sense of failure or fault. Incest victims did not always take on the role of the slut, and the girls victimized by this reputation had various backgrounds. But those incest victims who did fall into this role could give credibility to the reputation of all girls treated as tramps.[65]

By the 1970s the women's movement had called into question other assumptions about coercive sex. The National Crime Survey reported annual statistics on sexual assault, placing this for the late 1970s at around 4 percent per year. But this included only forcible rape or attempts at forcible rape. Many women found themselves exposed to a range of coercive tactics, with no clear demarcation between a date or steady boyfriend asking for more and more familiarity and then demanding it. A national sample for the late 1970s, which used a broader definition of coercion (including verbal coercion and intimidation without the use of force) found much higher rates, ranging from 7 to 9 percent annually. These proportions applied to girls 13 to 19 in 1978, then older in the subsequent years as the study followed the same young women.[66]

Contrary to the widely assumed profile of rape victims as black and lower class, the author wrote, "no significant differences in prevalence of sexual assault are noted by either social class or race." The study also undermined other broadly held assumptions about coerced sex, that strangers took advantage of girls who made themselves vulnerable by wandering into strange surroundings. Overwhelmingly, when girls were coerced into sex, it was with someone they knew, someone about their own age, and most often the boyfriend or date of the girl. Some evidence from the study also pointed to the higher likelihood of coercion as girls became women, as they left home for work or college. But the author concluded that "[w]ithout a doubt, the dating situation provided the setting in which most female adolescents were sexually assaulted in the late 1970s."[67] She might have changed "steady" for "dating" in this conclusion. Boys came to expect, and ask, for more intimacy as relationships became more serious.

## The Persistence of the "Slut"

Within the context of a revolution in sexual morality, the girl who has few sexual boundaries should no longer be a pariah but a heroine. As we have seen above, however, the major change of the 1960s was not the spread of permissiveness but of permissiveness with affection along with an intensification of the steady complex. In a world where girls and boys formed couples and shared study time and status along with sex play, a girl who had the reputation of stealing boyfriends or simply of providing intercourse for "free" still faced ostracism and hostility from other girls.

As always, reputation—even suspicion—mattered more than the actions of the girls labeled as sluts. Naomi Wolf recalled that in high school she and her middle-class friends experimented sexually with the boys they knew. Yet her friend Dinah had to bear the slut label. If not sexual transgression, then what earns the title slut? Wolfe points to one of the underlying realities that creates adolescence—bodies that are changing rapidly but not at the same rate for everyone. Young teenaged girls whose breasts develop early soon find themselves set apart from their peers. Her friend Dinah, white but poor, made no attempt to slouch or hide behind her school binders. "There was no visual language in our world for a poor girl with big breasts walking tall, except 'slut.'" More important to the slut label than changing bodies, however, was status. Girls new to a school, girls from a marginal group, girls set apart for any reason—in other words, girls without cliques or "tribes"—always had the greatest likelihood of further marginalization as a sexual outlaw. If they seemed to offer some threat to the existing steady system, then the label of slut became almost inevitable.[68]

The steady complex fostered the marginalization of some girls in another way. As we saw in the last chapter, after the 1920s homosocial relations became attenuated as the steady relationship demanded more time and emotional investment. Going steady meant not only greater likelihood of sexual experience but also less involvement with other peers. Research shows that those girls most involved with boyfriends had less connection to same-sex groups. This was not necessarily the case for boys. Sexual experience may have raised the status of boys in their peer groups. Girls, however, abandoned networks of girls in favor of mixed groups and gave up time with girlfriends in favor of time with boyfriends. Boys and girls alike seem to have given more credibility to the judgments of boys regarding status. This may have resulted in less sense of connection among girls generally. With more of their social life and status wrapped up in their relations to boys, girls had little sense of solidarity with other girls. Slut shaming became one practice that gave girls greater cohesion as a group.[69]

## Pregnancy and Venereal Disease

By the late 1950s and early 1960s, two of the risks of unmarried sexuality—pregnancy and venereal infection—seemed far less threatening. One of the common assumptions about the 1960s is that the sudden appearance of the birth control pill led to the sexual revolution. This idea assumes that technological change drives culture. It also overestimates the availability of the pill. Until 1970, even college students had access to the pill only on campuses where health service physicians saw fit to provide birth control services to single women. Eight states prohibited sale of birth control until 1965's *Griswold* case before the

Supreme Court established that birth control came under an individual's right to privacy. The great majority of adolescents and young adults had to face the possibility of pregnancy with a combination of traditional contraceptives, chance, and abortion. By the 1970s, federal funding for family planning for the poor, continued training for doctors by Planned Parenthood, legalized abortion, and legalization of oral contraceptives for adolescents, combined to give young people more options for managing fertility.

Yet in spite of the slow pace of change in contraceptive availability, the demographics of pregnancy changed in surprising ways before the 1970s. Pregnancy among teenagers declined after 1957 and continued to decline steadily until the early 1980s. While legalized abortion and even oral contraceptives can account for some of this decline, the drop began before either of these became easily available to teenagers. Probably traditional methods of birth control—including clandestine abortion—and improving sex education account for much of this shift. Yet, from 1960, the number of women who became mothers outside of marriage began to rise, doubling from 15 percent of births in 1960 to 31 percent in 1970. The portion of births to single women probably grew as an effect of the overall rapid decline in birth rates during the period of the "baby bust"—as families declined in size, the children of single women became a larger portion of all children. But other trends joined in a major shift in the social organization of pregnancy. More and more teenage girls and young adult women decided to carry pregnancies to term without marrying the father of the child. By the early 1970s, 87 percent of mothers who gave birth out of wedlock kept their children; among teenagers, this group stood at 94 percent of out-of-wedlock births. In a period when marriage lost popularity, single motherhood gained. African American girls had always looked more to support from family for help in raising a child out of wedlock rather than giving the child up for adoption. But by the 1960s white girls made the same choice much more readily—so much so, in fact, that by the late 1960s, pregnancy homes began to close and the pool of white babies for adoption declined precipitously.[70]

In the case of sexually transmitted infection and disease (referred to as venereal disease [VD] until the 1990s) medical technology caused a remarkable change in attitudes. The development of penicillin in the 1940s led to a direct assault on sexually transmitted infections (STIs). The death rate from syphilis plummeted, from 10.7 per 100,000 in 1940 to 0.2 in 1970. As early as 1957, cases of gonorrhea had dropped to 127 per 100,000. Sexually transmitted diseases (STDs) seemed on the road to extinction or at least insignificance. Through the 1960s and 1970s, treatment for "the clap" (gonorrhea) became widely available and so easy that calculations about the risks of VD began to play an ever smaller part in thinking about sex. A doctor practicing in the Haight Ashbury section of San Francisco in the late 1960s wrote that no stigma attached to clap among the young and that he frequently saw hippies who had contracted gonorrhea repeatedly. In this case, the counterculture placed complete trust in the efficacy of conventional medicine.[71]

But even in the years when they had seemed eradicated, STIs persisted. From the low-point of 1957, both syphilis and gonorrhea began to increase in frequency. From 1965 to 1975 cases of gonorrhea tripled. In 1972 Dr. David Smith wrote that "in California last year there was more gonorrhea than all other reportable communicable diseases combined." By 1979 gonorrhea stood well ahead of the chicken pox as the most widely spread communicable disease in the United States. Syphilis was number three on the list. From our perch in the twenty-first century, we tend to think of the experience of STDs in the 1960s and 1970s as a lull before the storms of the 1980s. But the deadly epidemics of the last decades of the century came on a rising tide of venereal infections.[72]

## Conclusion

For most people, the idea of a sexual revolution carries an assumption about the attitudes and behaviors of girls. When we see that premarital, pre-engagement sex became more openly accepted during the 1960s, we can conclude that a relatively rapid shift took place among girls and young women in their attitudes toward sex play, including intercourse. But, rather than seeing this as a shift in which girls adopted the attitudes of boys, the evidence leads us to another conclusion—boys adopted attitudes more like those of girls. By the 1960s, majorities of adolescents, male as well as female, took for granted that affection and permissiveness were linked. With the spread of the steady complex in the Depression and in the 1940s, long-term relations allowed couples to nurture the affection and commitment that gave both partners confidence to move toward greater physical intimacy. The proportion of girls and young women who had premarital sex, and who admitted to it, grew steadily until the 1970s as a result of the growing acceptance of steady relationships.

The social organization of heterosexual conviviality continued to develop in the direction it had taken since the Depression. Going steady—now replaced with "the relationship"—not only remained the major feature of adolescent sexuality; more adolescents also participated in it and gave it more of their time. Going steady probably began, on average, earlier than it had in the 1950s, but more strikingly it extended beyond college into early adult years. Cohabitation made the transitory relationships of adolescents even more like companionate marriage. Even though marriage remained the destination of most young adults, the traditional ideal of chastity until marriage declined as even a stated belief let alone a common practice. By the late 1960s cohabitation often became, explicitly, trial marriage.

The availability of contraception had important long-term consequences, but these were shaped by adolescent attitudes towards affection and relationship. Birth control became more effective and more readily available by the 1970s, and, along with legal abortion, made pregnancy less likely as an unintended consequence of intercourse. But teenage pregnancy had already gone into a decades-long decline by the 1970s. STDs had also begun a long period of decline earlier than the 1960s.

The most remarkable changes of this period may have been in the prospects for gay and lesbian youth. With shrinking social space because of the high school practice of going steady, by 1970 homosexual adolescents could begin to see media coverage of gay issues and images of gay people. The shift toward gay pride and acceptance, with a slow beginning in the 1970s, looked more like a minority civil rights movement than a part of a generalized sexual revolution. But if we want to apply the term *revolution* with confidence, we should append it to the gay rights movement beginning in 1969.

## Notes

1. Linda Prentiss [pseud], "Papers of Linda Prentiss" (hereafter Prentiss papers), 1962–1967, Schlesinger Library, Radcliffe Institute, March 2, 1962; May 23, 1963; and April 20, 1962; Rachel Rafael [pseud.], "Rachel Rafael Diaries" (hereafter Rafael diaries), 1974–1976, January 15, 1975, and November 10, 1974; and Prentiss papers, Mary 23, 1962; February 3, 1967; and January 27, 1974. Joan Brumberg, *The Body Project: An Intimate History of American Girls* (New York: Vintage Books, 1998).
2. Rafael diaries, January 15, 1975, and November 10, 1974; Prentiss papers, Mary 23, 1962, and February 3, 1967.
3. Prentiss papers, November 4, 1962, and September 22, 1963.
4. Rafael diaries, November 14, 1974, and December 1, 1974.
5. Prentiss papers, May 14, 1967.
6. Rafael diaries, March 27, 1977, and May 18 and 20, 1977.
7. Prentiss papers, August 27, 1967.
8. Rafael diaries, January 5, 12, and 17, 1978.
9. "The Second Sexual Revolution," *Time*, January 24, 1964; Jane Gerhard, *Desiring Revolution: Second-Wave Feminism and the Rewriting of American Sexual Thought, 1920 to 1982* (New York: Columbia University Press, 2001), 86; and David Allyn, *Make Love, Not War: The Sexual Revolution, an Unfettered History* (Boston: Brown & Co., 2000), 50.
10. Susan Maria Ferentinos, "An Unpredictable Age Sex, Consumption, and the Emergence of the American Teenager, 1900–1950" (PhD diss., Indiana University, 2005), 233, http://wwwlib.umi.com/dissertations/fullcit/3204295; Alan Petigny, *The Permissive Society: America, 1941–1965* (New York: Cambridge University Press, 2009), 110–128; Gerhard, *Desiring Revolution*, 86; John Heidenry, *What Wild Ecstasy: The Rise and Fall of the Sexual Revolution* (New York: Simon & Schuster, 2002).
11. Rafael papers, January 15, 1975.
12. Eliot Margolies, "Joy Ride," *Cowbird*, accessed July 11, 2014, http://cowbird.com/story/92888/Joy_Ride/?uiid=widget-97417583-92888.
13. Helen Harmon Weis, "Helen Harmon Weis Papers," 1936–1943, Schlesinger Library, Radcliffe Institute, August 30, 1939; and Helen F. Southard, "The Challenge of Choice for Youth" (New York: Association Press, 1964; pamphlet rpt. from YWCA magazine, May 1964), n.p.
14. "Median Age at First Marriage, 1890–2010," *Infoplease.com*, accessed July 11, 2014, http://www.infoplease.com/ipa/A0005061.html.
15. Joan Biren, interview by Kelly Anderson, Voices of Feminism Oral History Project, February 27, 2004, 22–24, http://www.smith.edu/libraries/libs/ssc/vof/transcripts/Biren.pdf; and Bruce L. Paisner, "Deans Will Study Parietal Rules, May Propose Reduction in Hours," *Harvard Crimson*, September 24, 1963, http://www.

thecrimson.com/article/1963/9/24/deans-will-study-parietal-rules-may/. Rachel Rafael, who went to Wellesley in the late 1970s, recalls that the parietal rules had changed dramatically by then, although students still mocked the earlier "three legs" rule by speculating how one could manage lovemaking and meet the letter of the law (personal communication with the author); and Beth Bailey, *Sex in the Heartland*, (Cambridge, MA: Harvard University Press, 2002), 7–8.

16. Tyler Olkowski, "The Great Harvard Sex Scandal of 1964," *The Harvard Crimson*, May 29, 2014, http://www.thecrimson.com/article/2014/5/29/harvard-sex-scandal-1964/?page=1; and Bailey, *Sex in the Heartland*, 78–79, 80–104.

17. Henry Levin, *Where the Boys Are* (MGM, 1960); Elizabeth Pope, "Is Going Steady Going Sexy?" *McCall's*, May 1957, 132–133; also see Sidney Katz, "Going Steady: Is it Ruining Our Teenagers?" *Maclean's* 108, no. 52 (December 25, 1995): 66.

18. W. J. Cameron and W. F. Kenkel, "High School Dating: A Study in Variation," *Marriage and Family Living* 22 (February 1960): 74–76; Robert R. Bell and Jay E. Chaskes, "Premarital Experience among Coeds, 1958 and 1968," *Journal of Marriage and Family Living* 32, no. 1 (1970), 82; and Martin Whyte, *Dating, Mating, and Marriage* (New York: De Gruyter, 1990), 24.

19. Michael Gordon and Randi L. Miller, "Going Steady in the 1980s: Exclusive Relationships in Six Connecticut High Schools," *Sociology & Social Research* 68, no. 4 (July 1984): 467–471, 473, 475.

20. Svend Riemer, "Courtship for Security," *Sociology and Social Research* 45 (July 1961): 423–424.

21. Gordon and Miller, "Going Steady," 470.

22. Gordon and Miller, "Going Steady," 471; note that almost 60 percent said that exchange of gifts marked beginning of going steady; Riemer, "Courtship and Security"; Google, Google N-Gram Viewer, "Going Steady." http://books.google.com/ngrams 2012. As late as the 1960s sociologists used the term crush as describing a homosocial relation when it had long lost this meaning for teenagers.

23. Bell and Chaskes, "Premarital Experience," 84.

24. Nora Johnson, "Sex and the College Girl," *Atlantic*, November 1959, 59; on the changes in American standards, and for more precise definitions, see Ira Reiss, *Premarital Sexual Standards in America: A Sociological Investigation of the Relative Social and Cultural Integration of American Sexual Standards* (Glencoe, IL: Free Press, 1960), 130, 158, 220.

25. David Boruff, "The Quiet Revolution," *Esquire*, July 1961, 98; Gael Greene, *Sex and the College Girl* (New York: Dial Press, 1964); John H. Gangon and William Simon, "Prospects for Change in American Sexual Patterns," *Medical Aspects of Human Sexuality* 4 (January 1970): 103; and "Harvard Men Lack Sex Sophistication," *The Harvard Crimson*, March 18, 1964, http://www.thecrimson.com/article/1964/3/18/harvard-men-lack-sex-sophistication-pharvard/.

26. Winston Ehrmann, *Premarital Dating Behavior* (New York: Henry Holt, 1959), 130–133.

27. Ira Robinson, Karl King, and Jack O. Balswick, "The Premarital Sexual Revolution among College Females," *Family Coordinator* 21 (April 1972): 190, 192.

28. John DeLamater and Patricia MacMorquodale, *Premarital Sexuality: Attitudes, Relationships, Behavior* (New York: Plenum, 1987), 59, 72–73, 91; and Patricia Y. Miller and William Simon, "Adolescent Sexual Behavior: Context and Change," *Social Problems* 22, no. 1 (October 1974): 65.

29. Tom W. Smith, "The Sexual Revolution?" *Public Opinion Quarterly* 54, no. 3 (Fall 1990): 416–417.

30. Melvin Zelnik, John F. Kantner, and Kathleen Ford, *Sex and Pregnancy in Adolescence* (Beverly Hills, CA: Sage, 1981), 47, 65.

31. Daniel Yankelovich, *The New Morality: A Profile of American Youth in the 70s* (New York: McGraw-Hill, 1974); John Gagnon in Gregory Baum and John Coleman, eds.,

*The Sexual Revolution* (Edinburgh: T&T Clark, 1984); and Ira Reiss, "The Sexual Renaissance: A Summary and Analysis," *Journal of Social Issues* 22 (April 1966): 125.

32. Reiss, "Sexual Renaissance," 125.
33. Phillips Cutright, "The Teenage Sexual Revolution and the Myth of an Abstinent Past," *Family Planning Perspectives* 4, no. 1 (1972): 30; William Simon, John H. Gagnon, and A. Berger, "Beyond Fantasy and Anxiety: The Coital Experiences of College Youth," *Journal of Youth and Adolescence* 1, no. 3 (1972): 216; and Gangon and Simon. "Prospects," 103.
34. Ira Robinson, Ken Ziss, Bill Ganza, Stuart Katz, and Edward Robinson, "Twenty Years of the Sexual Revolution, 1965–1985: An Update," *Journal of Marriage & Family* 53, no. 1 (February 1991): 219.
35. Boruff, "The Quiet Revolution," 98; Bailey, *Heartland*, 203–204, has noted that cohabitation, less colorful than many of the challenges to the sexual status quo in the 1960s, may have brought more fundamental change; David R. Shumway, beginning with his introduction and then in his section on intimacy, discusses the development of "the relationship" as the dominant concept for interpersonal intimacy; David R. Shumway, *Modern Love: Romance, Intimacy, and the Marriage Crisis* (New York: New York University Press, 2003); John F. Cuber and Peggy B. Harroff, *Sex and the Significant Americans: A Study of Sexual Behavior among the Affluent* (New York: Penguin, 1966); and Riemer, "Courtship and Security."
36. Allyn, *Make Love*, 96–98; and Eleanor D. Macklin, "Cohabitation in College: Going Very Steady," *Psychology Today* 8, no. 6 (November 1974): 53, 55.
37. Bailey, *Heartland*, 202–204; and Editors of Fortune, *Youth in turmoil* (New York: Time-Life, 1969), 42.
38. J. L. Simmons and Barry Winograd, *It's Happening: A Portrait of the Youth Scene Today* (Santa Barbara, CA: Marc-Laird, 1966), 115.
39. Macklin, "Going Very Steady," 56; and Barbara J. Risman, Charles T. Hill, Zick Rubin, and Letitia Anne Peplau, "Living Together in College: Implications for Courtship," *Journal of Marriage and the Family* 43 (February 1981): 77–83.
40. Simmons and Winograd, *It's Happening*, 106; Allyn, *Make Love*, 100–102; and David E. Smith, "Sexual Practices in the Hippie Subculture," *Medical Aspects of Human Sexuality* (April 1972): 142–151.
41. Evelyn Mills Duvall, *Facts of Life and Love for Teen-agers*, new rev. ed. (New York: Association Press, 1956), 100–103; and Catherine S. Chilman, *Adolescent Sexuality in a Changing American Society* (Washington, DC: Department of Health, Education, and Welfare, 1978), 57–58.
42. Greene, *Sex and the College Girl*, 133–134; and A. Shostak, "Oral Sex: New Standard of Intimacy and Old Standard of Troubled Sex," *Deviant Behavior* 2 (1981): 127.
43. John Paul Brady and Eugene E. Levitt, "The Scalability of Sexual Experiences," *Psychological Record* 65 (1965): 275–279.
44. Rafael papers, May 20, 1974, and January 5 and 12, 1975.
45. Brady and Levitt, "Scalability," 275–279; and John H. Gangon and William Simon, "The Scripting of Oral-Genital Sexual Conduct," *Archives of Sexual Behavior* 16, no. 1 (1987): 1–25.
46. Various, "Kinsey Era Correspondence Collection," Letters, Kinsey Institute for Research in Sex, Gender, and Reproduction, 1939–1959, F. B., September 30, 1955; S. D., June 2, 1954, and October 19, 1957.
47. Gagnon and Simon, "Scripting oral Sex"; and Ehrmann, *Premarital Dating*.
48. Gagnon and Simon, "Scripting Oral Sex," 15, 17; and Ira Robinson, Karl King, and Jack O. Balswick, "The Premarital Sexual Revolution," 190–192.
49. Ira Robinson et al., "Twenty Years," 218.
50. Biren, "Voices of Feminism," 12, 14, 21.
51. Ibid., 23, 24, 27.

52. David Carter, *Stonewall: The Riots that Sparked the Gay Revolution* (New York: Griffin, 2011), 19–20; William Sadler, *Adolescence Problems: A Handbook for Physicians, Parents, and Teachers* (St. Louis: C. V. Mosby, 1948), 175; and John C. Spurlock, "From Reassurance to Irrelevance: Adolescent Psychology and Homosexuality in America," *History of Psychology* 5 (February 2002): 38–51.
53. Chilman, *Adolescent Sexuality*, 68.
54. Donald Webster Cory, *The Homosexual in America: A Subjective Approach* (New York: Greenberg, 1951), xiv; Carter, *Stonewall*, 19; and Alan P. Bell and Martin S. Weinberg, *Homosexualities: A Study of Diversity among Men and Women* (New York: Simon and Schuster, 1978), 250.
55. Biren, "Voices of Feminism," 30.
56. Chilman, *Adolescent Sexuality*, 68; and Carter, *Stonewall*, 20.
57. Bell and Weinberg, *Homosexualities*, 123, 126; and Jon Barrett, "Going Steady," *Advocate*, no. 835 (April 10, 2001): 36–40.
58. Bell and Weinberg, *Homosexualities*, 126; and John D'Emilio, *Sexual Politics, Sexual Communities: The Making of a Homosexual Minority in the United States, 1940–1970* (Chicago: University of Chicago Press, 1998), chap. 3.
59. Bailey, *Heartland*, 179–184.
60. Janice M. Irvine, *Talk about Sex: The Battles over Sex Education in the United States* (Berkeley: University of California Press, 2002), 49; and Smith, "Sexual Revolution?," 417; and "An American Family," *Wikipedia*, accessed July 9, 2013, http://en.wikipedia.org/wiki/An_American_Family.
61. Anne Moody, *Coming of Age in Mississippi* (New York: Dial, 1968), 111–112.
62. Ibid., 164–171.
63. Rachel Devlin, "'Acting out the Oedipal Wish': Father-Daughter Incest and the Sexuality of Adolescent Girls in the United States, 1941–1965," *Journal of Social History* 38 (Spring 2005): 609–633; and Alayne Yates, *Sex without Shame: Encouraging the Child's Healthy Sexual Development* (New York: Morrow, 1978), 114, 120, 121, 192.
64. Judith Lewis Herman and Lisa Hirschman, *Father-Daughter Incest* (Cambridge, MA: Harvard University Press, 1981), 100, 103; and Julia Penelope Stanley and Susan J. Wolfe, *The Coming Out Stories* (Watertown, MA: Crossing Press, 1980), 197–198.
65. Yates, *Sex without Shame*, 120; and Herman and Hirschman, *Father-Daughter Incest*, 100.
66. Suzanne Ageton, *Sexual Assault among Adolescents* (Lexington, MA: D.C. Heath, 1983), 25, 34.
67. Ibid., 31, 27, 40, 41.
68. Naomi Wolf, *Promiscuities: The Secret Struggle for Womanhood* (New York: Fawcett Columbine, 1998), 66.
69. Patricia Y. Miller and William Simon, "Adolescent Sexual Behavior: Context and Change," *Social Problems* 22, no. 1 (October 1974): 58–76.
70. Constance Nathanson, Dangerous Passage: The Social Control of Sexuality in Women's Adolescence (Philadelphia: Temple University Press, 1991), 27, 29–30; and James W. Reed and John C. Spurlock, "Young and Pregnant: Teenage Pregnancies in the United States," in Adolescent Sexuality: A Historical Handbook and Guide, ed. Carolyn Cocca (Westport, CT: Praeger, 2006), 31–44.
71. Allan M. Brandt, *No Magic Bullet: A Social History of Venereal Disease in the United States since 1880* (New York: Oxford University Press, 1987), 170–172; and Smith, "Sexual Practices," 150–151.
72. Smith, "Sexual Practices," 150; and Brandt, *Magic Bullet*, 174, plus chart in the appendix.

# 5

# CONTROLLING YOUTHFUL BODIES

Birth control and legal abortion, along with the Title IX–driven honesty about pregnancy, seemed by the mid-1970s to promise that adolescent sexuality could become far safer and treated with deliberate reason. By then most adolescents expected that sex play would be part of their lives. Everyone else seemed to expect it, too. Even the sex act had diversified, becoming more "polymorphous," with oral–genital sex added to the adolescent sex-play repertoire. Girls who engaged in "pre-premarital" sex—intercourse with partners who were not marriage prospects—might still seem unsettling, perhaps because this mirrored the freedom boys had always enjoyed. Even the first glimmer of acceptance of sexualities that were not "straight" had appeared. Like popular music, adolescent sex play merged the cultures of the middle class and the working class, white and black.

Taken together, these changes could seem like the radical consequences of the revolutionary era in American sexuality. We might better apply the more sedate term *modernization* to these changes. The underlying social organization of adolescent sexuality remained recognizably the same as the one that existed in the 1950s. If anything, the "relationship"—couples in short-term, committed, physically expressive relations—became more general among adolescents, and more taken-for-granted. As queer youth began to lead more open lives, their distinctive sexualities began to conform to the relationship model. Openness about sex gave adolescents opportunities to discuss their anxieties, fears, hopes, passions. Even issues around sexual coercion became more open. Like many pursuits in the postwar era, sex play was on its way to becoming more diverse, more widely accepted, far more frequently and openly discussed, and less difficult and dangerous.

Or so it seemed. By the early 1980s sexual panics dominated the U.S. media, with conflicts raging over adolescent bodies, especially the bodies of girls. At a time when sexual information and understanding of contraception might have become more valuable and more readily available than ever before, a coalition of conservative organizations attempted to eliminate sex education or else use it to promote chastity among teenagers. Another sexual panic crossed the political divisions of Democrats and Republicans, who worried about children giving birth to children and that teenage mothers reproduced and spread a culture of poverty. Even the sex act itself, which—with a little planning and precaution—had seemed a source of safe and clean fun, became dangerous. First, because of Herpes simplex virus and, then, more chillingly, because of HIV, sex play could be harmful, even deadly.

As the century ended, adolescent Americans could find sexual images everywhere they looked—in movies, advertising, and television. But at the same time they received stern warnings that sex was both dangerous and immoral. The contradictions within American culture that swirled around sexual issues gave rise to new scripts that served as variations on the theme of the relationship.

## Changing Bodies

We have seen that twentieth century adolescents have typically struggled with the rapid changes coming into their physical and social lives after puberty. By late in the century new sources of counsel became available. In 1963 Elizabeth Winship, the children's book editor for the *Boston Globe*, began writing an advice column for young readers. With syndication in 1970, readers across the country could benefit from the "good sense and stable judgment" featured in her column. Anxious, angry, or frightened adolescents wrote to "Ask Beth," sending far more letters than she could possibly feature in print. She managed, however, to identify themes that spoke to the largest cross section of readers. The letters to the columnist offer a tour of late-twentieth-century adolescent concerns about the stresses of life—about parents, about other adolescents, about relationships, and about sex. Teenagers who wrote to "Ask Beth" mirrored the adult confusion on display in Ann Landers' columns. At the same time that adolescent sexuality seemed a mystery to adults, it also mystified most adolescents.[1]

If balance and good sense prevailed in "Ask Beth," another genre, common in the late twentieth century, offers a counterpoint with personal stories with sharper emotions. Adolescents and young adults produced a flood of "Zines," typed up (sometimes handwritten) by one person or at most a few friends, Xeroxed, and circulated by mail or person to person. The writing was always raw, the illustrations unabashedly personal. The youth who wrote Zines asserted their own voice, often consciously rejecting the tamer, deferential tone of the kind of young person who asked Beth Winship for help. One girl wrote that in high school she used to read the major circulation magazine *Seventeen*. "It always made me feel like I was missing out on something. . . . All the girls in Seventeen are happy and perfect and no one ever feels alienated or lost. That's the magazines [*sic*] biggest mistake: all teenagers feel alienated, no matter what. I'm convinced."[2]

That sense of alienation probably begins when adolescents suddenly feel like they inhabit a body they don't know. For boys and girls alike, physical changes almost inevitably caused discomfort and confusion. Even though expert opinion had seemingly accepted masturbation, "Ask Beth" received a steady supply of letters, mainly from boys, wondering if it is normal ("yes," Beth assured them) or how much could be considered healthy. One 14-year-old admitted to masturbating frequently and to being unable to control it, so that his penis engorged even in the gym shower and in other public places. Teen ambivalence about masturbation persisted into adulthood, of course. In the 1990s, *Seinfeld* episodes could reliably make nervous humor using masturbation as a plot device.[3]

Sometimes girls also asked about masturbation, but far more often girls wrote about changes in their bodies. The "Ask Beth" collection contains many folders devoted to breasts. Girls who still had small breasts wrote about feeling unattractive, and girls whose breasts developed quickly felt awkward and often had questions about bras. As we have seen, early development for boys usually manifested as increased height and more muscle, something that they could make use of in school sports. For girls, rapid development generally worked the opposite way. Tall girls might tower over other 12- and 13-year-olds at an age when blending in is far more desirable. And rapid breast development would bring mainly unwanted attention to girls. Leora Tanenbaum recalled how suddenly it seemed that boys in her junior high school began to make remarks about her and try to snap her bra or touch her chest. A girl with many friends might pass through this phase with little pain. But a girl with few friends, or one new to a school, could easily find herself shunned and marginalized, with no real protection from the remarks of boys and the resentment of other girls jealous of the boys' attention.[4]

For some girls, bodily changes could become everything. Many letters to "Ask Beth" dealt with weight. One girl managed to overcome an anorectic phase only to gain 100 pounds. When thin, she had a nice wardrobe and felt like she had lots of friends, and an attractive teacher gave her special attention. But with the weight gain, friends apparently abandoned her and the teacher ignored her. Writers in the Zines also cast a critical eye on body issues and recounted personal struggles with ideals of beauty. Amanda Burr recalled looking at pictures of "waspy girls" and wondering "why my life was not like that." At 15, one girl "swallowed the Beauty Myth whole. I felt fat—obese even (at 5'5" and 130 lbs)— and developed a hatred of my body that I have yet to fully shake." Another girl ate to forget the pain caused by her abusive father. She echoed the pain that we have noted from girls' writings since the 1920s. "I gained weight, and at the worst time: high school, when what you look like is what you are."[5] Overweight girls in some cases compensated for their low self-perceptions by becoming more sexually adventurous, trying to attract some form of approval.

Even normal physical changes could quickly become the most important theme in a person's life. One Zine writer recalled her "(hellish) junior high school days" when, "if a boy really wanted to hurt a girl, all he would have to do was sniff the air and say 'hmmm. it smells in here. hey (girl's name), close your legs!" Joan Jacobs Brumberg used the diary of "Sarah Compton" to illustrate the pressures faced by teenage girls as boys paid closer and closer attention to their bodies, using the 1 to 10 rating system or making lewd suggestions in classroom notes or in front of other boys. Even a boy Sarah had once considered a friend became verbally abusive, publicly calling her names and asking her in the school hall, "'Do you want to make love, or just fool around?'" "[He] talks like he is going to rape me," she wrote, "and that's really scary."[6]

Perhaps the most common confusion of the teens who wrote to "Ask Beth" concerned how to socialize with other teens. Does he like me? How do I ask her out? When a 14-year-old wrote to ask how she could attract a boy's attention, Beth answered, "Flirt." In a 1984 column a broken-hearted girl asked how she could recapture a boy who had gone out with her for two weeks, telling her, "things 'weren't working out.'" "Don't feel rejected," Beth counseled. "Nothing is wrong with you. A relationship just didn't work out." Another girl wrote that she broke up with a boy but then wanted to go back with him, but he had begun dating another girl. Or a girl exchanged gifts with a boy, only to have hers suddenly returned. Then another boy asked her out. But she still liked the first boy. "What should I do?"[7] For these girls facing the confusion of their first relationships, the stakes seemed high. On a personal level, they were right. They were facing the transition from childhood to adolescence.

## Heterosexual Relationships

Adolescent sexuality in the last decades of the century appeared in many respects the way it had at mid-century—only more so. During the junior high years, most boys and girls began some socializing with opposite-sex partners. This meant a slow transition from single-gender groups to mixed groups and even some one-on-one dating. A study from the mid-1980s found that students began dating at about 14 years old. Within a year they began going steady, usually around 15 years old. Most students went steady at some point and most went steady repeatedly, with 2.5 times the average for both male and female adolescents. They probably still exchanged gifts to mark the beginning of the steady relationship. A study by the Alan Guttmacher Institute published in the mid-1990s still showed serial monogamy as the typical relationship pattern for teenagers. Also, first intercourse, and most subsequent teen intercourse, happened within one of these steady relationships.[8]

For most adolescents the major struggles of life came from working out relationships with other adolescents of the opposite sex. But this challenge grew as relationships with same-sex peers declined in importance. The crush culture of the early twentieth century allowed girls and young women to explore their emotions with other girls. Boys could engage in physical play with other boys that might also involve both emotional and sexual desire. Youth today still spend a great deal of time with other youth of the same gender, and they probably share secrets more readily with close same-sex friends than with boyfriends or girlfriends. But mixed-sex socializing becomes normal very early for teenagers today. Girls spend 10 hours a week talking on the phone to boys, and boys invest 5 hours the same way. Even before mid-century, the accepted norm for adolescent relationships shifted to the steady couple. For most boys and girls, beginning to date means leaving their single-sex groups and socializing in mixed-sex groups. As dating becomes more serious, girls tend to be more distant from their close friends—telling secrets and offering support shifts from girlfriends to their steady boyfriends.[9]

Boys have retained stronger homosocial networks than girls. Michael Kimmel has identified "bros before hos" as one of the basic assumptions in what he calls "guyland." Terms of slander commonly used by adolescents such as *faggot* or *gay* make the boy's ethic seem homophobic. In fact, what boys fear is to appear at all feminine. Kimmel quotes David Mamet: "What men need is men's approval." If anything, boys need the approval of other boys even more. Spending too much time with girls, even girlfriends, may leave some boys suspect of being effeminate.[10]

The transition to mixed-gender socializing, and giving up special friendships, probably held more trauma for some young adolescents, especially girls, than others. When a girl is in eighth grade, one girl wrote in a Zine in 1994, "your best friend is fucking God." By the time girls and boys reached ninth grade, dating had usually begun and those earlier passions had to be forgotten or at least rejected. A 10th-grade girl wrote of the girl she had loved since eighth grade: "We don't hang out much anymore. She wants a best friend that wears make-up and wants to try out for cheerleading. She likes boys. . . . I gave her my heart but she has lost it somewhere on the varsity football field." One girl whose admiration and desire for older girls reads like a textbook example of "hero worship" wrote to Beth Winship, "I'm 14. Since I was 7 I can remember sometimes having confusing feelings for other girls, mostly older. I've never had a boyfriend. How do you know if you are a lesbian. I don't want to be one." A Zine writer recognized that her love for other girls violated her peers' expectations: "So when I liked boys, I'd engross in that boy cos I knew that was 'normal' (to society's standards) and I'd soon 'lose' my virginity to a boy and be normal and happy like in all those teen magazines." She realized that she had embraced heterosexuality as a way to fit in.[11]

Even though having a boyfriend or girlfriend seemed like a heterosexual rite of passage, the arrangements on the individual level remained fluid and could seem ambiguous. By the 1980s terms like *dating"* or *being a couple* or even *go out* might carry the same weight that *going steady* had in earlier decades. Sixteen-year-old

Becky Bain recalled sitting in a car with a boy she had a crush on in 1998, trying to think of something to say. Finally, he asked, "Do you wanna go out?"

"Do you mean out of the car?

"No, you know—go out." Then she realized that he'd finally asked her to become his girlfriend. "That's all it takes back in high school. Now we were a couple."[12]

When sociologist Lillian Rubin asked one high school girl what she meant by "commitment," she replied, "[W]e won't date anybody else as long as we're together. That's a commitment, isn't it?" This might seem rather shallow, except that studies of going steady since the 1940s had shown that relationships might last relatively short periods. As they had since mid-century, these committed couples dominated the social lives of most teens as the century closed.[13]

Even if "going out" could seem casual, relationships had important consequences. Courtship still played a major role in adolescent sexuality. Steady commitments could turn into engagements. A study from the 1990s linked higher self-esteem to going steady. The importance of relationships—the high stakes involved—may have added to the stress of life for teenagers. The dating and rating regime of the 1920s had brutally made clear the few winners and many losers of the popularity game. But going steady raised the stakes of any individual relationship. Zine writers often expressed the ambiguity served up by the steady complex. "Like when I desire someone there is this thing where I am freaking out that maybe they don't like me the same amount back," wrote one girl from the mid-1990s. Beth Winship would have advised her to settle down, act rationally. But, in the Zine world, cool counsel rarely prevailed. The girl continued narrating her tactics for managing her chaotic emotions: "I do this cool chain-smoking [sic] don't say anything don't look into each others [sic] eyes let's just get stoned thing because it's all about control and I've got lots of it ONLY FUCK THAT FOR REAL."[14]

In traditional or classic dating, frequency of going out had as much importance as dating people with good credentials (attractive and with enough resources to bear the costs of dating). But a steady relationship linked the social life and status of two people, and also imposed the real or imagined opportunity costs of forgoing other possible partners. Even in seventh- and eighth-grade girls discussed boys constantly, "drooling over" them as one Zine writer recalled. The sense of these discussions was that having a boyfriend is the key to social success. By the time girls reached high school, a heterosexual relation seemed essential. Having a relationship determined who you were as part of the peer culture.[15]

The couple culture that begins early in the teen years seemingly culminates near the end of the senior year in the prom night, like the one shown in figure 5.1. Mary Ellen Mark, who has documented proms with her photographs since 1986, writes of the prom as "a rite of passage that has always been one of the most important rituals of American youth." Francine Pascal, a writer of young adult fiction, goes further, calling it "the quintessential glory of high

**FIGURE 5.1** Even at the end of the century, the prom continued as an important experience in the lives of most high school aged youth. Prom, 1993, Homer L. Ferguson High School, Newport News, VA.

*Source*: Used by permission of Galon Morgan.

school." For many American youth, only the wedding day will match the prom in importance. Even for young people who were not socially very active in high school, finding a date for the prom could mean achieving one of the significant goals of high school. Johnnie B. Baker had to scramble for his date, taking his cousin when the girl he asked turned him down at the last minute. "There was no limo involved," he wrote, only a friend's car. He met up with other friends, swearing them all to secrecy about his date's identity. In the end, it was a successful evening of dressing up, dancing, passing time with friends, and staying out late. The important thing was to participate.[16]

## The New Sexual Orthodoxy

Once children began to go out they had other decisions to make. Even as the country moved beyond its putative sexual revolution, many of the adolescents writing to "Ask Beth" wondered how far to go physically, and how soon. One girl had trouble with the traditional good-night kiss: "Whenever I kiss my dates goodnight, they always use their tongues. What am I supposed to do with mine?" In 1973 a girl wanted to know if she should pet with boys if she's not really serious. A 15-year-old girl "[r]espectfully" wondered how fast boys should be permitted to go around the bases. Some of her friends "say that letting a boy feel you up is no big deal. . . . Do you think it's wrong to do it on the first date? When a girl first goes to second base with a boy shouldn't she only allow him to touch her on the outside of her shirt?" A pair of 10-year-old girls tried to prepare for the world of male attentions by playing at boyfriend/girlfriend. One of the girls recalled that after watching the popular television show *Love American Style*, they practiced by having the "boy" seduce the "girl" into revealing her breasts. "We could tell the goal was to fully expose the breasts, and probably to touch them too, but we didn't know what exactly should be touched, how to touch or what more should happen with the touch, so our action just ended."[17] Everything about physical intimacy could be confusing for adolescents.

By the 1980s, however, a new set of sexual standards—what anthropologist Michael Moffatt called the "new sexual orthodoxy"—had evolved for older adolescents. The college students Moffatt wrote about considered sex fundamental to their lives, and good sex (for heterosexuals this meant intercourse to orgasm) had gained the status of an entitlement. Overwhelmingly, almost universally, students who shared their sexual narratives in Moffatt's study believed that sex should come with strong emotions—love, romance, some form of deep connection. Even those who admitted to enjoying casual sex still assumed that the best sex existed within a caring relationship.[18] The new sexual orthodoxy grew out of the value placed on sexual pleasure in 1960s and 1970s, yet in most respects this sexual culture had developed as a consequence of the steady complex and the high value that girls and young women placed on permissiveness with affection. By the 1970s and 1980s, this had already become the assumption of most college-age adolescents, and younger teenagers had adopted it by the 1990s.[19]

Many teenagers came to assume that sex, or even just losing their virginity, was a prerequisite for "normal" adolescence. Writing in the mid-1980s, Moffatt concluded that among college-age students, the value of virginity was "as dead as a dodo." The shift in the value of virginity had begun long before. Sometime in the 1970s a girl wrote Beth Winship that "these days it seems that there isn't 1 virgin over 14. I was totally shocked this year when I started finding out how many of my close friends have been to bed with 1 or 2 guys!"[20] What was new was not that girls had sex as teenagers, but that they had sex at younger ages and with boys they had no plans to marry. From the 1970s into the 1980s, the largest increases in sexual activity came from younger girls, with up to a quarter of 15-year-olds reporting intercourse. Sex posed greater risks for the young, especially girls. They were less likely to use birth control, and if they continued to be sexually active their risks of pregnancy became much greater than those for girls who became sexually active later. Similarly, risk of STDs was much higher for younger girls. Since young girls typically began intercourse with older boys, they may have experienced more coercion than did older girls. A turn of the twenty-first-century survey found that 10 percent of first intercourse for teenage girls was not consensual, but this rose to 18 percent for girls 14 or younger.[21]

In the decades following an upheaval in sexual standards, combined with a steady increase in sexual activity and decline in the age when that activity began, heterosexual intercourse could seem like "no big deal," "nothing to get excited about." For boys, virginity had never held any "exchange value" and maintaining it made no difference except among the most earnestly religious groups. Sex could not begin soon enough. After a 12-year-old boy lost his virginity to a 15-year-old friend at a party, he gained an immediate boost in status. "People thought I was suddenly mature enough to carry on a conversation." A 14- year-old boy wrote to "Ask Beth" if his 16-year-old girlfriend was being unreasonable in resisting going all the way. "I think by 16 yrs. old it is odd to still be a virgin. She says I'm jumping the gun with her." Even though girls grow more quickly than boys do in early adolescence, boys in many cases have moved ahead in terms of physical desire. Boys usually begin masturbating years before girls do, and they do much more of it than girls do. Carnal desire may be wide awake for the male youth who finally convinces his girl (or any girl) to have sex. Even if the experience turns out like one of the truncated sex scenes in *Fast Times at Ridgemont High*, at least the experience is undeniably sex.[22]

But for many young people, having sex and gaining sexual pleasure turned out to be quite different experiences. For girls, carnal desire may wait for carnal knowledge—they discover their sexual selves by having sex. Girls frequently report that their partners talked them into sex for the first time—he "told me I was beautiful"—or pressure them into it. Social pressure appears to have a decisive role for a far larger portion of girls than for boys. Alcohol continued to play a supportive role in teen sex, and often it took the lead. "Over and over," writes sociologist Lillian Rubin, "girls talked about getting so drunk or stoned that they couldn't remember the next day what had gone on the night before." "I was drunk. He was drunk," one senior said as she discussed having sex with a boy she barely knew, in a bathroom during a party. No wonder that many of the girls who Sharon Thompson interviewed in her study of first intercourse reported, "It was something that just happened."[23]

In many cases, the "something that just happened" was not very satisfactory for girls. By the 1980s petting might seem pointless if intercourse was possible, so the exploration of one another's bodies that can heighten the intensity of intercourse for a couple was often missing. This, combined with both inexperience and anxiety, often led to encounters far less exciting or important than expected. "It wasn't that I didn't like it," one girl told Sharon Thompson. "It was just kind of a letdown." Or as another said, "There was nothing I really liked about it." Lillian Rubin found only one teenager in 10 of those she questioned who described their first experience as pleasurable. More commonly she heard terms like *overrated, disappointing, a waste, awful, boring, stupid, empty, ridiculous, awkward, miserable*, and *unmemorable*. One girl recalled that after her boyfriend had pressured her into having sex for the first time, "I was really disappointed because I expected it to be a beautiful thing. I felt so dirty afterwards."[24]

Most teenagers—three-fourths in the case of girls—had sex first with a steady partner. Continuing the trend we have noted since the 1940s, love, affection, some sense of an ongoing regard had replaced marriage or even engagement as a warrant for physical intimacy. "We love each other," said a 16-year-old from Columbus, "so there's no reason why we shouldn't be making love." This simple formula—a statement of permissiveness with affection—carried important consequences. Compared to girls who began having sex with casual partners, girls whose sex lives debuted with steady partners had higher self-esteem, lower likelihood of depression, and higher likelihood for using contraception. These girls also probably had more sex. As in the 1950s college populations, in the 1990s girls with steady partners were more sexually active. And these relations likely had the best chance for good sex. Both Lillian Rubin and Sharon Thompson found that mutual regard could lead to the kind of sexual exploration and progressive intimacy that had the best chance for heightened sexual pleasure.[25]

"I don't have a single friend who is not having sex, though most of them are not promiscuous," a 16-year-old told interviewers in the 1990s. Her friends had sex with steady boyfriends, even if they, like her, did not enjoy the experience. Steady dating provided the setting for first intercourse and often for the first sexual relationship. This continued even for students away at college. In his 1980s fieldwork and survey of students at Rutgers University, Michael Moffatt found that the majority of students in his study practiced "sex that was one-on-one, heterosexual, in private, conventional in technique and caring in emotional style. In other words, for the most part, modern American suburban sex in its adolescent variant."[26]

## Race and Class

Class and race made less of a difference in adolescent sexuality at the end of the 20th century than at the beginning. But race and, even more, class, still mattered. Black and white girls during the 1990s, for instance, began to diverge in their sexual experiences around age 14. By age 17, 52 percent of white girls, but 67 percent of black girls, had become sexually active, although this difference tended to diminish as they grew older. Even so, this difference could have large consequences, because earlier sexual activity also predicted less likelihood of using contraception and greater likelihood of both STIs and pregnancy. White girls, however, had more sexual partners, often had briefer sexual encounters, and were more likely to have sex more frequently. Hispanic females, on the other hand, tended to have the most "traditional" sex lives. They had less early sex and, like white girls in the 1950s, their first intercourse tended to be with fiancés. But differences in sexual trajectories could be measured in far fewer months by the end of the century than at mid-century. Many differences—age at first intercourse, likelihood of pregnancy, number of partners—became less evident, or even disappeared, in comparisons of racial groups, when social class became a factor in the analysis. For adolescents, low socioeconomic status (SES) predicted significant likelihood of early and frequent intercourse, pregnancy, and teen parenthood.[27]

## Is it Sex?

The level of sexual activity for adolescents at the end of the twentieth century usually stands as proof that sexual attitudes and behavior have fundamentally changed. A poll in 1998 found that 53 percent of girls (and 41 percent of boys) believed sex before marriage was "always wrong." But this surveyed all teenagers—attitudes change with age. By 18, about two-thirds of girls and 75 percent of boys have had sex at least once. Even among youth who have had clear and unambiguous teachings about the sin of sex, sexual activity had become pervasive. A 1987 study by eight conservative Protestant churches found that 43 percent of these youth, all active churchgoers, had sex. Of course, these numbers do not tell complete stories. Having sex once makes a person, technically, sexually active. But during the 1990s Lillian Rubin found many young people who had intercourse for a period, then stopped, putting it off until marriage or until another steady relationship or indefinitely. "Sexually active" teens and even college students might lead relatively chaste lives.[28]

Or they might remain sexually "inactive" and yet have very lively sex lives. About as many evangelical youth had experimented with sex short of coitus as had experienced coitus. In the final decades of the twentieth century, adolescent sexuality generally moved toward finer distinctions in what constituted sex. As we have seen, investigations of sexuality had established a scale of intimacy, with kissing at the beginning and proceeding through petting and fondling to genital intercourse. The authors of a major survey of sexual life in the United States in the 1990s took for granted that adolescents still worked their way through these steps, and only after intercourse did they open themselves to oral–genital and anal sex.[29]

But, as should be clear from the last chapter, fellatio and cunnilingus had lost most of their exotic aura for adolescents well before the 1980s, and these acts may have appealed to teenagers and college students as at once more "hip" and more convenient. Both acts required less disrobing than intercourse, in instances where time might have been in short supply, and each could be performed in cramped spaces. These acts also seemed much safer. Although Herpes can be spread through oral–genital sex, leading to mouth sores, HIV has a lower likelihood of transmission via cunnilingus or fellatio. By the 1980s oral sex had become fairly common, with 40 percent of 17- to 18-year-old girls and one-fourth of 17- to 18-year-old boys having given oral sex. Studies in the early 2000s found even higher percentages who had engaged in oral sex, about 55 percent for both boys and girls. These studies tended to find a strong relationship between oral sex and intercourse—those who had already engaged in intercourse were more likely to also engage in oral sex (82 percent within the first six months). Even so, a separate study found that 16 percent of adolescents did not move on from oral sex to coitus. By the end of the 1990s, 10 percent of teenaged girls who considered themselves virgins in a Planned Parenthood study admitted to having given oral sex.[30]

As we saw in the last chapter, the "coitus equals sex" definition has held some weight with teenagers and even college-age youth since early in the 1960s. As one young woman put it, she and her boyfriend delayed having sex for six or seven months, but "dealt with our lust with lots of oral sex." A study from the 1980s found 12 percent of females at Harvard, and 17 percent at the University of North Dakota considered themselves "virgins" yet had engaged in oral sex. Michael Moffatt concluded that oral sex had become the solution to a whole range of issues within the new sexual orthodoxy. College women used it to preserve their virginity and avoid pregnancy; men used it as the penultimate form of petting and a means of ensuring the sexual pleasure of their partners.[31]

As Moffat showed with his fieldwork, adolescents in the mid-1980s made sexual pleasure a fundamental element of human life. Yet they defined "real sex" as heterosexual intercourse. In one of the narratives that Moffat used for his research, a college student recalled sexual relations with his high school girlfriend. They "made out a lot and even masturbated each other frequently," rubbed each other as though having intercourse but with their clothes on, and gave each other oral sex, and he inserted his penis between the girl's breasts. "Once we almost had sex," he went on, "we had all our clothes off and I was wearing a condom, we just started to do it and my mother called me to feed the damn dog." So, in spite of an active sex life with this girl, he concluded, "I never actually had sex with her." Distinguishing between sex acts and "real sex" was not a judgment about the pleasure of oral sex. Most men and many women found oral sex highly satisfactory. But oral sex did not inspire the guilt that vaginal intercourse could provoke in women; it did not carry the high stakes of "real" sex, and so demand the same high level of emotional involvement. Virginity, perhaps even technical virginity, had its own appeal. Into the 1980s young adults claimed to prefer potential marriage partners who had little or no sexual experience.[32] The shift toward abstinence-centered or abstinence-only sex education, and the rapid rise of evangelical Christianity in the public sphere, may have had the residual consequence of making oral sex more attractive.

## Lesbian and Gay Youth

"I'm 16 and a female," began one letter to Beth Winship. At a party the girl responded to a "pass" from another girl, and they spent two hours petting in one of the bedrooms. "I'm so confused because I have to admit that I actually enjoyed it. . . . Could I be bisexual? . . . At this point, what do I do?" Adolescent sexuality, confusing enough for young people with abundant cultural models, posed even more challenges for queer youth. A study from the early 1990s found that six percent of teenaged girls and 17 percent of boys reported some "homosexual encounter." Gay and lesbian adolescents still had to embrace an identity outside the mainstream, come out to themselves and perhaps to others. And beyond these personal issues of identity lay the frightening possibilities of relating to other young people. Yet in the final decades of the twentieth century, gay and lesbian youth began to shape their own version of the "new sexual orthodoxy," one in which their own desires and sexual pleasure became fundamental to their lives. As these adolescents with marginalized identities felt freer to have their own sexualities, they also moved closer to the sexual values of other adolescents.[33]

The Stonewall riot in 1969 and the Gay Pride movement that followed marked the beginning of an expanding awareness and acceptance of sexual minorities. By the opening of the twenty-first-century terminology stretched to include a larger range of youth. LGBT, standing for lesbian, gay, bisexual, transgendered persons (with the initials sometimes moved around) embraced as many marginalized sexualities as possible, although the term *queer* also came to stand in for sexualities and personal identities not contained within the notion of heterosexuality. But recognition and acceptance did not proceed quickly or easily. When one girl wrote to "Ask Beth" in the early 1980s that she felt no attraction to boys, Beth responded, "[T]here is the possibility you are going to be gay" and not to worry about it. For this reasonable response Beth Winship received a flood of letters chiding her for encouraging this girl to become a lesbian or informing her that homosexuality could be cured.[34]

Perhaps in reaction to the visibility of gay liberation, a conservative, largely evangelical movement began to exploit and promote antigay sentiment in the country. In the late 1970s, anti-discrimination legislation was challenged in cities across the country, culminating in an unsuccessful initiative in California that would have banned homosexuals from teaching in public schools. During the 1980s disapproval of homosexuality remained high and actually increased. Among first-year college students support for laws prohibiting homosexuality peaked in 1987.[35]

Although media gave steadily more coverage to gay issues into the 1990s, the majority of "out" gay high school boys reported harassment. "Some of the jocks won't sit next to me in class, and I get called 'faggot' and 'queer,'" said one high school boy. Even those who were not harassed could still feel "like you're the only gay person on the entire planet," as recalled a lesbian from Louisville. The sense of isolation, the threat of harassment, and the absence of clear, positive cultural cues mean that most gay youth "experience life at a certain distance and in a state of constant vigilance."[36] No wonder many struggled to accept their own homoerotic desire.

Andrew Solomon recalls that he always knew his desires were "exotic, and out of step with the majority." By the late 1970s, as his teenage years and the dawning of sexuality approached, "the nonconformity of same-sex desires thrilled me—the realization that what I wanted was even more different and forbidden than all sex is to the young. . . . I nonetheless thought that if anyone found out I was gay, I would have to die." Solomon endured harassment on his school bus, even after his mother intervened, "I was merely called 'faggot' on the bus and at school, often within hearing distance of teachers who raised no objections. That same year, my science teacher told us that homosexuals developed fecal incontinence because their anal sphincters were destroyed."[37]

Gay children and adolescents often entered a period of self-questioning, during which they attempted to both live a "normal" life and to pass as heterosexual. At 13, Andrew Solomon purchased a *Playboy* to study the women's bodies to try to "resolve my discomfort with female anatomy." A few years later he even entered a sex therapy clinic in an effort to achieve heterosexuality. Brandon, in the early 1980s, recognized his feelings for other boys and men but decided to "sequester" them. "I decided to try dating and I explored the drawers where my father hoarded his Playboys. . . . I delved into anything manly"—Little League, Boys Club, basketball, books about cars and engines. He had his first date at age 15, but when the girl became sexually aggressive he felt no arousal. "I try to go out with girls in order to hide my homosexualness [sic] from the public," one senior wrote to Beth Winship.[38]

Girls with homoerotic desire faced many of the same issues. Sharon Thompson found that many teenaged girls believed that their lack of attraction to boys was a personal problem. They have sex with several guys to try to spark a desire for boys. One girl remembered denying her attraction to girls by exaggerating her interest in boys. She "talked dirty" and made herself available for sex. "People thought I was a real nymphomaniac. I found myself having sex with boys to prove I wasn't gay."[39]

Even those who crossed the personal Rubicon of revealing their desires likely faced further struggles. Almost all would face harassment from peers in high school. Adults often treated gayness as a passing phase. When one teenager went to talk to a field hockey coach who was rumored to be lesbian, the coach told her that she "was just nervous around boys and should make an attempt to be around them more." Another girl, still a virgin, came out to her parents as a lesbian. "'You haven't had sex with a man,' they responded, 'you haven't had sex with a woman—how do you know you're a lesbian?'" Most gay youth in the 1990s came out first to a friend but at the risk of losing the friendship. And gay teens who came out to their parents risked being kicked out of their home. Studies in the 1980s and 1990s showed gay youth at increased risk for homelessness, drug abuse, suicide, sexually transmitted infections (STIs), and even pregnancy.[40]

Still, as the century moved toward its close, queer sexualities became more visible and more information was available to adolescents in search of self-understanding. The Gay Liberation movement stressed the political value of leaving the closet, of being "out, loud, and proud."[41] The average age of coming out dropped from the mid-20s during the 1970s to about 16 by the end of the century. Richard, for instance, played "straight" until he was 15, "but I became very depressed and got to the point where I was thinking about suicide right before I came out. I came out as a last resort to get help." Richard was fortunate—both his parents and his guidance counselor were supportive. Rebecca Harvey recalls her sense of isolation as a 14-year-old in 1984, realizing that she might have desires that did not fit with her family's values. She looked for cues wherever she could find them: "Sensing that I had reached the limit of what I could learn from 'Donahue' shows and desperate to end my isolation, I mustered up the nerve to go to a bookstore to find a biography of Martina Navratilova, the only other queer woman of whom I had heard." About the same time, another 14-year-old "JoAnne," growing up in York, Pennsylvania, managed to find information about homosexuality in her school library to help her define her own sexuality. One writer for a Zine quickly found useful information to help her sort out her feelings when she realized that she only liked boys who looked like girls. By the early twenty-first century Rebecca Harvey would write, with her colleague Linda Fish, "Youth today are more likely to know adult gay and lesbian people, to have a sense of a queer community, and to see positive (or at least not totally negative) images of themselves in the media."[42]

As the age of coming out steadily declined in the late twentieth century, a distinctive gay identity emerged from the shadows for American youth. Young people could begin to have sexual lives that were not entirely dominated by the need for secrecy. By the turn of the century the Internet played a role in connecting lesbian and gay youth, and a growing network (800 by 2001) of youth groups gave teenagers opportunities to discuss issues of relationships, dating, and sex. A writer in the *Advocate* remarked that "gay teens are not only coming out younger every year, they're also leading openly gay dating lives with a panache that would surprise gay people only 10 years their senior."[43]

The adolescent sexuality that began to form for queer youth looked in many ways like adolescent heterosexuality. Young gay people wanted to date, to go steady, and to attend the prom. Gay sexuality never mimicked heterosexuality, but adapted elements of it. Gender norms, for instance, even though greatly vitiated since mid-century, still shaped heterosexual relations. Boys still paid for dates, by and large, and typically took the aggressive role. The limitations of these gendered norms for homosexual youth were aggravated because gay youth often still had to delay the beginning of dating and so had fewer years to sort out how to make their adolescent sexuality work. Lesbians faced similar issues. As girls tried to negotiate relationships with other girls, heterosexual practices could cause confusion. Like other adolescents, lesbians might spend time together without knowing if they were just hanging out or actually dating. But for heterosexual couples, there still existed an established ritual of flirtation, one in which the boy asked and the girl responded.[44]

At least in some places, gay and lesbian youth at the turn of the century felt free to have sexual lives more or less like their straight peers. One 17-year-old living in Milwaukee in 2001 had come out at age 15 and already had been in three relationships, the longest lasting five months. "I have two lesbian friends who are never apart. Like, if you say one of their names, you say the other. That's just how it is." As early as 1980 an openly gay boy in Rhode Island had gone through a court challenge to enable him to attend prom with a boyfriend. By the 1990s the prom came within the reach of more and more gay couples. Aaron, a Rhode Island teen, delayed coming out until 11th grade. He chose an openly gay boy to confide in. The two became a couple and attended the senior prom together. Even in Nashville, surrounded by the Bible Belt, Tonya and her girlfriend decided to attend prom together. They had to hire a lawyer to challenge their high school's prohibition. But the district relented. When Tonya and her partner appeared on stage for the ritual presentation of couples, they received "the most astounding round of applause."[45]

## Sexual Panics

As the new sexual orthodoxy crystallized in the last decades of the twentieth century, adolescent sexuality became an issue for adult authorities. The recognition that adolescents became sexually active at younger ages had already provoked strong reactions from defenders of traditional morality. Movements coalesced to combat the perceived threat of sex education. But by the 1980s, new issues arose that challenged elites across the liberal/conservative divide. Adolescents seemed to threaten not only themselves but also the social fabric. Pregnancy, sexually transmitted disease, and new sexual practices all demanded attention and action from social professionals, moral elites, and even politicians.

At a time when adolescent sexuality captured the attention of the media and the general public, other issues remained in the shadow. Feminists and social professionals had already raised alarms over coercion and violence against children, but these gained little general attention until late in the century. Relations among adolescents, especially the harsh treatment of girls by other girls, remained an understated issue in discussions of adolescence.

## Sex Education

During the 1960s, many adults perceived the media-driven attention to adolescent sexuality in terms of moral crisis. Religious leaders and parents began to mobilize in response to these perceptions, and moved to intervene in the one area that seemed key to teenage sexual freedom, school-based sexuality education (SBSE). Some of the most conservative groups in the country, including the John Birch Society, joined in a concerted effort to delegitimize SBSE. These groups charged SBSE as "smut," "immoral" and "a filthy communist plot." By the end of the decade, 40 states had "sex ed" controversies brewing. The pregnancy panic of the Reagan years undoubtedly emboldened the reformers who believed sexual education should be eliminated or at least reformed to emphasize the danger of sex. Although school districts could set their own standards, by 1980 only three states and the District of Columbia *required* school districts to provide sex education. Very few politicians had any desire to appear to favor encouraging teenage sex, especially within an atmosphere of panic about pregnant 14-year-old girls.[46]

By the mid-1980s, however, the rapid spread of AIDS changed attitudes and the public debate. Ronald Reagan's Surgeon General, C. Everett Koop, called for sex education for children as early as the third grade. Activists who had formerly opposed SBSE changed tactics and now worked to move districts away from comprehensive sex education toward programs that emphasized abstinence. Congress, in the 1981 "Family Life Act," had already given federal support to programs that promoted abstinence for teens. States went further. Virginia's legislature, for instance, in the late 1990s reinstated the state's requirement for SBSE but also required that the curriculum present premarital abstinence and marital fidelity as moral obligations. Many conservative organizations provided their own sex education materials. A congressional study from early in the twenty-first century found these curricula riddled with false and misleading information about the effectiveness of condoms, the consequences of abortion, and the risks of sexual activity. Curricula such as "Choosing the Best" attempted to inject panic into the discussion of sexual issues. A video packaged with the material portrayed a student asking about having sex before marriage. "The student's teacher then responds, 'Well, I guess you'll just have to be prepared to die. And you'll probably take with you your spouse and one or more of your children.'"[47]

By the 1990s the federal government placed its stamp of approval on abstinence programs. In 1996 legislation provided $50 million annually from 1998 to 2000 to fund these programs. By the end of the century only about 10 percent of school districts required comprehensive sex education programs that dealt with all options for a sexual life, abstinence included. About 45 percent of students lived in districts that had programs that stressed abstinence, and another third of students lived in districts where abstinence was treated as the only legitimate sexuality outside of marriage. At a time when more and more teenagers were becoming sexually active, and at earlier ages, the high school curriculum that dealt with sexuality frequently presented sexual imperatives that most students had, or would, reject. Abstinence-preferred or abstinence-only education may account for what appeared to be a growing popularity for oral sex and technical virginity. In other respects, however, the abstinence message seems to have left teenagers less capable of dealing with the demands of their social environments. One study demonstrated that while abstinence education had no impact on if or when adolescents began sexual activity, students in these programs were less likely to use birth control when they did begin.[48]

Thanks to sex education curriculum that revolves around scare tactics and abstinence, discussion of a healthy sex life became more and more rare. Outside of school, those same discussions were also absent. As the century closed, media, music, fashion, and the expectations of friends all exerted new pressures for adolescents to become sexual. One family therapist reflected on the "bizarre dynamic whereby young people are overexposed to sexuality on one hand while also having this occur in an educational, moral, emotionally and interpersonally responsible vacuum." By the early 1990s, television was awash with sexual themes, references, and innuendo. By one estimate, teenagers saw 14,000 references to sex every year. A writer for *Mother Jones* pointed out that movies, TV, and popular music portrayed "a sexual universe that has little room for either 'values' or 'choices.'" In the world shown on the screen "the beautiful people are having [sex] all the time." And, they take it for granted. Sex educator Debra Haffner told an interviewer that in the pop culture version of sex, there is no discussion of birth control or possible difficulties with STIs. In fact, there is no discussion at all. "It just happens."[49]

## Children Having Children

"I'm am in terrible trouble and I don't know where to turn" a pregnant 14-year-old wrote to "Ask Beth." The risk of pregnancy had always counted as one of the dangers of early sexual activity, but by the late 1970s it seemingly had become not only a personal problem but a national calamity as well. In the mid-1970s, about 10 percent of teenaged girls became pregnant each year and about 6 percent gave birth; one-third of illegitimate births were to teenagers. Congressional hearings called attention to teenage pregnancy, leading to the establishment of an Office of Adolescent Pregnancy Programs. In 1978 Joseph Califano, President Carter's secretary of health, education, and welfare identified it as a major domestic issue. A 1986 Children's Defense Fund television ad asked, "What does it mean to be pregnant at 15? At 14? At 13?" From the mid-1970s through the early 1990s, the number of articles in major magazines on the problem of teen pregnancy grew in number every year, with more than 200 by 1990.[50]

The phrase "children having children" became the catchphrase of the media obsession with pregnant 14-year-olds. This narrative, however, ignored demographic shifts in the United States. As noted earlier, the high point for teenage parenthood came in 1957, at 97.3 births per 1,000 girls 12 to 20. From the 1960s into the mid-1980s, in tandem with the greater availability of birth control and then of abortion, the birthrate for teenagers declined by nearly half (to 51.7 per 1,000 in 1983). While childbearing for young teens, 10 to 14, increased by 22 percent during roughly the same period, this accounted for only 2 percent of births to women younger than 20. In contrast, two-thirds of teenage mothers were 18 or 19.[51]

Rapid changes in adolescent sexuality, especially for girls, seemed to drive the teen pregnancy panic of the late twentieth century. More girls became sexually active as teenagers, with the most rapid increases taking place in the 1970s. In 1972 Title IX outlawed the discriminatory practices that kept pregnant girls (and even teachers) away from school. Suddenly pregnancy seemed far more common just because it was far more visible. Pregnancy was also not the underlying problem for many teenagers; rather, by 1980 half of these girls were unmarried and so had to rely far more on government programs for support than married mothers. This shift toward teen illegitimacy, in turn, resulted from the decision of teen mothers to keep their children rather than give them up for adoption. From 1962 to 1975, 19 percent of never-married white women and 2 percent of never-married black women gave up babies for adoption. In the subsequent two decades, the percentages for white women fell to 8 and then 3 percent, and for black women, declined by half. By the 1970s adoption agencies could no longer keep up with the demand for available infants, and waiting lists grew as did the willingness of white adoptive parents to take children of other races. The sexual panic also seemed to have a racial bias. In 1983, 4 of 10 births to white teenaged girls were out of wedlock; for black girls, the unwed accounted for 9 of 10 births. The perception of crisis over teenage pregnancy slowly abated in the late 1990s and early 2000s as report after report showed teenage pregnancy declining.[52]

## Sexually Transmitted Diseases

Even if pregnancy gained the headlines first, another sexual panic soon displaced it—this one not specific to teens and not disproportionately a problem for girls. The Herpes simplex virus (HSV) has been known for millennia and is quite common. Depending on the strain, the virus can cause primarily oral (HSV-1) or genital (HSV-2) sores. The usual means of transmission is through sexual contact, so the infection had been considered one of the minor STIs. But by the 1980s the virus—especially HSV-2—began to appear frequently among young white adults. The virus symptoms varied greatly. "Some have herpes almost continuously," a physician told the *New York Times*, "others never suffer anything after their first infection. . . . Some victims suffer such extreme pain during a recurrence that they can scarcely walk; others feel nothing more than soreness." At a time when syphilis and gonorrhea seemed on the brink of extinction, Herpes brought venereal disease roaring back into the consciousness of sexually active youth. The virus was highly infectious, and even clinical studies seemed to support the view that the disease could be transmitted casually, via toilet seats or hand towels.[53]

As late as 1981, Herpes seemed to have had a minor impact on adolescents. "Gonorrhea is probably the most commonly contracted venereal disease," according to a *New York Times* article that named several other diseases that were similar. "The Health Department also sees an occasional case of syphilis and, lately, an increase in the number of cases of herpes simplex II." The article profiled Cathy Sullivan, who worked on Long Island, as a "V.D. investigator" for the state of New York, contacting teenagers about possible exposure to sexually transmitted diseases (STDs). Once she had a report on a young person with an infection, she went to work tracing the boy's or girl's partners. For teens 16 or older, she called the home. When parents answer, "I just say that I'm a friend of theirs from school and I would like to talk to them; that usually gets past the parent and there isn't any problem." But for younger teens, she went directly to the school, to meet the children in person, in an effort to win their confidence. The goal in every case was to help the teenager get treatment.[54]

In 1981, no treatment for Herpes existed other than some palliatives, and even today there is no cure. Since those carrying the disease could spread it when not obviously symptomatic, transmission accelerated. As the disease spread quickly, so did public reaction. A year after the V.D. investigator story, Jane Brody wrote in the *New York Times* that HSV-1 and HSV-2 "are now believed to cause more illness than any other group of viruses." The article repeated the estimate that 20 percent of American adults had the infection. She quoted a microbiologist at Hershey Medical School who stated that infection increased by half a million cases each year "We will soon have 30 million cases, and the chances of getting infected by an occasional sexual partner keep increasing."[55]

*Time* magazine undoubtedly fixed the contagion in the minds of Americans with its August 1982 cover story, "The New Scarlet Letter." "'With herpes, every new case is added to the pool,' says Dr. Yehudi Felman, a New York City VD specialist. 'The increase is exponential after a while.'" The article mainly reported the experiences of Herpes sufferers, of their adjustment to their new condition, and of how the disease changed their lives. Those who contracted the disease after casual sex had their whole lives to regret their bad luck or bad judgment. Those uninfected who wanted to continue to seek casual sex had to find new strategies for protecting themselves. But even though health specialists in the early 1980s speculated that Herpes would curtail or even reduce casual sex, no reliable studies showed any strong impact. One physician who worked with thousands of adolescents in the course of a year told the *New York Times*, "We are continuing to see tremendous amounts of sexual activity among adolescents. The big problem is still that they're not using the contraceptive resources that are available." "I just don't think it's going to happen to me," a ninth grader told *Washington Post* reporters when they asked her what she did to guard against STIs. "I'm not going to worry about it," she said.[56]

The Herpes epidemic, although serious and in some cases devastating, rarely proved more than a complication for the lives of sufferers. But the AIDS crisis, coming hard on the heels of Herpes, made a far more profound impact on the sex practices of the generation coming of age in the 1980s. The disease first gained attention as a new affliction among gay men in Los Angeles, and reports of this appeared in the influential gay newspaper, the *New York Native*, in May of 1981. The *New York Times* carried its first story on the disease in July of that year. The retrovirus responsible for the infection was identified by researchers in the United States and France in 1984 and was named Human Immunodeficiency Virus (HIV). During the early 1980s the disease seemed mainly a concern for gay males and intravenous drug users, although the spread of the disease among heterosexual Haitians showed that the disease was not exclusively gay. In 1983, when *New York Times* reporters tried to weigh the impact on sexual practices of the new epidemics, neither Herpes nor AIDS seemed to have made much difference for young people. No doubt many assumed "it won't happen to me." As the decade wore on, however, and more cases of AIDS became well known, the presumption of indestructibility became more and more tenuous. Media attention to Ryan White, who contracted AIDS through a contaminated blood transfusion, gave an adolescent face to the epidemic. Ryan was diagnosed in 1984, at age 13, and had to endure expulsion from school and then a lengthy legal battle to reinstate him. He died in 1990 just before his graduation from high school.[57]

The potential problems of unmarried pregnancy, together with the health risks of Herpes and AIDS, may have shifted attitudes toward early intercourse for a portion of American youth. By 1994 an Alan Guttmacher Institute survey found that about one-third of teenagers believed "sex before marriage is always a mistake," not because of moral scruples but from fear of health risks. These attitudes seemed to translate into real-life decisions. A trend became evident by the turn for the century for teenage boys, and to some extent girls, to delay the beginning of sex. By 2000 teenagers used birth control more effectively, and more and more adolescents—teenagers and college-aged—made the decision to either remain virgins or else to give up intercourse for long periods.[58]

## Hooking Up

Hooking up became widely known by the late 1990s. Although more typically a college practice, the culture of hooking up has influenced younger adolescents and young adults as well. A study from the early 2000s noted that hooking up, while it appears as the norm for socializing, still applies only to a minority of students. The practice varies widely from place to place and even from one experience of it to the next. The gender imbalance at colleges, where the majority of students are female, works in favor of male students who wish to have physical relations without relationships. Settled, steady relationships are often rare. Sometimes, the college students have regular boyfriends or girlfriends who are out of school or go to other colleges. In the absence of long-term relationships, more and more college youth socialize in groups. At the end of the evening, some couples form. These temporary couples often become physically intimate, sometimes moving on to what an earlier generation would have called petting, or even to oral sex or intercourse. Wherever it goes physically, the hook up carries no implication of further involvement.[59]

The hookup may point to a basic shift in adolescent sexuality, at least for college students. Sex play without emotional connection probably has wide appeal, because it removes much of the confusion demanded of making and maintaining a relationship. Many college women who participated in the hookup culture that became current in the 1990s agreed that hooking up, and often providing oral sex, was easier than making small talk. One young woman recalled in a Zine why she had preferred fellatio, beginning in eighth grade. Even kissing "would have been too intimate, and frankly, too gross. Cocksucking entailed little face-to-face contact, almost no pain or small talk, no fear of disease . . ." Although this could seem demeaning—another form of male dominance—the writer felt that it worked in the opposite way. "Sucking cock, you felt important. No longer acted upon, above or below the waist, now you were the actor, the doer instead of the 'do-ee,' or worse the 'done-to.' . . . Fellatio put you in the driver's seat." A mental health professional at a major university has referred to this same attitude among the young women who talked with her about giving oral sex to male basketball players—they felt in control of these athletic superstars.[60]

The hook-up culture arose within the context of longer-term relationships of the kind we have seen dominating adolescent sexuality for more than half of the century. On many college campuses, formal dating almost disappeared by the late 1990s in favor of group socializing. Consequently, hooking up became much more prominent because of its sharp contrast with what seems like the only other kind of heterosexual socializing available, settled relationships—couples "joined at the hip."[61] From this point of view, the pervasiveness of hooking up in college makes better sense. In high school, members of dating (steady) couples do not readily consider one another marriage partners. But in college, marriage becomes a real possibility. Hooking up—a dalliance relation, to use the sociological term from the 1930s—may allow college youth to put off more serious commitments until they have finished school and established careers.

## Slut Bashing

In 1980 "Ask Beth" received a letter from a 15-year-old who had moved to her high school only two years before. "I feel very insecure," she wrote, "because of 'popular kids' who are really *mean* to me." Although we expect young people to be overly sensitive to others during their teenage years, this young girl provided a list of actions by other students: they called her "ugly names," pushed and shoved her, threw food and books at her, spread rumors about her, and even printed T-shirts with obscenities about her. Much worse than the harshness incidental to high school social life, this describes the kind of bullying directed at girls labeled as sluts.[62]

Some girls could adopt the slut label and use it as an identity that set them apart from a world they already felt alienated from. But for most girls, having "slut" applied to them meant loss of friendship and marginalization at a time when belonging to a group can feel like the most important goal of life. Sexually adventurous girls risked this kind of marginalization. "Ask Beth" heard from one girl who wrote about being "Hot to Trot." After a period of sexual experimentation, she admitted to having earned a "terrible reputation." "Nobody wants anything to do with me & now even my best girl friends are starting to look down on me" even though they are all sexually active.[63]

For most girls, the slut reputation had little to do with outsized sexual experience. In separate investigations, Leora Tanenbaum and Emily White found that the girls who had been labeled as sluts in high school or college had no consistent sexual history. Some recalled being highly promiscuous, but others remained virgins—and all shades in between. As we have seen in earlier chapters, girls who develop early, who look different from their peers, may endure teasing that can turn into name-calling. The long-term decline of homosocial networks among girls may have fostered the growth of slut bashing. If boys take an interest in the lone girl, then she might acquire a reputation whether she is sexually active. If she attracts someone else's steady boyfriend—or if she is perceived to do it—then other girls feel free to shun and verbally abuse her. Boys also use slut bashing to maintain a double standard of moral judgment. Girls can still be condemned for their sexuality, while boys have impunity. And while it seems that the slut identity is applied to a single girl in a school, a much wider portion of girls are vulnerable to the damage that rumor can bring them. A study from the 1990s revealed that two of five girls have had rumors spread about them.[64]

## Abuse

Giving currency to the slut identity are those girls whose sexuality may be a compensation for abuse. One girl recalled being sexually abused by a babysitter for four years, and then becoming sexually very free even in early middle school: "[I]t wasn't conscious or deliberate. It was something I did because I felt I was supposed to." In high school she already had a reputation so decided that brief sexual encounters could do her no harm. "This whole time I craved a boyfriend, a long-term relationship, which I never had," she told Leora Tanenbaum. Other girls willingly embraced the slut identity, or retrospectively gave themselves that name as they looked back from early adulthood. Violet wrote in a Zine that "to try to have an ongoing 'thing' was a sick farce." For her, embracing the slut identity gave her relief from her own self-loathing. "I became a slut," she wrote, "because my father beat me, made me feel like nothing." Many of the writers in the girl Zines illustrated with their own stories the link between abuse and risky sexual behavior.[65]

In a 1988 article psychologist David Finkelhor described some of the consequences that come with the trauma of abuse, particularly sexual abuse. Children violated by an adult might transform their sense of worth into their value as a sexual object. Their feelings of betrayal, toward the abuser or toward those whose collusion made the abuse possible, coexisted with a sense of "evilness, worthlessness, shamefulness, guilt." "Dixie LaRue" wrote of this transformation, of living in a world that is "a big place, ablaze with multicolors . . . Then someone you love, someone you trust, someone's tobacco breath is too close. And the world is no longer full of color." She recalled pushing her "innocence to a bottom where it could not be further burgled." Rather than find the vulnerability to establish friendships and begin a relationship, it seemed far easier for Violet to abuse alcohol and have sex with someone who would never become part of her life. "Basically, everyone was a one-nighter, even if we fucked several different times . . ." "Ultimately," she concluded, "this is how the world is divided: people who have been severely abused as children, and people who haven't."[66]

Probably no more than a tiny minority of girls labeled as sluts actively took that name for themselves and engaged in sexual behavior that matched their imagined role. Abuse cannot explain risky behavior, since traumatic sexual experience can lead to a wide variety of behaviors. Depression, dependency, hostility, a sense of powerlessness are all possible responses to childhood abuse. Boys who had been abused may have become eager to exercise control themselves. Or girls and boys could withdraw and reject any kind of intimacy. The testimony of victims shows the range of responses. When, at age 12, a girl tried to seek help from her sister after being molested by her brother-in-law, she became the object of her sister's accusations: "So from then on I just let my brother-in-law do as he pleased, because I was at fault." A high school girl who had been molested wrote that she could not enjoy "fooling around with someone. . . . I would freak out. see his [the abuser's] face, smell him like it was totally happening again."[67]

The results of abuse, particularly sexual trauma, in the lives of victims included personal problems of adjustment and difficulties in relationship. Lovemaking most often had to do not with love but with issues of control and self-worth. These personal problems might strike us as merely unfortunate if they applied to a tiny, singularly unfortunate minority. But a 1985 national survey, using random sampling, found 26 percent of women and 16 percent of men reported childhood sexual abuse. The common impression of social workers and counselors is that these percentages might, if anything, be low. Abuse has not come as a result of looser sexual morality. The 1985 survey found that the highest level of reporting came not from the youngest cohort, but from women 40 to 49, who would have experienced violation in the 1950s. Childhood sexual trauma has been a persistent element of adolescent sexuality.[68]

Sexual coercion by peers has also become visible as an issue for girls late in the century, but an issue clouded by changes in the sexual culture. During the 1950s and 1960s the growing proportion of teenagers engaging in sexual play seemed simply a response to the urgency of desire and the dwindling value placed on virginity. From the 1970s onward, the wider culture seemed complicit in the eroticization of adolescence. Middle-class teenagers and college students late in the century assumed that a vibrant social life could only come with an active sex life. Yet most sexually active teens, but more girls than boys (73 vs. 50 percent) cited social expectations when asked why they decided to have sex for the first time. This youthful sexual culture appeared to work in the interests of the boys and young men who pressured their girlfriends for more and more physical intimacy. Feminist authors had already begun to raise awareness of the ways that coercion could operate at a cultural level as well as at the level of physical force. By the 1980s, physical force also had emerged as a matter of growing public concern.[69]

Coercion has become difficult to discuss because it is now so common. Harassment is widespread if not pervasive. Two seventh-grade girls talked about the pressure they felt from boys:

ANNIE: "It happens to everybody! You hear girls talking and its, 'Oh, yeah, her too, me too,' and nothing is being done!"
KATY: "They talk about your body parts, they cop a feel, they drop pencils to try and look up your dress. It's like mildly raping someone."[70]

Boys who feel free to treat girls this way may believe that they can go further. "Recently I went to a party," a 12-year-old wrote to Beth Winship. "Later on in the party a boy grabbed me and shoved me into a closet. He slipped off my clothes and had sexual intercourse with me. I didn't scream because I enjoyed it. . . . I feel guilty and don't know what to do." Even though she had been assaulted, the girl's experience of desire confused her, leaving her feeling guilty. Sharon Thompson has written that many girls discover sexual desire later than do boys and find it more confusing. Most girls have also lost the possibility of casual caresses from other girls, something that in earlier decades could have given them a sense of their sexual selves. Even heterosexual petting has become less common. Discovering arousal in sexual situations with boys may leave girls confused about the possibility of consent.[71]

Confusion about desire, and about the boundaries of coercion and consent, made any discussion of appropriate behavior difficult. When "Ask Beth" in the early 1980s wrote about "date rape," a new term for the era, she received the following, signed "A parent." "From reading your column today, a guy who had pressured a girl into having sex could think he was guilty of rape. So could the girl." This parent joined others in chastising Beth Winship for publicizing a major problem for adolescent girls. A variety of studies in the 1980s and 1990s found that a high percentage of girls—almost 20 percent—had been victimized during dates and suffered either physical abuse or psychological harm. One phone survey even found 5 to 11 percent of girls 18 and under assaulted by peers *each year.*[72]

The message of these studies, and of Beth Winship, was that rape cast a shadow over all of adolescent sexuality, no matter how normal it seemed. Sexual assault typically occurred on dates, and was committed by the girl's date or boyfriend. One frightened 15-year-old girl wrote to Beth Winship about going home to meet the parents of a boy she had been dating for three months. But the parents were not at home. "He took me up to his room, locked the doors, shut the lights and put me on the bed. I wanted so much to stop him, but I couldn't. He told me I'd like him a whole lot more and I did. . . . [H]e wanted to prove his feelings." In the girl's report, she could not stop the boy—and this may well have been the case. But her account seems to say that she felt as though she had no choice. And, she continues in her letter that she knows he will marry her. We can clearly see the confusion of this girl, who knew that what happened was wrong, but felt that she was somehow culpable, and at the same time that her belief in romance and marriage would ultimately be vindicated.[73]

We might expect a 15-year-old to be confused about her actions and the meaning of such an incident. But consider this account from a senior at Rutgers University who met someone at a fraternity "and when he went to drive me home, he decided to kidnap me to his apartment. . . ." Scared and drunk, she decided to sleep with him "to get out of there." She concluded, "It could have been a very bad experience. I was lucky." Like Yvonne Blue 50 years before her, this college girl saw her own drunkenness and bad judgment as the real problem: "When I get drunk I get myself into these spots like you would not believe."[74] Coercion, or even rape, does not enter her discussion. For many young women, the line between coercion and consent seemed vague.

As early as the 1970s it was becoming clear that coercion and violence played a role in the sex lives of a significant portion of adolescents and young adults. Feminists had identified fear of rape as a major issue in the lives of women, with 400 rape crisis centers opening by 1976.[75] In Michael Moffatt's fieldwork at Rutgers University, 10 percent of college women described some form of coercive sexual debut. A 1987 study found almost half of college women had experienced some form of sexual coercion, ranging from giving in to sex play to rape. Peggy Reeves Sanday studied the case of Laurel, at the University of Pennsylvania, who went to a fraternity party where she drank and used LSD. When she woke up naked, a fraternity member took her upstairs where she was gang-raped. By 1985 more than 75 incidents of gang rape had been identified at colleges across the country. In many cases young women felt they were at fault, or were intimidated by harassment from female as well as male peers. Although their inebriation made them incapable of real consent, they were subjected to the argument that drinking at, or just attending a fraternity event, made them available for sexual use.[76]

For some boys, the trauma of abuse may have predisposed them to become abusers themselves. A boy whose father had beat him remembered seeing his father beat a prostitute he had brought home. "Afterward, I felt like I was ready to try my hand at sex. . . . I raped a girl." The honesty of this account stems from the willingness to admit sexual assault and rape, something that seemed too difficult for most adolescents. We now know that abuse of boys, including coerced sex, had continued under institutional protection during much of the twentieth century. Scandals erupting in the Roman Catholic Church in the United States, in the late 1990s and again in the new century, showed that abusive relations of priests with boys under their authority or guidance had been endemic. Even more recent revelations have shown that Boy Scout leaders took advantage of boys in their care. Taken together, these institutional revelations suggest that tens of thousands of boys may have been sexually abused during the twentieth century. We can only imagine the wide range of impacts this may have had on the general relations of adolescents to one another.[77]

Sexual coercion probably became no worse as the century ended, but at least consciousness of it expanded. As litigation continued to claim compensation for victims, institutions moved slowly toward policies to protect minors. In a 2002 conference of Catholic bishops, the president of the conference Wilton D. Gregory III confronted his colleagues: "We are the ones who allowed priest abusers to remain in ministry and reassigned them to communities where they continued to abuse," he said. "We are the ones who worried more about the possibility of scandal than bringing about the kind of openness that helps prevent abuse." And while incest and acquaintance rape continue as widespread problems, family professionals—therapists, social workers, psychiatrists—at least understand now that the issues exist and require attention and intervention.[78]

## Conclusion

The final decades of the century seemed to provide opportunities for adolescent sexuality to be treated with honesty by adolescents as well as adults. Instead, adolescent sexuality was politicized in efforts to control the bodies of youth. Both the pregnancy panic and the STD epidemics that followed led to public policy, especially regarding sex education, that attempted to reverse the development of openness around sexual issues. The growing chorus of revelations regarding sexual violence, whether from date rape or sexual abuse of children, only began to be taken seriously in the early twenty-first century, and then slowly and unevenly. The revalorization of girlhood chastity by conservative groups evoked nostalgia for an imagined past of strangely unsexual adolescents. Television and other media, meanwhile, continued to provide a torrent of sexual images and ideas. The messages from the media joined the new purity movement in ignoring the reality of adolescent lives.

Meantime, adolescent sexuality continued to function as it had for more than half the century. American youth organized their social lives and physical intimacy through committed, even if short-term, relationships. Around the edges of this system, sexual violence, binge drinking, and hookups provided a chaotic contrast to the steady complex of companionate nonmarriages. Adolescents negotiated the chaos and the system and managed their responses to contrasting ideas and images streaming from their sex education curricula and the media.

## Notes

1. Dennis Hevesi, "Elizabeth Winship, Advice Columnist for Youths, Dies at 90," *New York Times*, October 28, 2011. http://www.nytimes.com/2011/10/28/us/elizabeth-winship-advice-columnist-for-youths-dies-at-90.html.
2. Amanda Burr, "(The Other) Teen Magazines," *Ben Is Dead* ("Very Essential Super Extra-Special Sassy Issue," Spring 1994), 41, box 2, Girl Zines Collection, Sophia Smith Collection, Smith College, Northampton, Mass. [hereafter Girl Zines].
3. Elizabeth C. Winship, "Ask Beth: Elizabeth C. Winship Papers," Schlesinger Library, Radcliffe Institute, Harvard University, Cambridge, MA, 1965–1994, MC570 [hereafter Ask Beth], Box 1, August 27, 1974; and Robert T. Michale, John H. Gagnon, Edward O. Laumann, and Gina Kolata, *Sex in America: a definitive survey* (New York: Warner, 1997), 162.
4. Leora Tanenbaum, *Slut!: Growing Up with a Bad Reputation* (New York: Perennial, 2000), 28–32.
5. Ask Beth, box 1, folder 3, July 28, 1983; Girl Zines: Burr, box 2, "Teen Magazines," p. 41; box 3, Giana, "Sex Diary of an Ugly Girl," *Bust*, 1 (Summer/Fall 1994), 28–30; box 1, folder 2, Violet I, "Scream of Love," *Abuse* #3, 40–41; and Susan Averett, Hope Corman, and Nancy Reichman, "Effects of Overweight on Risky Sexual Behavior of Adolescent Girls," NBER Working Paper 16172, The National Bureau of Economic Research, Cambridge, MA, July 2010, http://papers.nber.org/papers/w16172.
6. Girl Zines, box 2, folder 2, *Bitter Critter*, #1, 1996, 2; and Joan Jacobs Brumberg, *The Body Project: An Intimate History of American Girls* (New York: Vintage Books, 1998), 188–189.
7. Hevesi, "Elizabeth Winship"; Ask Beth, box 1, folder 3: June 26, 1983; box 1, folder 5, n.d., "Upset and Frustrated."
8. Michael Gordon and Randi L. Miller, "Going Steady in the 1980s: Exclusive Relationships in Six Connecticut High Schools," *Sociology & Social Research* 68, no. 4 (July 1984): 464, 467, 469, 471; 81.2 percent of females and 69.7 percent of males go steady in teen years; Alan Guttmacher Institute, *Sex and America's Teenagers* (New York: Alan Gutmacher Institute, 1994), 24.
9. Ami Flam Kuttler and Annette M. La Greca, "Linkages among Adolescent Girls' Romantic Relationships, Best Friendships, and Peer Networks," *Journal of Adolescence* 27, no. 4 (2004): 395–414.
10. Michael S. Kimmel, *Guyland: The Perilous World Where Boys Become Men* (New York: Harper, 2008), 47–48.
11. Nancy Nathan, "Dickless & Damaged," *Ben Is Dead* (Spring 1994), 51–53, Girl Zines, box 2, folder 1; n.a., *Alien Girl* #7, (1990s), Girl Zines Box 1, folder 3.
12. Becky Bain, "A Bad Omen," *Cowbird*, August 31, 2012, http://cowbird.com/author/becky-bain/#!/38702.
13. Lillian B. Rubin, *Erotic Wars: What Happened to the Sexual Revolution?* (New York: HarperPerennial, 1991), 61.
14. Martin Whyte, *Dating, Mating, and Marriage* (New York: de Gruyter, 1990), 39–40; Donna L. McDonald and John Paul McKinney, "Steady Dating and Self-esteem in

High School Students," *Journal of Adolescence* 17, no. 6 (December 1994): 557–564; and n.a., *Aphrodite's Trousers* #2 (mid-1990s?), n.p., Girl Zines, Box 1, folder 4.

15. On adolescent sexuality and market-like behavior, see Roy F. Baumeister and Kathleen D. Vohs, "Sexual Economics: Sex as Female Resource for Social Exchange in Heterosexual Interactions," *Personality and Social Psychology Review* 8 (2004): 339–363; and n.a., *Bitter Critter*, #1, 1996, 2, Girl Zines, box 2, folder 4.

16. Mary Ellen Mark, "Prom Night," *New York Times*, March 30, 2012, The Opinion Pages, http://www.nytimes.com/2012/04/01/opinion/sunday/prom-night.html?module=Search&mabReward=relbias%3Ar%2C%7B%222%22%3A%22RI%3A12%22%7D&_r=0; Francine Pascal was interviewed by Ira Glass for *Prom | This American Life*, June 8, 2001, accessed November 29, 2014, http://www.thisamericanlife.org/radio-archives/episode/186/prom?act=2; and Johnnie B. Baker, "My Prom," *Cowbird*, June 17, 2012, http://cowbird.com/story/29049/My_Prom/?uiid=widget-1376931424-29049. Johnnie B. Baker's prom took place at the Disneyland Hotel in 1984. One year before that, I chaperoned a prom at the same location.

17. Ask Beth, box 1, folder 1, January 29, 1983; box 1, folder 1, July 1973; box 1, folder 1 1970–79; Rivka Solomon, "Lust American Style," *Bust* #11 (Summer/Fall 1998), 30–31, Girl Zines, box 2, folder 8.

18. Michael Moffatt, *Coming of Age in New Jersey: College and American Culture* (New Brunswick, NJ: Rutgers University Press, 1989), 192–195, 202.

19. Correspondence with family therapist Tracey Lasloffy, PhD.

20. Ask Beth, box 1, folder 1, 1970–79, K.S.

21. Moffat, *Coming of Age*, 196; John H. Gangon and William Simon, "Prospects for Change in American Sexual Patterns," *Medical Aspects of Human Sexuality* 4 (January 1970): 107; Brent C. Miller, Cynthia R. Christopherson, and Pamela K. King, "Sexual Behavior in Adolescence," in *Adolescent Sexuality*, ed. Thomas Gulotta, Gerald R. Adams, and Raymond Montemayor (Newbury Park: Sage, 1993), 71; Richard Lincoln, Frederick S. Jaffe, and Linda Ambrose, *11 Million Teenagers: What Can Be Done about the Epidemic of Adolescent Pregnancies* (New York: Alan Gutmacher Institute, 1976); and J. C. Abma, "Teenagers in the United States: Sexual Activity, Contraceptive Use, and Childbearing, 2002," *Vital and Health Statistics* 23, no. 24 (2004), http://www.cdc.gov/nchs/data/series/sr_23/sr23_024.pdf, 7.

22. Stephen Buckley and Debbi Wilgoren, "Young and Experienced: Area's Teenagers Are Having Sex Earlier with Little Concern for Safety, Monogamy," in *Issues in Adolescent Sexuality: Readings from the* Washington Post *Writers Group*, ed. Frank C. Leeming, William O. Dwyer, and Diana P. Oliver (Boston: Allyn and Bacon, 1996), 8; Ask Beth, "Bummed out in Grosse Pointe," box 11, folder 2, August 3, 1982; and F. Rice, *The Adolescent: Development, Relationships, and Culture*, 10th ed. (Boston: Allyn and Bacon, 2002), 213.

23. Buckley and Wilogren, "Young and Experienced," 8, 10; Miller, Christopherson, and King, "Sexual Behavior in Adolescence," 61; Sharon Thompson, "Putting a Big Thing into a Little Hole: Teenage Girls' Accounts of Sexual Initiation," *Journal of Sex Research* 27 (August 1990): 343; and Jeffrey S. DeSimone, "Binge Drinking & Sex in High School," NBER Working Paper 16132, the National Bureau of Economic Research, Cambridge, MA, June 2010, http://www.nber.org/papers/w16132.pdf?new_window=1.

24. Thompson, "Putting a Big Thing," 344, 346; Rubin, *Erotic Wars*, 42–43; and Buckley and Wilogren, "Young and Experienced," 8.

25. Abma, "Teenagers in the U.S.," 1; Baumeister, "Sexual Economics," 349; Rubin, *Erotic Wars*, 60; Wendy D. Manning, Monica A. Longmore, and Peggy C. Giordano, "The Relationship Context of Contraceptive Use at First Intercourse," *Family Planning Perspectives* 32, no. 3 (May 2000): 104; Catherine M. Grello, Deborah P. Welsh, Melinda S. Harper, and Joseph W. Dickson, "Dating and Sexual Relationship Trajectories and Adolescent Functioning," *Adolescent and Family Health* 3, no. 3 (2003):

103–112; and Miller, Christopherson, and King, "Sexual Behavior in Adolescence"; and Thompson, "Putting a Big Thing," 352–356.

26. Donna Britt, "For Teens, a Revolution Gone Haywire," in Leeming et al., *Issues in Adolescent Sexuality*, 3; Manning, "Relationship Context"; and Moffatt, *Coming of Age*, 250.

27. Gail Elizabeth Wyatt, "Changing Influences on Adolescent Sexuality over the Past Forty Years," in *Adolescence and Puberty*, ed. John Bancroft (New York: Oxford University Press, 1990), 190; Abma, "Teenagers in the U.S.," 7; John E. Bates, Douglas B. Alexander, Sarah E. Oberlander, Kenneth A. Dodge, and Gregory S. Pettit, "Antecedents of Sexual Activity at Ages 16 and 17 in a Community Sample Followed from Age 5," in *Sexual Development in Childhood*, ed. John Bancroft (Bloomington: Indiana University Press, 2003), 206–237; and Alan Guttmacher Institute, *Sex and America's Teenagers*, 25.

28. Tanenbaum, *Slut!*, 20; and Rubin, *Erotic Wars*, 61, 63–64.

29. Rubin, *Erotic Wars*, 63–64; Edward Laumann, John H. Gagnon, Robert T. Michael, and Stuart Michaels, *The Social Organization of Sexuality: Sexual Practices in the United States* (Chicago: University of Chicago Press, 2000), 7.

30. Laura Duberstein Lindberg, Rachel Jones, and John S. Santelli, "Non-Coital Sexual Activities among Adolescents," *Journal of Adolescent Health* 43 (July 2008): 231–238; Paula K. Braverman and Victor C. Strasburger, "Adolescent Sexual Activity," *Clinical Pediatrics* 32 (November 1993): 658–668; and Amy Dickinson, "Teenage Sex," *Time* 154, no. 19 (November 8, 1999): 160.

31. N.a., "Ten True Stories about Bad Relationships," *Chatty Cathy*, #1 n.d. [1990s], n.p., Girl Zines, box 3, folder 8; John D. Williams and Arthur P. Jacoby, "The Effects of Premarital Heterosexual and Homosexual Experience on Dating and Marriage Desirability," *Journal of Marriage and Family* 51 (May 1989): 489–497; and Moffat, *Coming of Age*, 200–201.

32. Moffat, *Coming of Age*, 199–201; and Williams and Jacoby, "Effects of Premarital Experience."

33. Ask Beth, box 1, folder 3, February 15, 1983; and Braverman and Strasburger, "Adolescent Sexual Activity," 661.

34. Ask Beth, box 11, folder 2, December 1983.

35. Tom W. Smith, "The Sexual Revolution?" *Public Opinion Quarterly* 54, no. 3 (Fall 1990): 417; Chris Bull and John Gallagher, *Perfect Enemies: The Religious Right, the Gay Movement, and the Politics of the 1990s* ([S.l.]: Diane Pub Co, 1996), chap. 1.

36. Diane Raymond, "Homophobia, Identity, and the Meaning of Desire: Reflection on the Cultural Construction of Gay and Lesbian Adolescent Sexuality," in *Sexual Cultures and the Construction of Adolescent Identities*, ed. Janice Irvine, (Philadelphia: Temple University Press, 1994), 115–150; T. Allen, "Gay Students Speak Out," *Education Digest* 61 (November 1995): 24–30; and Sadie Van Gelder, "It's Who I Am," *Seventeen*, November 1996, 144.

37. Andrew Solomon, *Far from the Tree: Parents, Children and the Search for Identity* (New York: Scribner, 2012), 7–9, 11.

38. Solomon, *Far from the Tree*, 10–11, 14–15; Raymond, "Homophobia," 136; and Ann Heron, *One Teenager in Ten: Writings by Gay and Lesbian Youth* (Boston: Alyson Publications, 1983), 15–16; Ask Beth, box 11, folder 2, n.d.

39. Thompson, "Big Thing," 347–348; and Heron, *One in Ten*, 75–76.

40. Caitlin Ryan, Donna Futterman, and Kathleen Stine, "Helping our Hidden Youth," *American Journal of Nursing* 98, no. 2 (December 1998): 37; Van Gelder, "It's Who I Am," 144; Allen, "Gay Students Speak," 24–30; Ritch Savin-Williams and Richard G. Rodriguez, "A Developmental, Clinical Perspective on Lesbian, Gay Male, and Bisexual Youths," in *Adolescent Sexuality*, 91; Gary Remafedi, James A. Farrow, and Robert W. Deisher, "Risk Factors for Attempted Suicide in Gay and Bisexual Youth," *Pediatrics* 87, no. 6 (June 1, 1991): 869–875; Anthony D'Augelli and Scott L.

Hershberger, "Lesbian, Gay, and Bisexual Youth in Community Settings: Personal Challenges and Mental Health Problems," *American Journal of Community Psychology* 21, no. 4 (1993): 421–448; and Anthony D'Augelli, and Charlotte J. Patterson, eds. *Lesbian, Gay, and Bisexual Identities and Youth: Psychological Perspectives* (Oxford, UK: Oxford University Press, 2001).

41. Susan Maria Ferentinos, *Interpreting LGBT history* (Lanham, MD: Rowman & Littlefield, 2015).

42. Ryan, "Helping our Hidden Youth," 37, 64–64; Allen, "Gay Students Speak," 24–30; Linda Fish and Rebecca Harvey, *Nurturing Queer Youth: Family Therapy Transformed* (New York: Norton, 2005), 5–6; Heron, *One in Ten*, 9; and n.a., *Bitter Critter*, #2 1(1996), n.p. Girls Zines, box 2, folder 4.

43. Jon Barrett, "Going Steady," *Advocate*, no. 835 (April 10, 2001): 36–40; and Tina Tessin, *Gay Relationships* (New York: Putnam, 1989).

44. Craig Nelson, *Finding True Love in a Man-Eat-Man World: The Intelligent Guide to Gay Dating, Sex, Romance, and Eternal Love* (New York: Dell, 1996), 96; D. Clunis and G. Green, *Lesbian Couples: A Guide to Creating Healthy Relationships* (Emeryville, CA: Seal Press, 2005), 47; and Judith McDaniel, *The Lesbian Couples' Guide : Finding the Right Woman and Creating a Life Together* (New York NY: HarperPerennial, 1995), 30.

45. Barett, "Going Steady"; Leeming et al., *Issues in Adolescent Sexuality*, 19; Heron, *One in Ten*, 39–40; and Van Gelder, "It's Who I Am," 144.

46. Patricia Donovan, "School-Based Sexuality Education: The Issues and Challenges," *Family Planning Perspectives* 30, no. 4 (August 1998): 188–193, http://www.guttmacher.org/pubs/journals/3018898.html; and Irvine, Janice M. *Talk about Sex: The Battles over Sex Education in the United States* (Berkeley: University of California, 2002), 35.

47. Donovan, "School-based sexuality education"; S.D. White and R.R. DeBlassie, "Adolescent Sexual Behavior," *Adolescence* 27, no. 105 (Spring 1992): 103; Committee on Government Reform—Minority Staff Report, *The Content of Federally-Funded Abstinence Only Education Programs* (Washington, D.C.: U.S. House of Representatives, 2004), http://www.apha.org/apha/PDFs/HIV/The_Waxman_Report.pdf.

48. M.H. Thomas, "Abstinence-Based Programs for Prevention of Pregnancy," *Journal of Adolescent Health* 26, no. 1 (January 2000): 5–17; Linda Villarosa, "More Teenagers Say No to Sex, and Experts Aren't Sure Why," *New York Times*, December 23, 2003, Health and Fitness; "New Report Finds Federally Funded Abstinence-Only Programs Offer False, Misleading Information," December 3, 2004, http://www.guttmacher.org/media/inthenews/2004/12/03/index.html; and Pamela K. Kohler, Lisa E. Manhart, and William E. Lafferty, "Abstinence-Only and Comprehensive Sex Education and the Initiation of Sexual Activity and Teen Pregnancy," *Journal of Adolescent Health* 42, no. 4 (April 2008): 344–351.

49. Tracey Laszloffy, personal communication with the author; Catherine Chilman, "Promoting Healthy Adolescent Sexuality," *Family Relations* 39 (April 1990): 123–131; Laina Y. Bay-cheng, "The Trouble of Teen Sex: The Construction of Adolescent Sexuality through School-Based Sexuality Education," *Sex Education* 3, no. 1 (April 2003): 61–74; Moffat, *Coming of Age*, 194; Rubin, *Erotic Wars*, 68–69; Braverman and Strasburger, "Adolescent Sexual Activity," 661; "The (Sexual) Revolution Will be Televised," *Atlantic Monthly* 298, no. 2 (2006): 48; Jane D. Brown, Kelly Ladin L'Engle, Carol J. Pardun, Guang Guo, Kristin Kennevay, and Christine Jakcson, "Sexy Media Matter: Exposure to Sexual Content in Music, Movies, Television, and Magazines Predicts Black and White Adolescents' Sexual Behavior," *Pediatrics* 117, no. 4 (April 1, 2006): 1018–1027; and Nell Bernstein, "Learning to Love," *Mother Jones*, 20, no. 1 (1995), 44.

50. Hevesi, "Elizabeth Winship"; "Children Having Children," advertisement, http://www.youtube.com/watch?v=iZR0sL3FmOk; Maris Vinovskis, *An "Epidemic" of

*Adolescent Pregnancy? Some Historical and Policy Considerations* (New York: Oxford University Press, 1988), xii, xiv; and Kristin Luker, *Dubious Conceptions: The Politics of Teenage Pregnancy* (Cambridge, MA: Harvard University Press, 1996), 71, 75, 80.

51. Vinovskis, *Epidemic?*, 25–29; and Luker, *Dubious Conceptions*, 16.

52. Vinovskis, *Epidemic?*, 29 34–35; Luker, *Dubious Conceptions*, 2; Alan Guttmacher Institute, *Sex and America's Teenagers* (New York: Alan Gutmacher Institute, 1994), 50; Abma, "Teenagers in the U.S.," 3; Nina Bernstein, "Teenage rate of pregnancy drops in U.S." *New York Times*. New York N.Y., February 20, 2004. In 2000, the teen pregnancy rate in the United States was 84.5 per 1,000 females 15–19 years of age, about 27 percent lower than in 1990. The teen pregnancy rate for 15–17 year olds declined from 80 in 1990 to 54 in 2000, while for 18–19 year olds the teen pregnancy rate declined from 162 in 1990 to 130 in 2000.

53. Daniel Laskin, "Health." *New York Times*, February 21, 1982. http://www.nytimes.com/1982/02/21/magazine/health.html; John Leo, "The New Scarlet Letter," *Time* (August 2, 1982). http://www.time.com/time/magazine/article/0,9171,1715020,00.html.

54. Patricia Teasdale, "On the trail of V.D.—with tact," *New York Times* (December 13, 1981). http://www.nytimes.com/1981/12/13/nyregion/on-the-trail-of-vd-with-tact.html?scp=340&sq=herpes%20simplex&st=cse.

55. Jane Brody, "Herpes now blamed for more illness than any other human virus," *New York Times* (May 4, 1982). http://www.nytimes.com/1982/05/04/science/herpes-now-blamed-for-more-illness-than-any-other-human-viruses.html?scp=96&sq=herpes%20simplex&st=cse&pagewanted=1.

56. Leo, "The new scarlet letter;" Glenn Collins, "Relationships; of Herpes, AIDS and fear of sex," *New York Times* (July 18, 1983).

57. Jack Begg, "Word for word/nameless dread—20 years ago, the first clues to the birth of a plague," *New York Times* (June 3, 2001). http://www.nytimes.com/2001/06/03/weekinreview/word-for-word-nameless-dread-20-years-ago-first-clues-birth-plague.html?scp=386&sq=herpes%20simplex&st=cse; Glenn Collins, "Relations; of Herpes, Aids and Fear of Sex," *New York Times*, July 18, 1983, http://www.nytimes.com/1983/07/18/style/relationships-of-herpes-aids-and-fear-of-sex.html;" Ryan White, Wikipedia.

58. Alan Guttmacher Institute, *Sex and America's teenagers*; Abma, "Teenagers in the U.S.," 6; and Villarosa, "More Teenagers Say No."

59. Kathleen Bogle, *Hooking Up: Sex, Dating, and Relationships on Campus* (New York: New York University Press, 2008), 16, 23–29; and Glenn Norval and Elizabeth Marquardt, *Hooking Up, Hanging Out, and Hoping for Mr. Right: College Women on Dating and Mating Today* (New York: Institute for American Values, 2001), 20;

60. Dixie LaRue, "More than a Blow Job, it's a Career," *Bust* 1, no. 4 (Summer/Fall 1994), 14–15, Girl Zines, box 3; and Rebecca Harvey, personal communication with the author.

61. Glenn and Marquardt, *Hooking Up*, 15, 21; and Bogle, *Hooking Up*, 28, 29, 47, 63, 370.

62. Ask Beth, box 1, folder 2, April 29, 1980.

63. Ask Beth, Box 11, folder 3, n.d.

64. Tanenbaum, *Slut!*, 10, 113–114; Emily White, *Fast Girls: Teenage Tribes and the Myth of the Slut* (New York: Berkley Books, 2003), 9; Kimmel, *Guyland*, 47–48; and Michael Bamberg, "Form and Functions of 'Slut Bashing' in Male Identity Construction in 15-Year-Olds," *Human Development* 42 (2004): 331–353.

65. Tanenbaum, *Slut!*, 105; and Violet I., "Scream of love."

66. David Finkelhor, "The Trauma of Child Sexual Abuse: Two Models" in *Lasting Effects of Child Sexual Abuse*, ed. Gail Elizabeth Wyatt and Gloria Johnson Powell (Newbury Park, CA: Sage, 1988), 69–71; Dixie LaRue, "The World Moves," *Bust*, no. 5 (Winter/Spring 1995), 33; Girl Zines box 3; and Violet I., "Scream of love."

67. Finkelhor, "Trauma of Child Sexual Abuse," 75–77; and Ask Beth, box 11, folder 6, November 26, 1984, "Ashamed and alone;" Claire, Aphrodite's Trousers, no. 2 (1986) n.p., Girl Zines, box 1.

68. David Finkelhor, Gerald Hotaling, and Christine Smith, "Sexual Abuse in a National Survey of Adult Men and Women: Prevalence, Characteristics, and Risk Factors," *Child Abuse & Neglect* 14 (1990): 19–28. Note that this survey came out prior to the surge in reports of recovered memories. Erna Olafson, David L. Corwin, and Roland C. Summit, "Modern History of Child Sexual Abuse Awareness: Cycles of Discovery and Suppression," *Child Abuse & Neglect* 17 (1993): 7–24.

69. Miller, Christopherson, and King, "Sexual Behavior in Adolescence," 61.

70. Patricia Hersch, *A Tribe Apart: A Journey into the Heart of American Adolescence* (New York: Ballantine Books, 1999), 19.

71. Ask Beth, box 11, folder 3, n.d. "Enjoyed it while it Lasted"; and Thompson, "Big thing," 344–345.

72. Ask Beth, box 1, folder 3, August 11, 1983; Moffat, *Coming of Age*, 202; Annette U. Rickel and Marie C. Hendren, "Aberrant Sexual Experiences in Adolescence" in *Adolescent Sexuality*, 141–160; Jay G. Silverman, Anita Raj, and Karen Clements, "Dating Violence and Associated Sexual Risk and Pregnancy among Adolescent Girls in the United States," *Pediatrics* 114, no. 2 (2004): e220–e225.

73. Suzanne Ageton, *Sexual Assault among Adolescents* (Lexington, MA: D.C. Heath, 1983), 40–41; "Desperate," Ask Beth, box 11, folder 3.

74. Moffatt, *Coming of Age*, 216.

75. Estelle B. Freedman, *Redefining Rape: Sexual Violence in the Era of Suffrage and Segregation* (Cambridge, MA: Harvard University Press, 2013), 277–279.

76. Moffatt, *Coming of Age*, 202; Mary P. Koss, Christine A. Gidycz, and Nadine Wisniewski, "The Scope of Rape: Incidence and Prevalence of Sexual Aggression and Victimization in a National Sample of Higher Education Students," *Journal of Consulting and Clinical Psychology* 55, no. 2 (1987): 162–70; Peggy Reeves Sanday, *Fraternity Gang Rape: Sex, Brotherhood, and Privilege on Campus*, 2nd ed. (New York: New York University Press, 2007), 26, 33, 53.

77. Michael J. Baker, "Childhood Trauma," *Abuse Issue #3* (1990s), Girl Zines, box 1.

78. Laurie Goodstein, "Scandals in the Church; The Conference; Abuse Victims Lay Blame at Feet of Catholic Bishops," *New York Times*, June 14, 2002, http://www.nytimes.com/2002/06/14/us/scandals-church-conference-abuse-victims-lay-blame-feet-catholic-bishops.html?pagewanted=all&src=pm.

# CONCLUSION

In the early decades of the twentieth century, working-class youth and young adults surged onto the streets of American cities to escape family supervision and looking for a good time. Couples seemed to be everywhere, making sex play more public than ever before. A century later American youth are still making their own decisions about whom they want to play with, and how they want to play.

American culture at the opening of the twenty-first century affirmed the importance of sensual pleasure and the central role of sexuality, and did it with all the power of the media, old and new alike. Just like the exciting urban world of amusements at the turn of the twentieth century, contemporary culture provides abundant and often conflicting messages about sex. One example of this cultural confusion was a Candie's Foundation public service video that appeared in 2010 in which Mike "the Situation" Sorrentino, from the popular reality show *Jersey Shore*, and Bristol Palin, daughter of the 2008 Republican vice-presidential candidate, discuss premarital sex. The Situation counseled prudent delay ("pause before you play") and the use of birth control. Bristol Palin, herself a teenage mother, refused to recommend birth control and insisted that young people defer premarital intercourse.[1]

In spite of the confusing cultural messages, plenty qualify as good news about American youth. Although still high when compared to other industrialized nations, the U.S. birthrate for teenagers has continued to decline, and the use of birth control has become more widespread. Along with those who pause before they play are those who are not playing—yet. National surveys have shown an increase in the proportion of youth 15 to 24 who have never had sex—more than a fourth of both males and females. Sex among very young teenagers has also declined. And the large majority of girls continue to have intercourse first with someone with whom they have a long-term relationship. Considering what in the late twentieth century had seemed the inexorable rise in sexual activity, and the declining age of sexual debut, these trends suggest that youth are capable of prudence in their most intimate relations.[2]

Steady dating remains at the center of youthful sexuality. This provides the context for negotiations about physical intimacy, often including the use of birth control.[3] Going steady has become the gateway relationship for courtship, cohabitation, and engagement. But these intimate relations can also constrain friendships with others and even become abusive. A study from 2009 found that 29 percent of teenagers in relationships had experienced some form of psychological abuse, with 12 percent experiencing physical abuse.[4] Like the companionate marriages they emulate, steady dating relationships can foster reasoned intimacy or narrow and exploitive relations.

If, as I have argued, companionate sexuality—going steady or the steady dating of today—has been shaped by the interests of girls and young women, then surely the most important challenge to it has come from the hookup culture on college campuses where male interests are paramount. Hooking up has been discussed since the 1990s, but the phenomenon may simply be a more recent name for older practices. Older youth often have a period during which relative independence provides opportunities for some sexual experimentation, in earlier decades referred to as one-night stands, pickups, experiments, flings, or mistakes. College parties and housing provide the context for the hooking up. The semi-independent living of college students is so important that commuter students rarely participate in the hookup culture.[5] And even with the assumption that casual sex is intrinsic to college and desirable, no one really believes that the hookup can work without a lot of drinking.[6]

Controlling, or even limiting, intimacy has often been an objective for young men who wanted to avoid the emotional turmoil, or even just the time commitments, of a relationship. Hooking up does bear some similarity to the traditional dalliance relationships of classical dating during the 1920s. A 2012 article in *The Atlantic* suggested that women now want to devote the same kind of attention to their careers that men traditionally have. Hannah Rosin presented hooking up as a continuation of women's liberation, allowing young professionals to put off the demands of full-time relationships so they can build their careers. But sociologist Michael Kimmel cautions that this apparent sexual freedom for women comes within a thoroughly male-dominated context in which "claims of agency coexist with demands for compliance."[7] The prescriptive use of alcohol with the assumption that casual sex will follow means that "demands for compliance" may become coercive, that a passive acceptance of sex may be far from consensual. A recently completed study for a White House task force found that between a fifth and fourth of college coeds are victims of sexual assault. Headline-grabbing cases of rape give only a suggestion of the underlying, alcohol-fueled culture of coercive sex on college campuses.[8]

While youthful heterosexuality by mid-century settled into a pattern of domestic-like relations that remained recognizably consistent until today, homosexuality changed rapidly after about 1970. In the course of the last three decades of the century, gay, transgendered, and bisexual youth became far more visible. By the end of the century, in some places relationships between same-sex couples could be public.

My own experience seems relevant here. In 1998 I was faculty sponsor for a Gay-Straight Alliance at my university, a Catholic liberal arts college in small-town Pennsylvania. Although not far from Pittsburgh, Greensburg had no gathering place for its gay residents, and they were in most respects invisible. The students who organized the alliance acted in spite of the administration's reluctance and suspicion of the plan. The young women and men who founded the organization had faith in their goals and the persistence to meet the requirements to establish the new group. A wide variety of students quickly joined the alliance, both gay and lesbian students, but also those exploring sexual possibilities and self-identified heterosexual students who wanted to support their friends.

I advised the group for only a year or two, and like all student organizations it went through years of inactivity when student leaders were unavailable. But by 2005 the group was reconstituted, and after about a year of activity the leaders sponsored a public forum. One student after another talked about coming out and about their experience of coming to Seton Hill University. Many of them said that when they came out, their families supported them. One girl's mother and sisters told her, "Yes, we know, we've been waiting for you to tell us." The student speakers also found the university an open, welcoming environment. The suspicion provoked by the organization only a few years before had seemingly given way to acceptance and support. I later had a student speaker in one of my classes say that he had chosen my university because he wanted to go to a small college where there was an active gay–straight alliance.

The growing visibility and acceptance of LGBT people in my small university relate directly to larger changes in American life. The remarkable shift in the U.S. military from the "don't ask, don't tell" policy instituted in the Clinton era to the full acceptance of gay service members by 2011 runs parallel to the spread of legal marriage for gay and lesbian couples in many states. Although advocates for equality see more struggle ahead, the achievements of the last two decades would seem astonishing to an observer from any year in the twentieth century.

When Ritch Savin-Williams wrote about the "new" gay teenager early in the twenty-first century, he could almost have called his book the disappearance of the gay teenager. For many adolescents, sexual identity had become far less important. "Rather, teenagers are increasingly redefining, reinterpreting, and renegotiating their sexuality such that possessing a gay, lesbian, or bisexual identity is practically meaningless."[9] Although this has proceeded unevenly, the revolution among gay, lesbian, and queer youth has brought changes so rapidly that some of these adolescents can consider living as though their sexuality did not define their entire lives.

The future looks hopeful for greater acceptance of all kinds of sexualities, for reasonable attitudes among adults, and for responsible behavior among youth, about sex, birth control, and intimate commitments. But no one expects that future soon. Positive trends in the use of birth control and pregnancy come along with continued reports of abuse. Too many children and adolescents experience violence of some kind related to their sex lives, including sexual debut without consent. Too many young people are still made to feel ashamed of their sexual desire. I have spoken with gay students at my university who came out early to accepting families, and to others who grew up in subcultures, or areas of the country, where their emerging sexuality garnered only hostility. And slut shaming continues, whether to maintain the sexual double standard or class boundaries or as a response to claims of sexual assault. At least now we know more about sexual violence and the struggles of those who depart from heteronormative standards. Better understanding of sex and sexuality, and a growing willingness to discuss it, can become powerful forces for change.

## Notes

1. Candie's Foundation, *"The Situation" and Bristol Palin Talk Sex*, 2010, https://www. youtube.com/watch?v=UyWKlxNAh30.
2. Tara Parker Pope, "Well—the Myth of Rampant Teenage Promiscuity—NYTimes.com," *New York Times*, January 27, 2009, http://www.nytimes.com/2009/01/27/health/27well. html?_r=1&fta=y; and Richard Florida, "U.S. Teen Birthrates Are Down, But Still High in These States," *Theatlantic.com*, April 16, 2012, http://www.theatlanticcities. com/politics/2012/04/teen-birthrates-are-way-down-still-high-these-states/1735/.
3. Dana Frankoff, "Teen Girls: No Sex till We're Going Steady," *Psychology Today* 35, no. 6 (December 2002): 26.
4. J. Rosenberg, "One-Third of Teenagers Experience Abuse within Heterosexual Relationships," *Perspectives on Sexual and Reproductive Health* 34 (March/April 2002): 108, http://www.guttmacher.org/pubs/journals/3410802.html.
5. Michael Moffatt, *Coming of Age in New Jersey: College and American Culture* (New Brunswick, NJ: Rutgers University Press, 1989), 249; Barbara J. Risman and Rachel Allison, "Not Everybody Is Hooking Up at College—Here's Why," press release, Council on Contemporary Families, January 23, 2014, https://contemporaryfamilies. org/commuter-hookups/.
6. Jonathan Zimmerman, "Sexual Assault on Campus and the Curse of the Hookup Culture," *Los Angeles Times*, May 7, 2014, http://www.latimes.com/opinion/op-ed/ la-oe-adv-zimmerman-sexual-assault-college-hookups-20140508-story.html; and Owen Jennings, "Sober in the Animal House," *New York Times*, May 15, 2009, http:// well.blogs.nytimes.com/2009/05/15/sober-in-the-animal-house/?_php=true&_ type=blogs&partner=rss&emc=rss&_r=0.
7. Michael Kimmel, "Is It the End of Men, or Are Men Still in Power? Yes!," *Boston University Law Review* 93 (2013): 694.
8. Nina Burleigh, "Confronting Campus Rape," *Rolling Stone*, June 4, 2014, http://www. rollingstone.com/politics/news/confronting-campus-rape-20140604; and Jonathan Zimmerman, "Sexual Assault on Campus and the Curse of the Hookup Culture,"

*Los Angeles Times*, May 7, 2014, http://www.latimes.com/opinion/op-ed/la-oe-adv-zimmerman-sexual-assault-college-hookups-20140508-story.html. California has led the way with a new (2014) law that requires positive consent to sex acts. How this will change campus hookup culture remains a matter of speculation as this book went to press. Connor Friedserdorf, "Sex and the Class of 2020: How Will Hook-ups Change?," *The Atlantic*, October 18, 2014, http://www.theatlantic.com/politics/archive/2014/10/what-sex-on-campus-will-look-like-for-the-class-of-2020/381572/.

9. Ritch Savin-Williams, *The New Gay Teenager* (Cambridge, MA: Harvard University Press, 2005), 1.

# INDEX